Storytime Around the Curriculum

A Comprehensive Early Childhood Curriculum Presented Through Literature

BOOK I AIR · WATER · WEATHER · SUN

written by

Linda W. O'Berry   **Robin G. Little**   **Ann W. Fields**

Illustrations by Robin G. Little

Story O'Mimus illustrations by

Ed Mann

Copyright © 1993.   Linda W. O'Berry, Robin G. Little, Ann W. Fields

Published by **Pp** PARTNER PRESS INC.
Box 530124
Livonia, MI 48153-0124

ISBN 0-933212-03-8

Printed in the United States of America.

Distributed by:

Gryphon House
3706 Otis Street
Mt. Rainier, Maryland 20712
1-800-638-0928

To my parents, James and Milda Lamb, for teaching me how to use the simple things in life to make a day special.

. . . Linda

To my parents, Bob and Corny Gumbiner, for teaching me, as a child, to explore; as a teenager, to respect; as an adult, to care; and at all times, in all things, to have faith in God, family, friends, and myself.

. . . Robin

To my parents, Andrew and Peg Whitbred, who have given me the greatest gift of all—love.

. . . Ann

ACKNOWLEDGEMENTS

We would like to express our sincere appreciation to the many people who have made this book possible, who have believed in its purpose of encouraging a love of reading in children:

To those who have helped with the book production:

Liz Kobe, Dixie Hibner, and John Faitel, Publishers, for their faith and assistance;

Joyce King, Editor, for her enthusiasm and insight;

Terrie Stephens and Dave Poole, Photographers, for their expertise and flexibility;

Ed Mann, Artist, for his intuition and ingenuity;

Liz Cromwell and Dixie Hibner, authors of *Finger Frolics*, for granting permission to reprint selected fingerplays and poems. (The selections are indicated by an asterisk.)

To those friends and colleagues who have encouraged and supported us. We are especially grateful to:

Dorothy Krause, I.H.M., Josine Perez, S.S.N.D., Helen Francis, Judy McNeil, Carol Francis, Judy Biniasz, Phyllis Valus, Mardell Ammon, Laura Pishkur, Karen Kauffman, Connie Plante, and Robert Hoover.

To the hundreds of children who have touched our lives and taught us so much.

And to our families, for their time, patience, and understanding through all aspects of publishing:

Steve, Kara, and Scott
Dean, Kimberlee, Drew, Mom and Dad Little
Duke, Ashley, and A.A.W. III

TABLE OF CONTENTS

. . . ABOUT THIS BOOK

READ WITH THEM! READ WITH THEM! READ WITH THEM! Sharing the love of books with children instills the important message—reading is a natural and exciting part of everyday life.

As early childhood educators, we see storytime as a beginning. Books please the eyes and ears of children while stimulating their imaginations. Through literature, children can escape from the present, become someone else, learn more about their world and in the process discover themselves.

We believe a teacher's task is to encourage the learner's natural curiosity and provide experiences that invite children to explore and discover through active participation. Children need opportunities to verbalize their discoveries to a teacher who will listen and respond, be it through a simple nod or even silence.

In developing *Storytime Around the Curriculum*, we chose units that naturally arouse children's curiosity—Water, Air, Sun, and Weather. Each unit includes:

CONCEPTS to be explored

WELL-LOVED FEATURE STORIES reinforcing the unit concepts

PLANNING GUIDES organizing the activities into subject areas

STORY-RELATED ACTIVITIES integrating literature with language arts, math, science, health, social studies, and physical education

MISCELLANEOUS ACTIVITIES including recipes, center suggestions, and additional unit-related ideas

CREATIVE EXPERIENCES including art, drama, songs, poems, and action rhymes

ANNOTATED BOOKLIST recommending unit-related story and concept books

NOTE PAGES providing space for additional activities, books, or information

REPRODUCIBLES including multi-purpose activity sheets and patterns

As an added motivational feature, we have created an enchanting dinosaur, Story O'Mimus (Stor'-ee O-my'mus), who can come alive in the imaginative world of a young child. Children will be able to identify with his natural curiosity and mimic his love of learning.

We feel the combination of stories and related activities in *Storytime Around the Curriculum* will instill a life-long love of books and learning.

Linda W. O'Berry, Robin G. Little, Ann W. Fields

THE STORY MIMIC

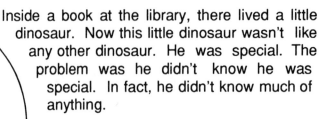

Inside a book at the library, there lived a little dinosaur. Now this little dinosaur wasn't like any other dinosaur. He was special. The problem was he didn't know he was special. In fact, he didn't know much of anything.

Day after day, he waited with all the other dinosaurs in his book for someone to come along and take him off the shelf. The library was always filled with all sorts of readers looking at books, but no one ever seemed to want to look at *his* book.

The little dinosaur knew he was different—all the other dinosaurs in his book stayed very still and never made a peep. But his legs fidgeted and sometimes the horn on his nose itched. Do you know that one day just after he arrived, someone folded the corner of his page—right where his tail was. Poor little fellow, he cried for days but couldn't seem to get anyone's attention.

Just about the time he was ready to give up all hope, he got a funny feeling in his tummy—you know, just like you get when your mom drives over a big bump in the road. He couldn't bear the thought of being disappointed, so he tried to pretend it wasn't really happening, but sure enough his book was being moved from the shelf.

"*Dinosaurs of Long Ago*, just what I've been looking for," said a little voice. She turned the pages carefully and seemed to be reading words.

"Words," thought the little dinosaur, "that's it, if she'll just read the words on my page, I might understand why I'm stuck here." He thought she'd never get to him, it seemed like it was taking forever.

Finally she turned the page and looked straight into his sad eyes. At that moment, he *knew* he was special.

"You're the dinosaur I've been looking for," exclaimed the little girl. "I knew if I kept reading books that one day I'd find you."

The little dinosaur's heart pounded anxiously as the little girl began reading the words on his page.

"Although dinosaurs lived millions of years ago, Story O'Mimus will live on and on in the hearts of boys and girls for years to come."

"Story O'Mimus," whispered the little dinosaur, "Is *that* my name?"

"Pardon me?" said the little girl, looking all around her. "Oh, I'm so happy I found you," she exclaimed. "I bet you can help me learn about dinosaurs."

Now, Story O'Mimus understood why he'd been put in a book. When people read books, they can learn about all sorts of things.

"Would you help me so I can be as smart as you are?" asked Story O'Mimus.

"Sure," said the little girl, "but more importantly, I will teach you to read so you can help yourself."

The little girl kept her promise and came to help Story O'Mimus every day after school. It wasn't long at all until Story O'Mimus learned to read.

And to this day, Story O'Mimus loves to read—which brings to mind a puzzling question—how does he get those books?

Well, that answer we may never know for sure, but rumor has it that sometimes his bedtime stories last all night long!

Bookin' It Till Bedtime

Daytime, nighttime, anytime is book time! After introducing Story O'Mimus, recall the rumor that his bedtime stories lasted all night long. Plan a Bookin' It Till Bedtime Bash to celebrate books. (Featured in this section are some fun activities to enhance the bash.)

Story Snuggle

Encourage the children to choose their favorite book to share with their friends. After they have had a chance to tell why they made their selection, provide time for the children to snuggle up with a new found favorite.

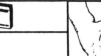

<u>Tricky Trivia</u>

Who was that dinosaur in the library? Whoever answers "Story O'Mimus" gets to ask the next question. Encourage the children to formulate questions to challenge each other with Story O'Mimus trivia. Not only is the game fun and challenging, but the children will be in the habit of looking and listening for details.

Examples: How many plates does he have down his back? (fourteen)

What is his favorite bedtime snack? (chocolate pizza)

How does he learn about his world? (reading)

Starry Story Nightshirts

Encourage the children to draw their favorite storybook characters on long, plain T-shirts using fabric paints. Glow-in-the-dark paint can add to the excitement.

Variation: Children paint the storybook characters on pillowcases and "dream the night away" with their favorite character.

Chocolate Pizza

⅔ cup butter or margarine
½ cup granulated sugar
½ cup brown sugar (firmly packed)
1 teaspoon vanilla extract
1 egg
½ teaspoon baking soda
½ teaspoon salt
1½ cups all-purpose flour
2 cups miniature marshmallows
¾ cup (6 oz.) jumbo semi-sweet chocolate chips

In a large bowl, cream together the margarine, granulated sugar, brown sugar, vanilla, egg, baking soda, and salt. Stir in flour. Spread the dough evenly over the bottom of an ungreased pizza pan. Pinch the edges to form a rim.

Bake at 375° for 10 minutes. Sprinkle the top with the marshmallows and chocolate chips and bake for an additional 5 to 8 minutes or until the marshmallows are melted and lightly browned. Cool and serve Story O'Mimus's favorite bedtime snack!

Mimic O'Mimus

(Tune: *The Muffin Man*)

Story O'Mimus says dance like me, dance like me, dance like me.

Story O'Mimus says dance like me.

Dance, dance, dance!

Children form a circle and take turns acting as Story O'Mimus, who stands in the center. "Story O'Mimus" performs an action for the others to mimic, such as shaking his tail, reading a book, or eating a friend.

Story O'Mimus, Mimus, Mimus

(Tune: *Miss Mary Mac*)

Story O'Mimus, Mimus, Mimus,
Carries his pack, pack, pack.
He has fourteen plates, plates, plates,
Up and down his back, back, back.

Count nineteen spots, spots, spots,
From head to tail, tail, tail.
When he stomps his feet, feet, feet,
His friends all wail, wail, wail.

Right on his snout, snout, snout,
He has one horn, horn, horn.
September second, second, second,
Was when he was born, born, born.

For a bedtime snack, snack, snack,
Before he reads, reads, reads,
It's chocolate pizza, pizza, pizza,
On which he feeds, feeds, feeds.

He is our friend, friend, friend.
No need to pout, pout, pout.
For Story O'Mimus, Mimus, Mimus,
Let's give a shout, shout, shout . . .
YEAH!

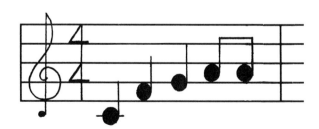

Stor - y O' Mi-mus

8

Five Little Dinosaurs

Five little dinosaurs tucked in bed.
One got a book and propped his head.
"Lights out!" called his mama
And then she said,
"No more reading! It's time for bed!"

Four little dinosaurs tucked in bed.
One got a book and propped his head.
"Lights out!" called his mama
And then she said,
"No more reading! It's time for bed!"

Three little dinosaurs tucked in bed.
One got a book and propped his head.
"Lights out!" called his mama
And then she said,
"No more reading! It's time for bed!"

Two little dinosaurs tucked in bed.
One got a book and propped his head.
"Lights out!" called his mama
And then she said,
"No more reading! It's time for bed!"

One little dinosaur tucked in bed.
He got a book and propped his head.
"Lights out!" called his mama
And then she said,
"No more reading! It's time for bed!"

No little dinosaurs reading in bed.
Then *Mama* pulled a book from under
   her head.
"Lights out!" called the dinosaurs,
"We heard what you said—
"No more reading! It's time for bed!"

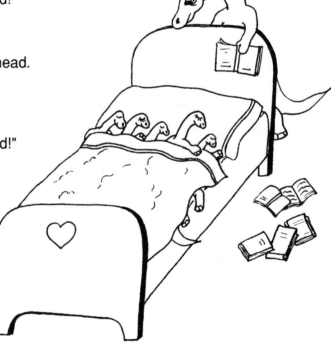

STORY O'MIMUS

asks

What is

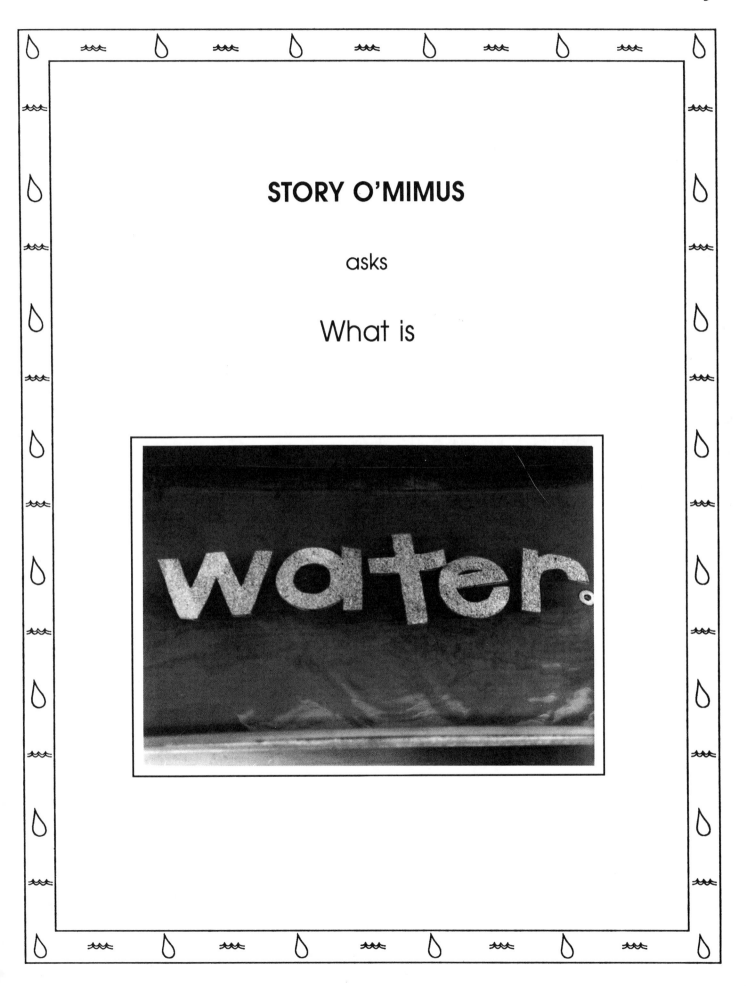

STORY O'MIMUS learns . . .

Water is needed by plants and animals to stay alive.

Water is all around.

Water is used in many ways.

Water has many properties.

Water needs to be conserved.

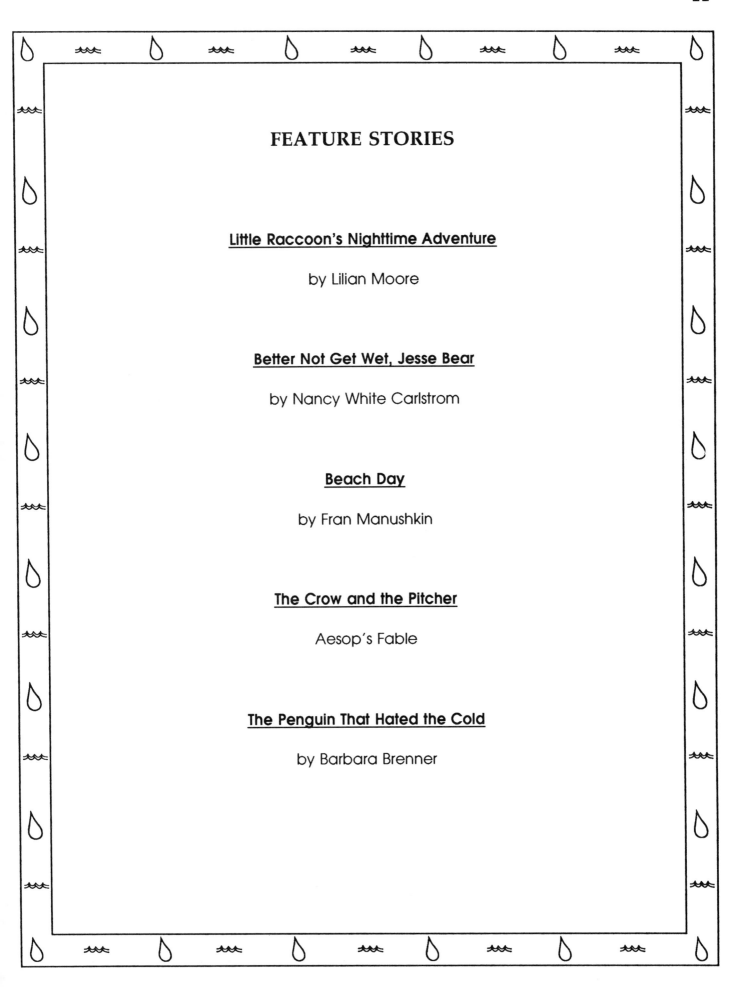

FEATURE STORIES

Little Raccoon's Nighttime Adventure

by Lilian Moore

Better Not Get Wet, Jesse Bear

by Nancy White Carlstrom

Beach Day

by Fran Manushkin

The Crow and the Pitcher

Aesop's Fable

The Penguin That Hated the Cold

by Barbara Brenner

PLANNING GUIDE

Feature Stories

LITTLE RACCOON'S NIGHTTIME ADVENTURE	Language Arts	Math	Science, Health, Social Studies	Motor
What Could It Be?	●			
Walk the Log			○	●
Puppet Play	○			●
Animal, Animal, Where Do You Live?	●		○	○
Is That Me I See?	○		●	
Musical Reflections	○			●
How Many in My Bag?		●		
Water Words from A to Z	●		○	
Jump the Stream				●
Rock Jumping	○	●		○
Hand Fishin'	●			○

BETTER NOT GET WET, JESSE BEAR	Language Arts	Math	Science, Health, Social Studies	Motor
Utensils with Holes			●	○
Act It Out	●			
Color It Wet	●			
Rhyme Time	●			
Slippery When Wet			●	
Fill It Up		●		○
Squirt a Shape		○		●
Never Swim Alone			●	
Drip, Drip, Drop	○	●		
Chant and Sort	●	○	○	
Will It Fit?		●		○
Dry or Drip			●	
Water Timer Race		●	○	○
Picture It Wet	○	●		○
Wet's the Word	●			
Floating Pebble Toss	○	○		●
Money Scoop		●		

Instructional Focus: ● = Primary   ○ = Secondary

BEACH DAY	Language Arts	Math	Science, Health, Social Studies	Motor
Wonderful Water			●	○
Car Wash	●	○		
Wet Sand, Dry Sand			●	○
What Will We Wipe With?		○	●	
What's Up?		○	●	
What's Missing?	●			
Did It Disappear?			●	
Size Match		●		
Water Movers		○	●	○
May I Have Your Order?		●		
Water Viewer			●	○
Water's Gone, Salt's Left			●	
Sink or Swim			●	
The Wet Look			●	
Water Safety			●	○
Shells, Shells		●		

THE CROW AND THE PITCHER	Language Arts	Math	Science, Health, Social Studies	Motor
It's Heavy!		○	●	
'Round and 'Round the Pebble		○		●
Thirst Quencher	○	○	●	
Bulge or Spill?			●	
Sink or Float			●	
Pass It Along		○		●
Water Magnifier			●	
Caw, Caw	○	●		
Ping Pong Spill Relay				●
Waterbreaker			○	●
Tip the Scales		●	○	
Read How It Happened	●			○

THE PENGUIN THAT HATED THE COLD	Language Arts	Math	Science, Health, Social Studies	Motor
Rescue Pablo			●	
Penguin Dive	●			○
Pablo, Put the Kettle On			●	○
Toss the Bottle				●
Water Solutions	○		●	
Geometric Ice		●		
Melt Down, Inch Up		●	○	
Enough Icebergs		●		
Clay Challenge			●	○
Boats, Boats, Boats		○		●
Penguin Pleasures	○	●		
Frozen Shapes			●	○
Count and Carry		○	●	○
Let's Go Fishing	●	○		○
Crunchy, Mushy Carrots		○	●	
Pablo's Opposites	●			○
Fish Pond		●		

MISCELLANEOUS	Language Arts	Math	Science, Health, Social Studies	Motor
Will It Fall Apart?			●	
What's That I Hear?	●			○
Sandbox Play				●
Frogs in a Pond				●
Sink or Float Gelatin	○	●	○	○
Water Play	●			
Knock 'Em Down				●
Clean Up			●	○
Sailing Ships	○	●		○
Man Overboard				●
Tug of War				●
Freeze	○			●
Where's the Salt?			●	

LITTLE RACCOON'S NIGHTTIME ADVENTURE

written by Lilian Moore

illustrated by Deborah Borgo

Western Publishing Company, Inc. (Golden Book)

ISBN 0-307-10255-6/ISBN 0-307-68255-2 (lib. bdg.)

adapted from

Little Raccoon and the Thing in the Pool

Summary:

This heartwarming story tells about a little raccoon who is sent to the stream to get dinner. Once there, Little Raccoon comes face-to-face with the thing in the pool, which the other forest animals have warned him about. After trying to scare it away without success, Little Raccoon hurries home to seek his mother's advice. She encourages him to return to the stream and try smiling at the thing. He does and finds that the thing in the pool was only his reflection.

What Could It Be?

During the first reading of the story, stop before the thing in the pool is revealed. Ask the children to guess what the thing in the pool could be. Encourage them to share their ideas before reading the story's ending.

Walk the Log

Children pretend to be Little Raccoon walking across the pool on the log, represented by a balance beam or a line on the floor. As they become confident crossing in different ways, such as forward, backward, and sideways, challenge them to cross as quickly as possible without falling. Aluminum foil can be placed under the beam for the children to see their reflections as they cross.

Puppet Play

Ask the children to recall the animals in the story. Provide materials for them to make a puppet of their favorite character. (Patterns are provided on pages 309–312.) These can be used with props (frown, stone, stick, and smile) to reenact the story.

Animal, Animal, Where Do You Live?

Place a string on the floor to represent a pond. Name animals that live in the water and others that do not. When an animal is named that lives in the water, the children jump into the "pond." Compile a list of those animals that live in the water. Ask the children to draw a picture of their favorite. The pictures can be displayed on a bulletin board or in a class book.

Is That Me I See?

Ask the children what the thing in the pool turned out to be. Gather them around a water table or small pool to see their reflections. Ask them to look for facial features, body movements, and clothing colors. Challenge the children to find their reflections in other places, such as windows or doors.

Musical Reflections

Children take turns pretending to be Little Raccoon crossing the log, represented by a balance beam or a line on the floor.

One child, acting as the reflection, faces the "log." As music is played, the "Little Raccoon" walks to the center of the "log," stops, and performs an action. The child who is on the "log" when the music stops becomes the new "reflection."

How Many in My Bag?

Choose small objects, such as little blocks or fish-shaped crackers, to represent crayfish. Put some "crayfish" into a bag. Ask the children to estimate the number of "crayfish" that were "caught." The child with the closest guess can be the next one to fill the bag.

Water Words from A to Z

Ask the children to brainstorm water-related words for each letter of the alphabet. Compile an alphabetical list.

Examples: A - alligator
           B - bathtub
           C - canoe

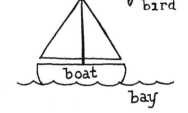

Jump the Stream

Place two strings on the floor to represent the banks of a stream. Challenge the children to jump over the "stream." Gradually widen the "stream" until all of the children have "fallen" in.

Rock Jumping

Cut several paper rocks and write a different numeral on each. Place them into a "stream" that has been made on the floor. Have the children take turns following oral directions.

Examples:

Jump to the 3 and then to the 5.

Jump on a rock and name the numeral.

Variation: Use this activity to review beginning sounds, sight words, letters of the alphabet, colors, or shapes.

Hand Fishin'

Fill a basin or pail with water. Muddy the water with a squirt of black tempera paint. Drop several items into the water. The children fish with their hands, using their sense of touch to identify the objects. Encourage them to describe their "catch."

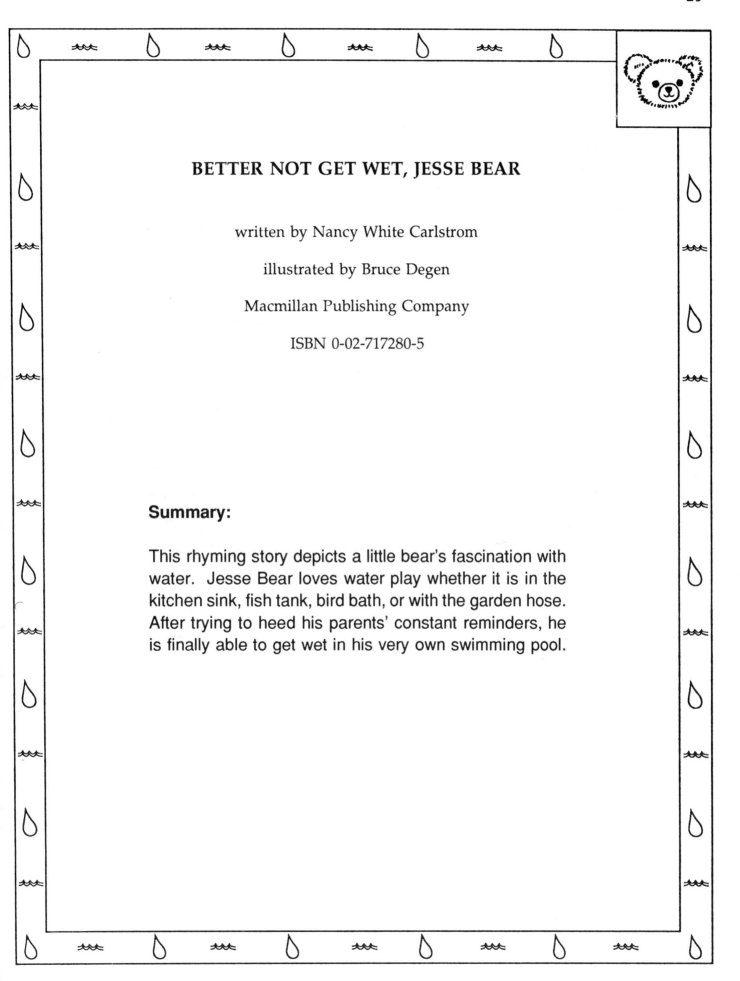

BETTER NOT GET WET, JESSE BEAR

written by Nancy White Carlstrom

illustrated by Bruce Degen

Macmillan Publishing Company

ISBN 0-02-717280-5

Summary:

This rhyming story depicts a little bear's fascination with water. Jesse Bear loves water play whether it is in the kitchen sink, fish tank, bird bath, or with the garden hose. After trying to heed his parents' constant reminders, he is finally able to get wet in his very own swimming pool.

Utensils with Holes

Provide a watering can similar to Jesse Bear's, other utensils that have holes (colanders, strainers, funnels, etc.), and a large container filled with water. Invite the children to freely explore the utensils in the water. Ask them to observe how the size and number of holes in the utensils affects the water flow.

Variation: Puncture holes in the bottom of plastic or cardboard containers to create homemade utensils for the children's use.

Act It Out

Ask the children what Jesse Bear did with water. The children take turns acting out their answers. Continue the charades with other water-related activities.

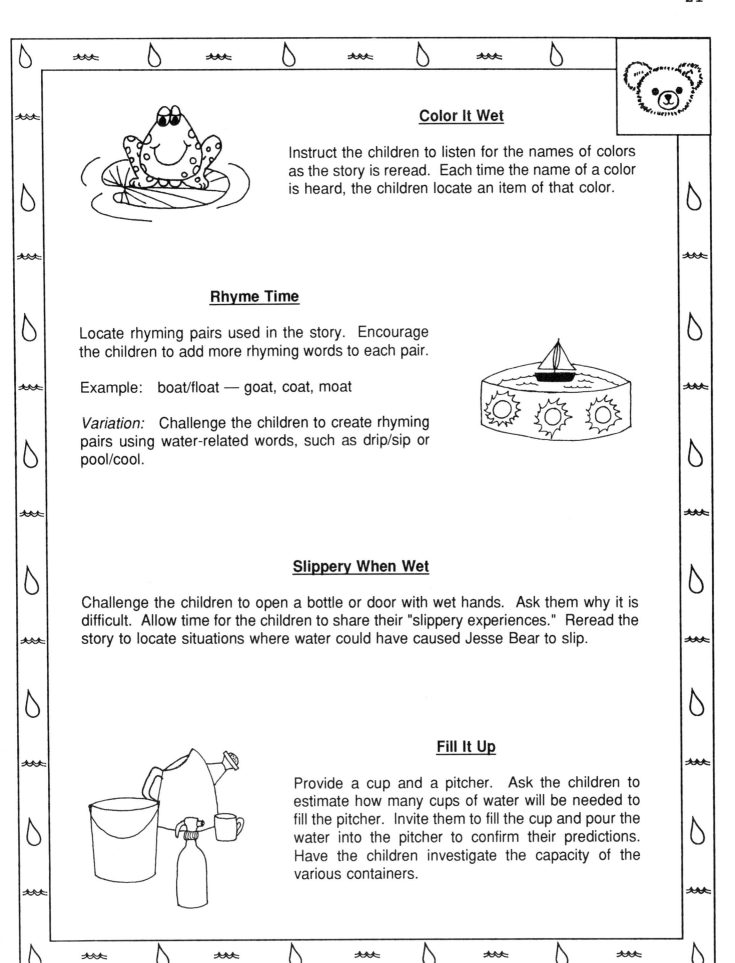

Color It Wet

Instruct the children to listen for the names of colors as the story is reread. Each time the name of a color is heard, the children locate an item of that color.

Rhyme Time

Locate rhyming pairs used in the story. Encourage the children to add more rhyming words to each pair.

Example: boat/float — goat, coat, moat

Variation: Challenge the children to create rhyming pairs using water-related words, such as drip/sip or pool/cool.

Slippery When Wet

Challenge the children to open a bottle or door with wet hands. Ask them why it is difficult. Allow time for the children to share their "slippery experiences." Reread the story to locate situations where water could have caused Jesse Bear to slip.

Fill It Up

Provide a cup and a pitcher. Ask the children to estimate how many cups of water will be needed to fill the pitcher. Invite them to fill the cup and pour the water into the pitcher to confirm their predictions. Have the children investigate the capacity of the various containers.

Squirt a Shape

Provide squirt bottles for the children to use during outside play. Encourage them to draw shapes on the sidewalk with the water in their bottles.

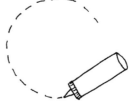

Never Swim Alone

Ask the children why Jesse Bear's parents stayed with him when he played in his pool. Discuss the reasons people should never swim alone. Allow time for the children to share their swimming experiences.

Drip, Drip, Drop

Identify water sounds in the story. Ask the children to create and repeat verbal patterns using two or more of the sounds. Encourage them to recreate the patterns visually with manipulatives or actions.

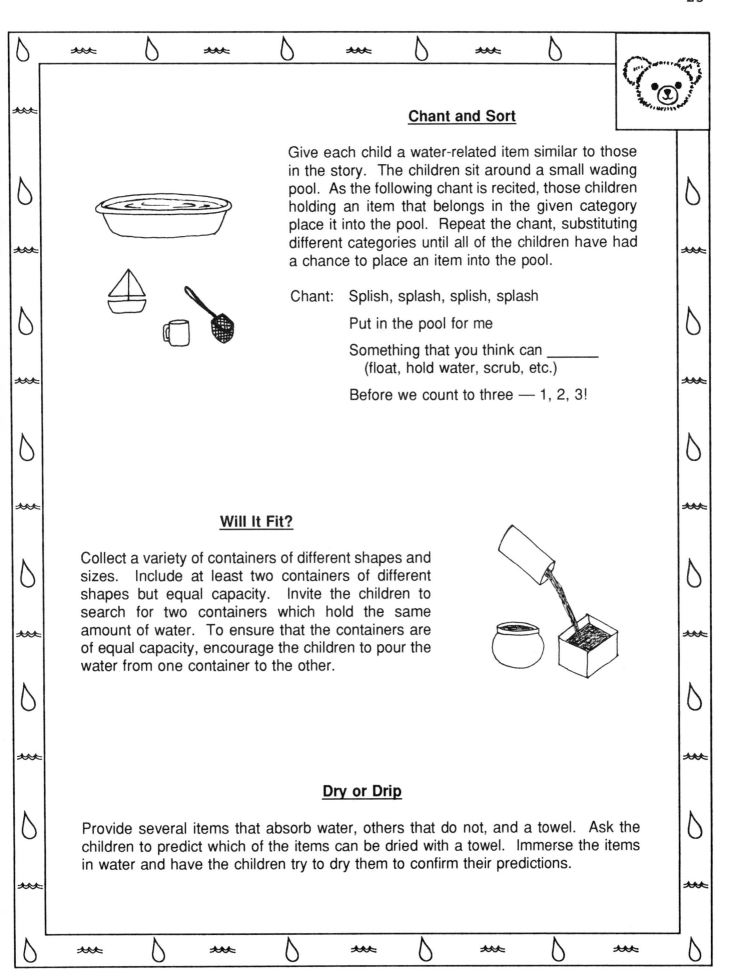

Chant and Sort

Give each child a water-related item similar to those in the story. The children sit around a small wading pool. As the following chant is recited, those children holding an item that belongs in the given category place it into the pool. Repeat the chant, substituting different categories until all of the children have had a chance to place an item into the pool.

Chant: Splish, splash, splish, splash

          Put in the pool for me

          Something that you think can _____
            (float, hold water, scrub, etc.)

          Before we count to three — 1, 2, 3!

Will It Fit?

Collect a variety of containers of different shapes and sizes. Include at least two containers of different shapes but equal capacity. Invite the children to search for two containers which hold the same amount of water. To ensure that the containers are of equal capacity, encourage the children to pour the water from one container to the other.

Dry or Drip

Provide several items that absorb water, others that do not, and a towel. Ask the children to predict which of the items can be dried with a towel. Immerse the items in water and have the children try to dry them to confirm their predictions.

Water Timer Race

Punch a hole in a jar lid and place it in a container of water. Challenge the children to perform a specific task before the lid sinks to the bottom of the container. (The lid might need a slight "push-start.")

Examples: How many cups of water can be transferred from one container to another without spilling?

How many pegs can be placed in a pegboard?

Picture It Wet

Recall the many ways Jesse Bear had fun with water. Ask the children to illustrate their favorite water activity from the story. Construct a graph, using their pictures.

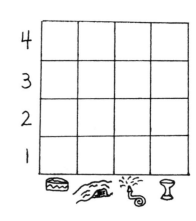

Wet's the Word

Give each child a small cup of water. Instruct the children to listen for the word "wet" as the story is reread. Each time they hear the word "wet," they sip water from their cups. Encourage the children to make their water last the duration of the story.

Floating Pebble Toss

Collect small styrofoam meat trays. Label each with a letter, numeral, shape, or word. Float the trays in a container of water. Challenge the children to toss a pebble underhand onto a tray, identifying the figure.

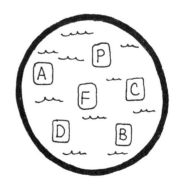

26

Money Scoop

Provide a fishbowl of water. Add pennies, nickels, and dimes. The children take turns scooping up coins with a small fish net. Ask them to sort and then count the number of pennies, nickels, and dimes in their "catch."

Variation: Children determine the value of their scoop.

BEACH DAY

written by Fran Manushkin

illustrated by Kathy Wilburn

Western Publishing Company, Inc. (Golden Book)

ISBN 0-307-02170-X/ISBN 0-307-60153-6 (lib. bdg.)

Summary:

This touching story tells of a little girl's special day with her family. In the morning she watches her daddy wash the car. The remainder of the day is spent at the beach with her mom and dad. They play in the water, walk on the beach, and collect shells. As the sun begins to set, the family heads for home. The little girl drifts off to sleep with the day's memories floating in her head.

Wonderful Water

Recall the ways water was used in the story. Ask the children how water affects their daily lives. Encourage them to illustrate the many uses of water.

Car Wash

Draw a large car on a chalkboard or make a gameboard using a laminated picture of a car. Write words on the car. Using a sponge, the children take turns wiping off the words they can identify.

Variation: Use this activity for alphabet, numeral, or shape recognition.

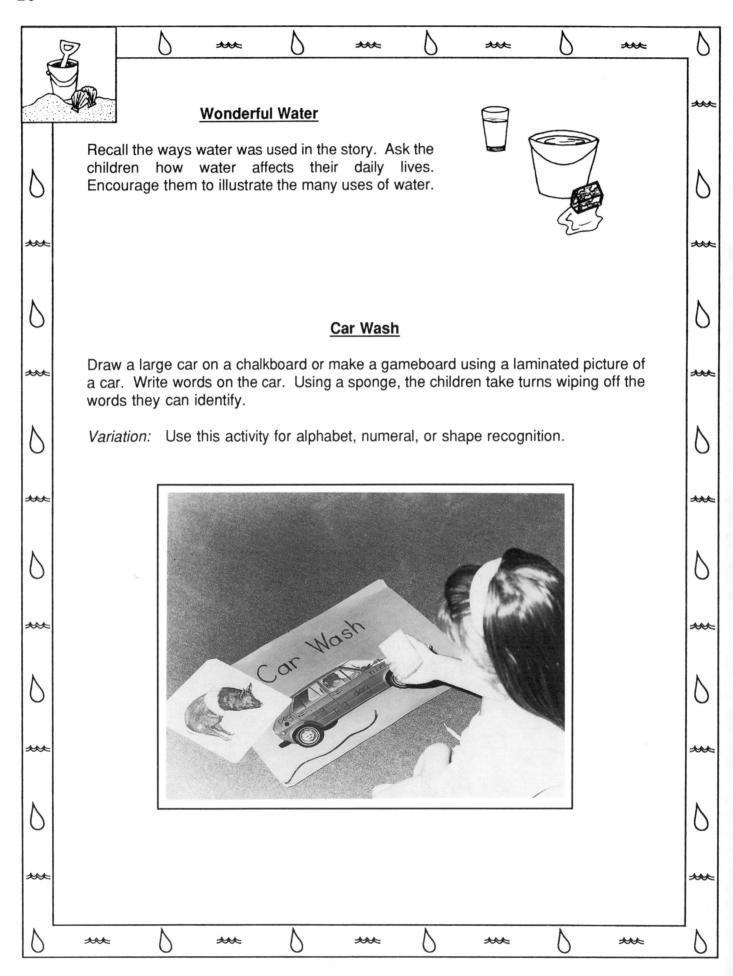

Wet Sand, Dry Sand

Provide two basins of dry sand. Add water to one of the basins until the sand is saturated. Ask the children to feel the sand in each basin and compare the texture, color, and temperature. Allow time for them to explore the many things that can be done with wet and dry sand.

What Will We Wipe With?

Ask the children why the little girl sat on a towel in the car. Provide an assortment of materials such as paper towels, waxed paper, sponges, newspapers, and a variety of cloth swatches. Spoon water onto a table to form small puddles. Have the children experiment wiping the spills to determine which materials absorb the most water.

Variation: Help develop little consumer minds by challenging the children to test different brands of paper towels to determine which brand absorbs the most water.

What's Up?

Using two identical sponges, saturate one with water. Place the sponges on opposite ends of a balance scale. The children observe the weight difference between the wet and dry sponge. Continue this activity using other materials such as washcloths, napkins, or sand.

What's Missing?

Place five or six beach-related items into a water table or wading pool. Allow time for the children to view the items before asking them to close their eyes. Remove one item and place it out of sight. Instruct the children to open their eyes to determine which item is missing. Repeat the activity, removing different objects.

Did It Disappear?

Provide several clear jars of water. Add a small amount of salt to one of the jars and shake. Ask the children to watch what happens to the salt. Provide other substances such as sand, pepper, sugar, or oil for the children to add to the remaining jars. Encourage them to discuss how each substance reacted with the water.

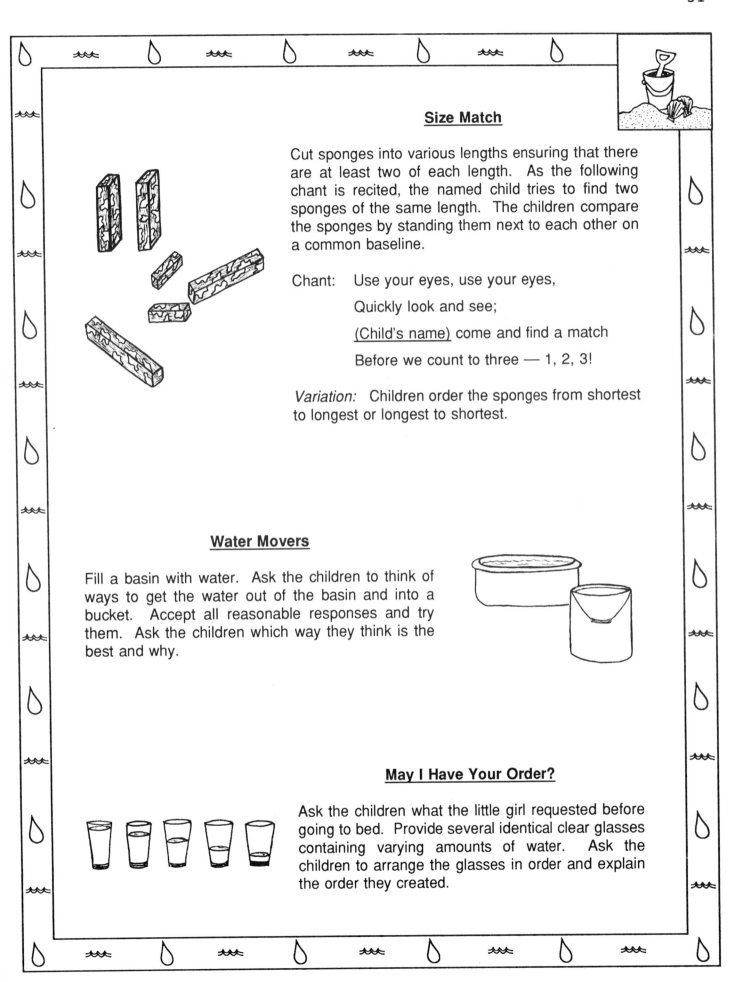

Size Match

Cut sponges into various lengths ensuring that there are at least two of each length. As the following chant is recited, the named child tries to find two sponges of the same length. The children compare the sponges by standing them next to each other on a common baseline.

Chant: Use your eyes, use your eyes,

Quickly look and see;

(Child's name) come and find a match

Before we count to three — 1, 2, 3!

Variation: Children order the sponges from shortest to longest or longest to shortest.

Water Movers

Fill a basin with water. Ask the children to think of ways to get the water out of the basin and into a bucket. Accept all reasonable responses and try them. Ask the children which way they think is the best and why.

May I Have Your Order?

Ask the children what the little girl requested before going to bed. Provide several identical clear glasses containing varying amounts of water. Ask the children to arrange the glasses in order and explain the order they created.

Water Viewer

Ask the children what they think the little girl saw when she looked under the water. Provide plastic wrap, cylindrical containers with the tops and bottoms removed (juice cans, plastic bottles, etc.), and rubber bands. Help each child place a piece of plastic wrap over one end of a cylinder and secure it with a rubber band. Invite the children to look through their viewers at the objects under the water.

Water's Gone, Salt's Left

Ask the children to recall how the beach water tasted to the little girl. Put some salty water in a shallow pan in the sun. After several hours, check the pan and discuss the findings. Let the children taste the salt that remains in the pan.

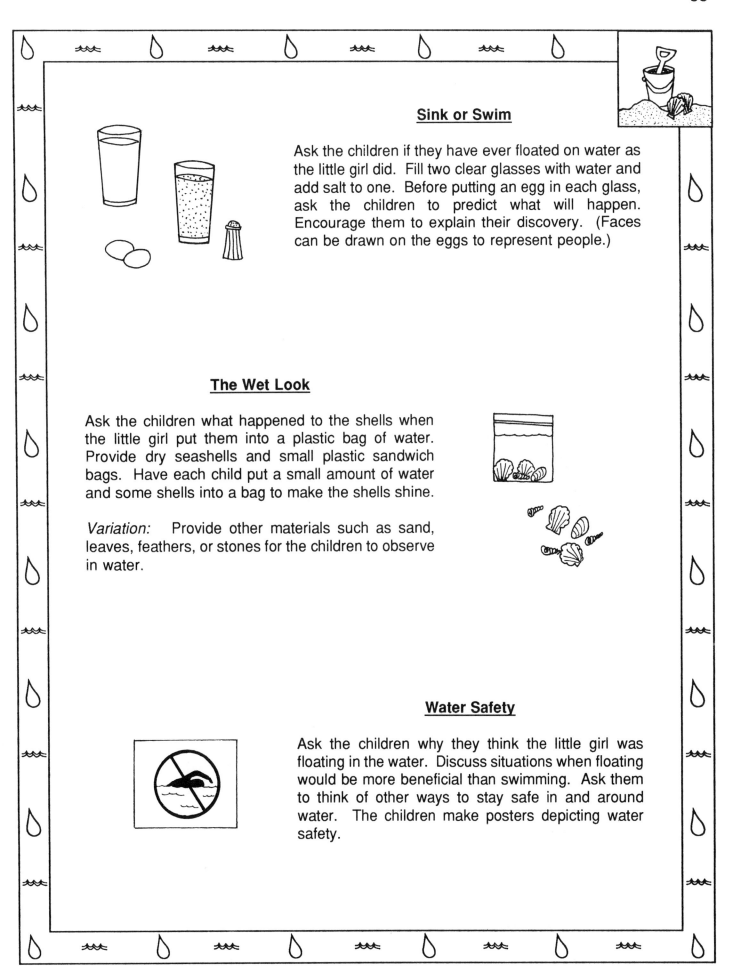

Sink or Swim

Ask the children if they have ever floated on water as the little girl did. Fill two clear glasses with water and add salt to one. Before putting an egg in each glass, ask the children to predict what will happen. Encourage them to explain their discovery. (Faces can be drawn on the eggs to represent people.)

The Wet Look

Ask the children what happened to the shells when the little girl put them into a plastic bag of water. Provide dry seashells and small plastic sandwich bags. Have each child put a small amount of water and some shells into a bag to make the shells shine.

Variation: Provide other materials such as sand, leaves, feathers, or stones for the children to observe in water.

Water Safety

Ask the children why they think the little girl was floating in the water. Discuss situations when floating would be more beneficial than swimming. Ask them to think of other ways to stay safe in and around water. The children make posters depicting water safety.

Shells, Shells

Provide five to ten seashells for each child. Working in pairs, each player places any number of the shells on the floor as the following chant is recited:

Shells, shells,

on the shore;

Are there less

or are there more?

One child then spins a spinner—one half labeled "more" and one half labeled "less." If the spinner points to "more," the child who has the most shells takes the opponent's shells. If the spinner points to "less," the child who has fewer shells takes the opponent's shells.

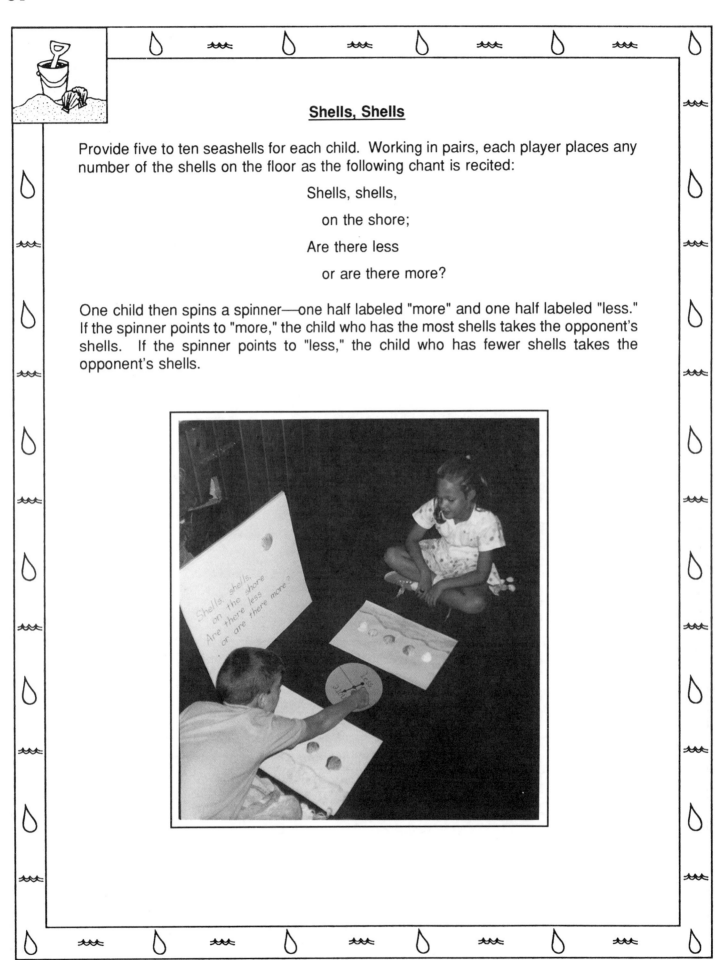

THE CROW AND THE PITCHER

Aesop's Fable

well-illustrated version included in

Tales from Aesop

Random House, Inc.

ISBN 0-394-82812-7

Summary:

This fable tells the story of a very thirsty crow who finds a pitcher of water. As he tries to take a drink, he realizes the water is too low for him to reach. Just as the crow is about to give up, he spies some pebbles nearby. The clever crow solves his problem by dropping pebbles into the pitcher until the water level rises high enough for him to get a drink.

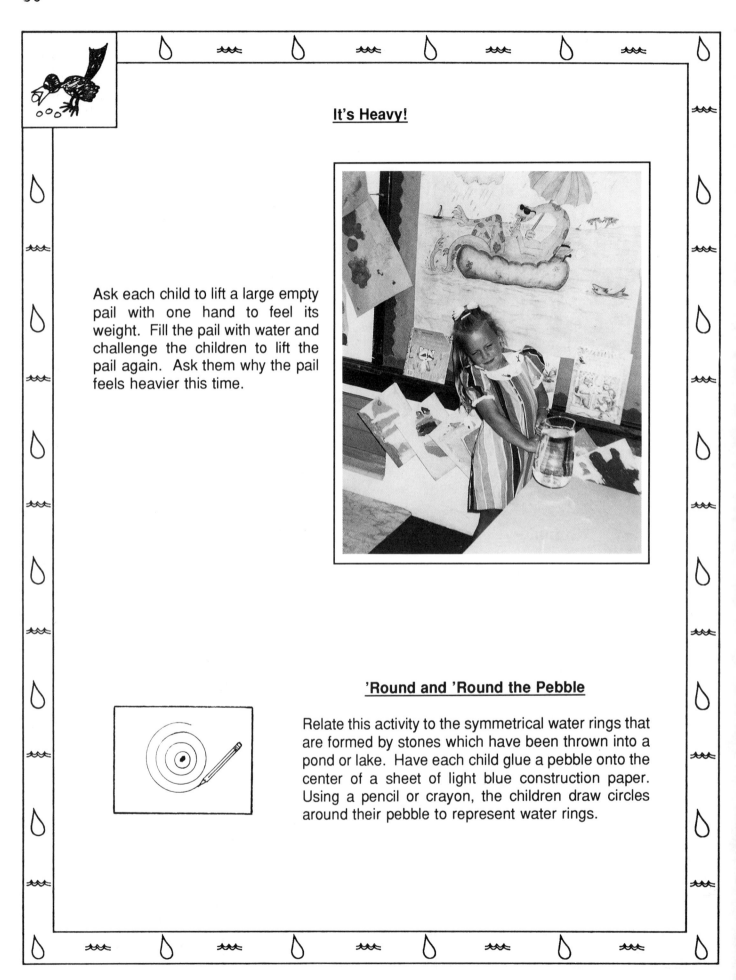

It's Heavy!

Ask each child to lift a large empty pail with one hand to feel its weight. Fill the pail with water and challenge the children to lift the pail again. Ask them why the pail feels heavier this time.

'Round and 'Round the Pebble

Relate this activity to the symmetrical water rings that are formed by stones which have been thrown into a pond or lake. Have each child glue a pebble onto the center of a sheet of light blue construction paper. Using a pencil or crayon, the children draw circles around their pebble to represent water rings.

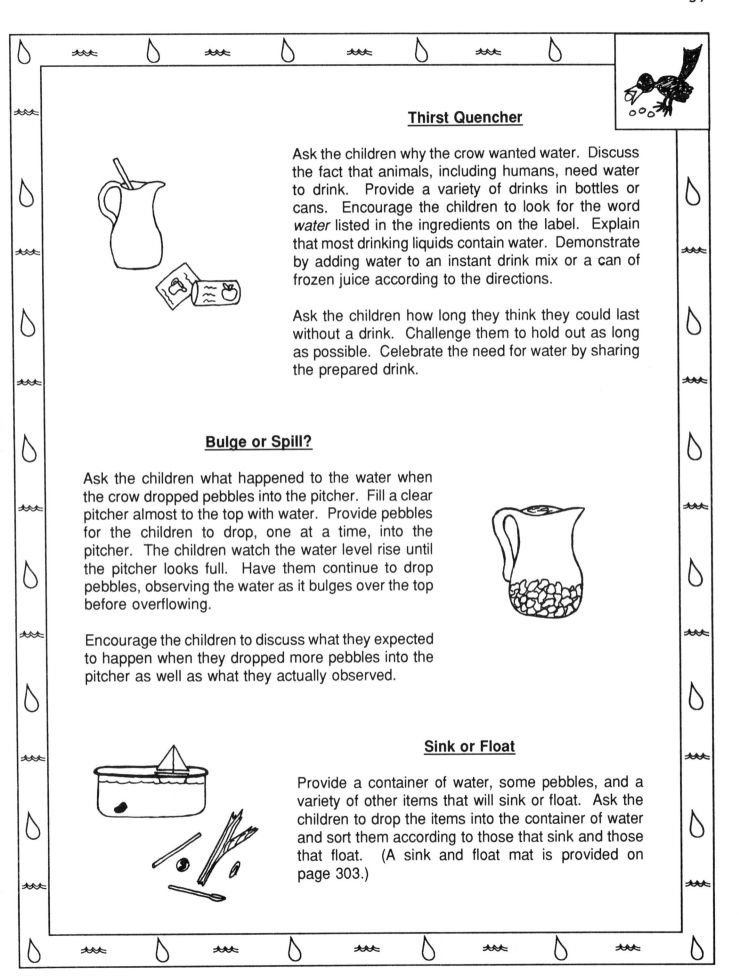

Thirst Quencher

Ask the children why the crow wanted water. Discuss the fact that animals, including humans, need water to drink. Provide a variety of drinks in bottles or cans. Encourage the children to look for the word *water* listed in the ingredients on the label. Explain that most drinking liquids contain water. Demonstrate by adding water to an instant drink mix or a can of frozen juice according to the directions.

Ask the children how long they think they could last without a drink. Challenge them to hold out as long as possible. Celebrate the need for water by sharing the prepared drink.

Bulge or Spill?

Ask the children what happened to the water when the crow dropped pebbles into the pitcher. Fill a clear pitcher almost to the top with water. Provide pebbles for the children to drop, one at a time, into the pitcher. The children watch the water level rise until the pitcher looks full. Have them continue to drop pebbles, observing the water as it bulges over the top before overflowing.

Encourage the children to discuss what they expected to happen when they dropped more pebbles into the pitcher as well as what they actually observed.

Sink or Float

Provide a container of water, some pebbles, and a variety of other items that will sink or float. Ask the children to drop the items into the container of water and sort them according to those that sink and those that float. (A sink and float mat is provided on page 303.)

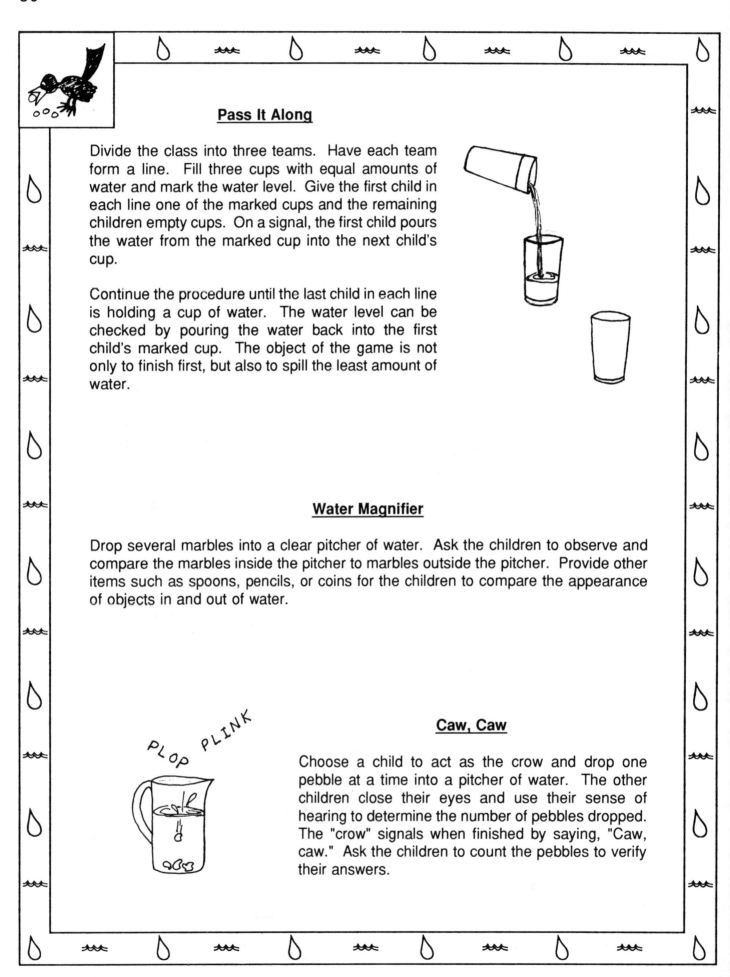

Pass It Along

Divide the class into three teams. Have each team form a line. Fill three cups with equal amounts of water and mark the water level. Give the first child in each line one of the marked cups and the remaining children empty cups. On a signal, the first child pours the water from the marked cup into the next child's cup.

Continue the procedure until the last child in each line is holding a cup of water. The water level can be checked by pouring the water back into the first child's marked cup. The object of the game is not only to finish first, but also to spill the least amount of water.

Water Magnifier

Drop several marbles into a clear pitcher of water. Ask the children to observe and compare the marbles inside the pitcher to marbles outside the pitcher. Provide other items such as spoons, pencils, or coins for the children to compare the appearance of objects in and out of water.

Caw, Caw

Choose a child to act as the crow and drop one pebble at a time into a pitcher of water. The other children close their eyes and use their sense of hearing to determine the number of pebbles dropped. The "crow" signals when finished by saying, "Caw, caw." Ask the children to count the pebbles to verify their answers.

Ping Pong Spill Relay

Divide the class into two teams. Provide each team with a plastic cup and two large containers—one filled with water and the other with many ping pong balls. Place the containers of water at the starting line and the containers of ping pong balls approximately 30 feet from the line. Give a cup to the first player on each team. On a signal from the starter, the players use their cup to scoop up water, run to their team's container of balls, pour the water into the container, then return to their team. The object of the game is to be the first team to raise the water level enough to spill all of the balls out of the container.

Waterbreaker

Divide the class into small groups. Provide each group with a cup of water and many pebbles. The children take turns adding one pebble at a time to the cup of water. The object is to drop the pebble into the cup, trying not to spill the water. Vary the water level each time the game begins.

Tip the Scales

Provide a balance scale and many identical sized cups with lids. Fill one cup with water and place it on the scale. Provide a variety of materials such as cubes, pegs, sand, or clay. Challenge each child to use one kind of item to fill a cup that will be heavier than the cup of water. The children verify their predictions on the balance scale.

Read How It Happened

Recall the events in the story. Have the children illustrate the events and sequence them to make a class book.

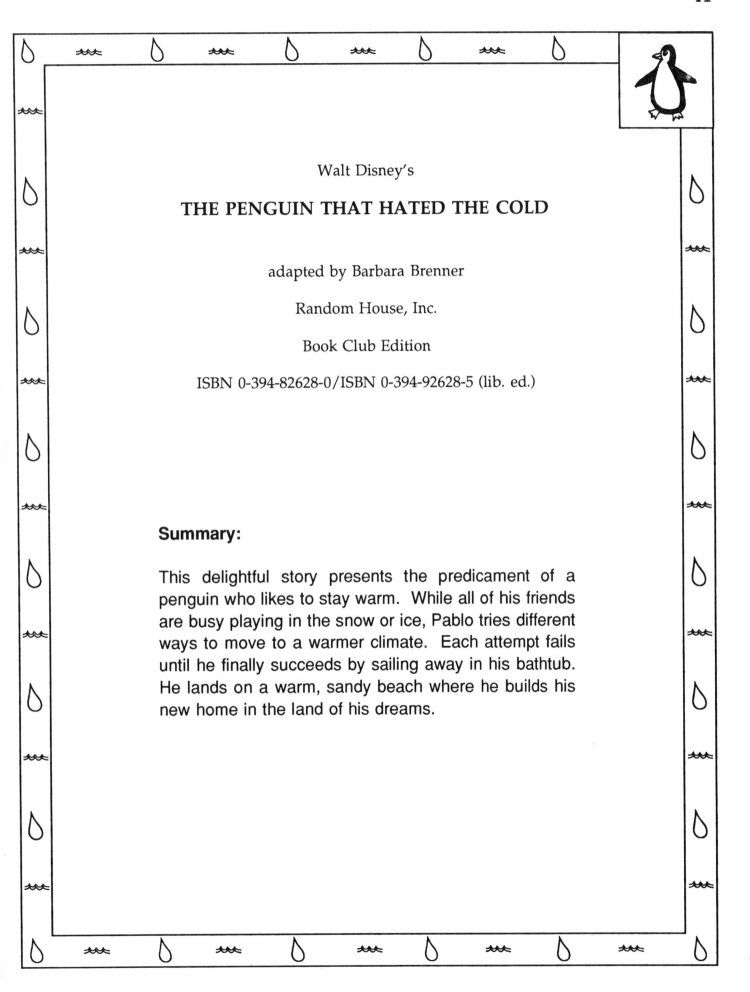

Walt Disney's

THE PENGUIN THAT HATED THE COLD

adapted by Barbara Brenner

Random House, Inc.

Book Club Edition

ISBN 0-394-82628-0/ISBN 0-394-92628-5 (lib. ed.)

Summary:

This delightful story presents the predicament of a penguin who likes to stay warm. While all of his friends are busy playing in the snow or ice, Pablo tries different ways to move to a warmer climate. Each attempt fails until he finally succeeds by sailing away in his bathtub. He lands on a warm, sandy beach where he builds his new home in the land of his dreams.

Rescue Pablo

Ask the children what Pablo's friends did to help him thaw when he was frozen. Use small plastic animals frozen in ice cubes to represent Pablo. Divide the class into small groups and give each a cup containing a frozen animal cube. Challenge each group to be the first to rescue "Pablo."

Penguin Dive

Lay craft sticks on a table to form a ladder. Write a word on each rung. Provide a penguin to climb the ladder. As a child correctly identifies a word, the penguin moves to the next rung. When the top of the ladder is reached, the child's penguin "dives" into a tub of water. (A small penguin pattern is provided on page 313.)

Variation: Children climb a class slide and land in a make-believe pool.

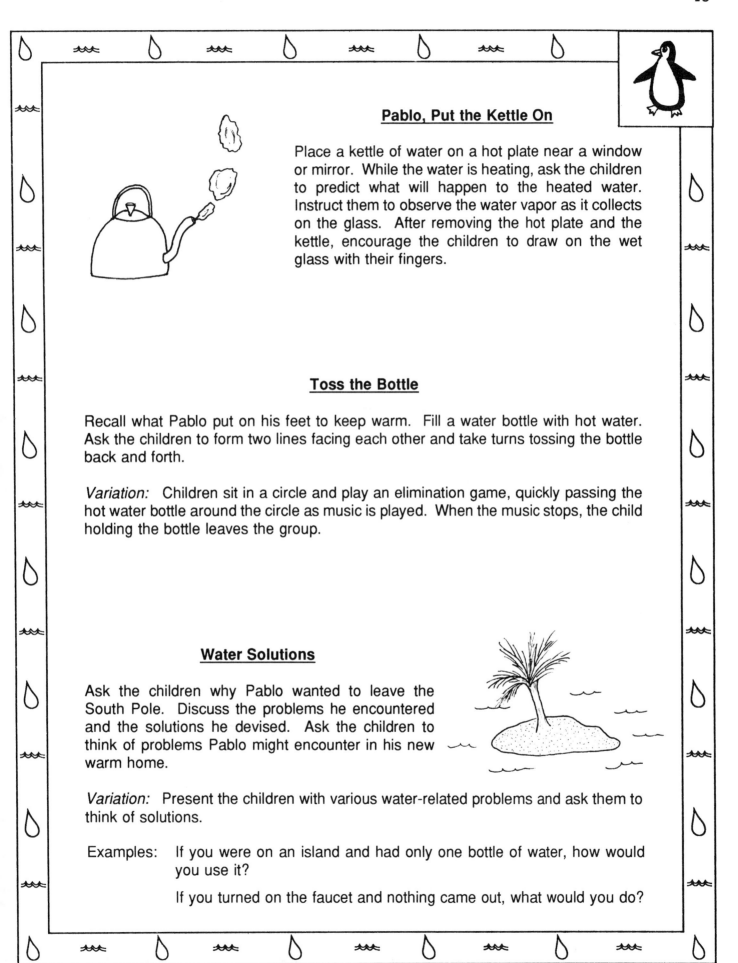

Pablo, Put the Kettle On

Place a kettle of water on a hot plate near a window or mirror. While the water is heating, ask the children to predict what will happen to the heated water. Instruct them to observe the water vapor as it collects on the glass. After removing the hot plate and the kettle, encourage the children to draw on the wet glass with their fingers.

Toss the Bottle

Recall what Pablo put on his feet to keep warm. Fill a water bottle with hot water. Ask the children to form two lines facing each other and take turns tossing the bottle back and forth.

Variation: Children sit in a circle and play an elimination game, quickly passing the hot water bottle around the circle as music is played. When the music stops, the child holding the bottle leaves the group.

Water Solutions

Ask the children why Pablo wanted to leave the South Pole. Discuss the problems he encountered and the solutions he devised. Ask the children to think of problems Pablo might encounter in his new warm home.

Variation: Present the children with various water-related problems and ask them to think of solutions.

Examples: If you were on an island and had only one bottle of water, how would you use it?

If you turned on the faucet and nothing came out, what would you do?

Geometric Ice

Freeze water in various containers to make cubes, cylinders, and cones. Remove the ice from the containers and ask the children to match the frozen geometric shapes to the original containers. Brainstorm other items that have the same shapes.

Examples:

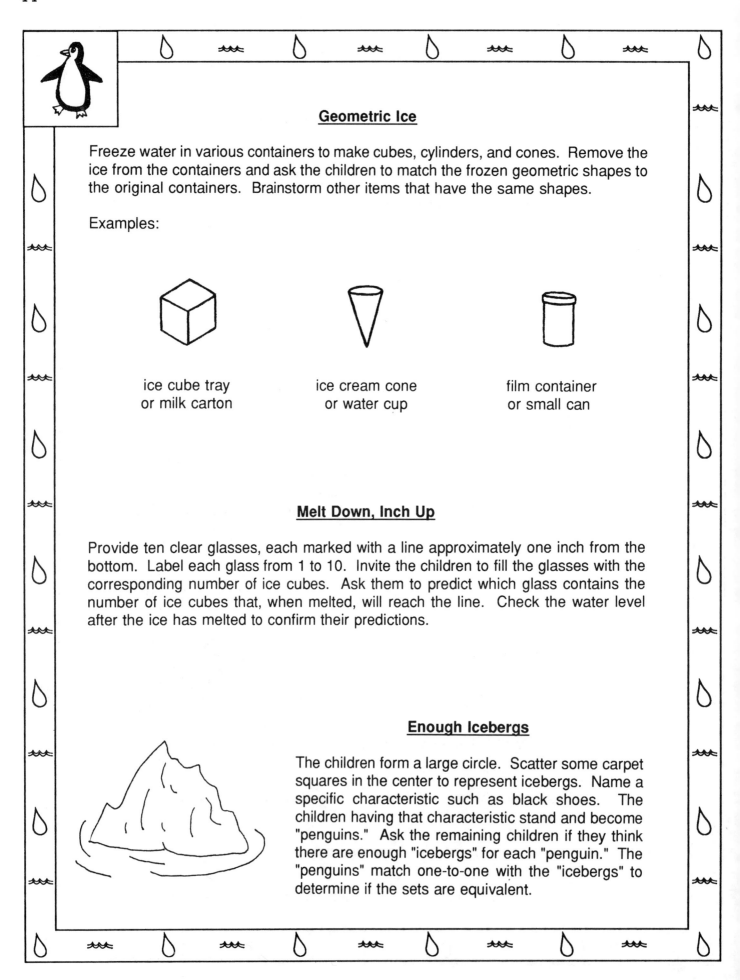

ice cube tray
or milk carton

ice cream cone
or water cup

film container
or small can

Melt Down, Inch Up

Provide ten clear glasses, each marked with a line approximately one inch from the bottom. Label each glass from 1 to 10. Invite the children to fill the glasses with the corresponding number of ice cubes. Ask them to predict which glass contains the number of ice cubes that, when melted, will reach the line. Check the water level after the ice has melted to confirm their predictions.

Enough Icebergs

The children form a large circle. Scatter some carpet squares in the center to represent icebergs. Name a specific characteristic such as black shoes. The children having that characteristic stand and become "penguins." Ask the remaining children if they think there are enough "icebergs" for each "penguin." The "penguins" match one-to-one with the "icebergs" to determine if the sets are equivalent.

Clay Challenge

Ask the children if they think a ball of clay will float or sink. Test their predictions by dropping a ball of clay into water. After watching the ball sink, challenge the children to mold a piece of clay into a shape that will float.

Boats, Boats, Boats

Provide a variety of materials such as wood scraps, milk cartons, styrofoam trays, straws, or craft sticks for the children to design their own boats. Challenge the children to move the boats without touching them (blowing on the boats, propelling them with egg beaters, swirling their hands in the water, etc.).

Variation: Challenge the children to make the tallest boat that will still float.

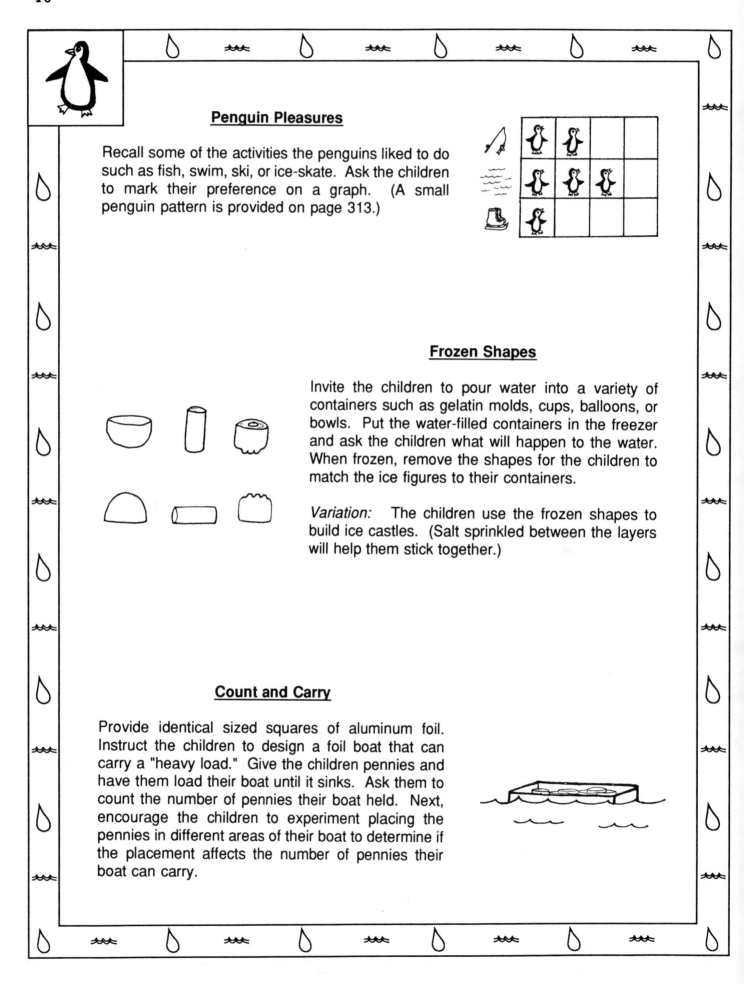

Penguin Pleasures

Recall some of the activities the penguins liked to do such as fish, swim, ski, or ice-skate. Ask the children to mark their preference on a graph. (A small penguin pattern is provided on page 313.)

Frozen Shapes

Invite the children to pour water into a variety of containers such as gelatin molds, cups, balloons, or bowls. Put the water-filled containers in the freezer and ask the children what will happen to the water. When frozen, remove the shapes for the children to match the ice figures to their containers.

Variation: The children use the frozen shapes to build ice castles. (Salt sprinkled between the layers will help them stick together.)

Count and Carry

Provide identical sized squares of aluminum foil. Instruct the children to design a foil boat that can carry a "heavy load." Give the children pennies and have them load their boat until it sinks. Ask them to count the number of pennies their boat held. Next, encourage the children to experiment placing the pennies in different areas of their boat to determine if the placement affects the number of pennies their boat can carry.

Let's Go Fishing

The children take turns pretending to be penguins fishing in the icy water. Provide many colored fish "swimming" in a container of water, a fishing pole, and color word cards. After a fish is caught, it is matched to the corresponding color word card.

Variation: This activity can be used to review letters or numerals.

Crunchy, Mushy Carrots

Cut carrots into small pieces. Put a portion of the cut carrots into a bowl of cold water. Cook the remaining pieces in one inch of boiling, salted water for 10 to 15 minutes. Ask the children to sample the raw and cooked carrots to compare the color, temperature, and texture.

Pablo's Opposites

Ask the children to complete the following sentences as they recall some of Pablo's experiences.

Most penguins like the weather <u>cold</u>, but Pablo likes the weather _____.

Pablo tried to ski <u>forward</u>, but the stove pulled him _____.

When Pablo tried to go <u>up</u>, he found himself coming back _____.

Most penguins play <u>outside</u>, but Pablo would rather play _____.

Pablo sailed in the <u>day</u> and even in the _____.

He had many clothes <u>on</u> until the sun made him take them _____.

Pablo hoped the tub would <u>float</u>, but the hole in the bottom made it _____.

Invite the children to create illustrations and assemble the pages into a class opposites book.

Fish Pond

Children work in pairs. Provide a bowl of fish-shaped crackers, two "ponds," and a teacher-made die (a cube with the sides labeled: +1, -1, +2, -2, +3, -3) for each pair. The children take turns rolling the die to determine whether to add or subtract crackers. The children may eat the crackers when they have accumulated five in their pond. A time limit can be set or play can continue until the bowl is empty. (A pond mat is provided on page 308.)

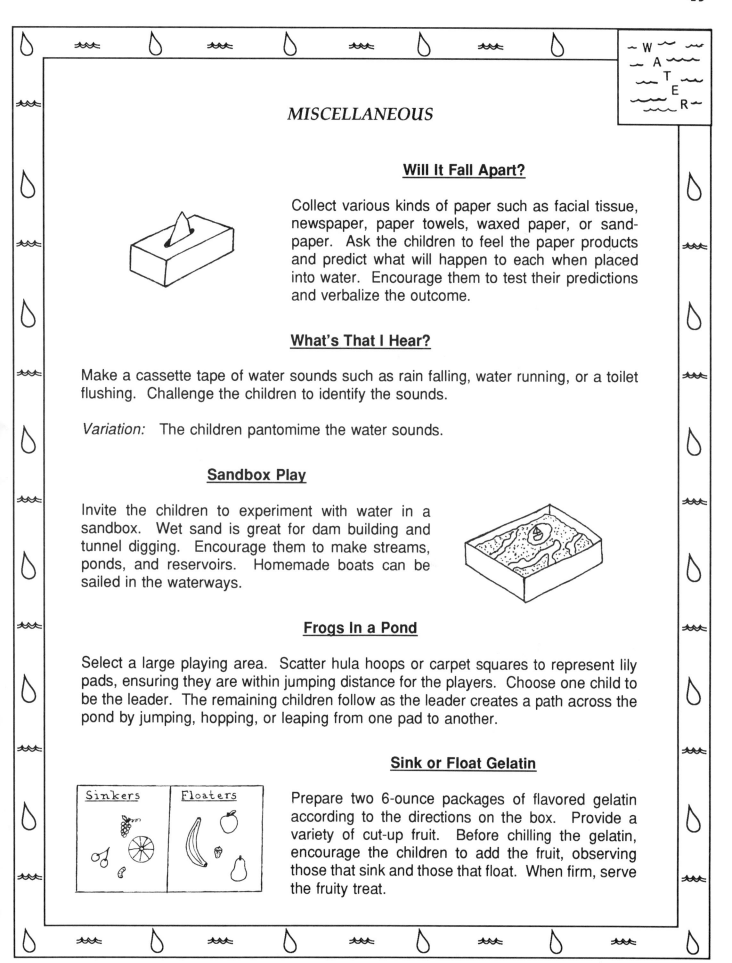

MISCELLANEOUS

Will It Fall Apart?

Collect various kinds of paper such as facial tissue, newspaper, paper towels, waxed paper, or sandpaper. Ask the children to feel the paper products and predict what will happen to each when placed into water. Encourage them to test their predictions and verbalize the outcome.

What's That I Hear?

Make a cassette tape of water sounds such as rain falling, water running, or a toilet flushing. Challenge the children to identify the sounds.

Variation: The children pantomime the water sounds.

Sandbox Play

Invite the children to experiment with water in a sandbox. Wet sand is great for dam building and tunnel digging. Encourage them to make streams, ponds, and reservoirs. Homemade boats can be sailed in the waterways.

Frogs In a Pond

Select a large playing area. Scatter hula hoops or carpet squares to represent lily pads, ensuring they are within jumping distance for the players. Choose one child to be the leader. The remaining children follow as the leader creates a path across the pond by jumping, hopping, or leaping from one pad to another.

Sink or Float Gelatin

Prepare two 6-ounce packages of flavored gelatin according to the directions on the box. Provide a variety of cut-up fruit. Before chilling the gelatin, encourage the children to add the fruit, observing those that sink and those that float. When firm, serve the fruity treat.

Water Play

Add items such as a watering can and plants, a doll bottle, empty detergent bottles, sponges, and rags to the housekeeping center. Encourage the children to role-play uses of water.

Knock 'Em Down

Place several non-breakable lightweight objects on large blocks or a table top. Challenge the children to spray water from trigger bottles to knock down the targets.

Clean Up

Give the children opportunities to wash things in their classroom such as tables, chairs, toys, or shelves. First, have them use only water. Then add soap. Ask the children to compare both ways.

Sailing Ships

14 hard boiled eggs
½ cup mayonnaise
14 slices of American cheese
½ teaspoon salt
½ teaspoon dry mustard

Cut the eggs in half lengthwise. Place the yolks in a dish and mash them with a fork. Add salt, dry mustard, and mayonnaise. Mix the ingredients together and use the mixture to fill the white halves. Cut the square slices of cheese in half diagonally. Attach toothpicks to the triangular slices of cheese to represent sails and insert them into the egg halves.

Man Overboard

Form two rows of chairs back-to-back to represent a boat. Provide enough chairs so that each child has a seat. Direct the children to stand. Remove one chair, then ask if there are more chairs or more children. As music plays, the children walk around the chairs. When the music stops, they quickly sit in the chair nearest to them. One child will be without a seat. The children shout, "Man overboard!" as the child pretends to swim away. The game continues until one child remains sitting in the "boat."

Variation: To ensure success for all, the game can be played allowing the child without a seat to sit on a classmate's lap. The game continues until each seat is occupied by two children.

Tug of War

Divide the class into two teams. Draw a river on the floor. Provide a tug of war rope and have each team hold an opposite end. On a signal, both teams pull, trying to make the other team "fall into the river." ("Tug a Tug," listed in the Well-Known Recordings can be played, if desired.)

Freeze

The children scatter around the room pretending to swim, skate, ski, or perform other water-related activities until a leader calls, "Freeze!" The children "freeze" until the leader calls, "Melt!" Play continues.

Variation: Substitute music. When the music is playing, the children remain in motion. When the music stops, they "freeze." ("Freeze," listed in the Well-Known Recordings can be played, if desired.)

Where's the Salt?

Ask the children how oceans and lakes differ. Locate bodies of water on a globe of the earth. Provide two bowls of water and add salt to one. Invite the children to taste the water in each bowl. Explain that most of the water covering the earth's surface is salty. Guide the children to discuss the need to conserve water.

ART

Wet Paper Creations

The children drip paint from a brush or squeeze bottle onto wet paper to create interesting designs.

Variation: Children chalk or paint on wet paper.

Crayon Resist

Suggest the children draw an underwater scene with crayons on white construction paper. Instruct them to press hard with the crayons. Apply a coat of diluted blue tempera or watercolor over the paper using a cloth or brush. The paint will be resisted by the crayon and will color only the background of the picture.

Sponge Painting

Children paint with wet or dry sponges that have been dipped in thickened tempera. Invite them to try different techniques. Patting gives an airy effect, while sweeping motions make bold lines.

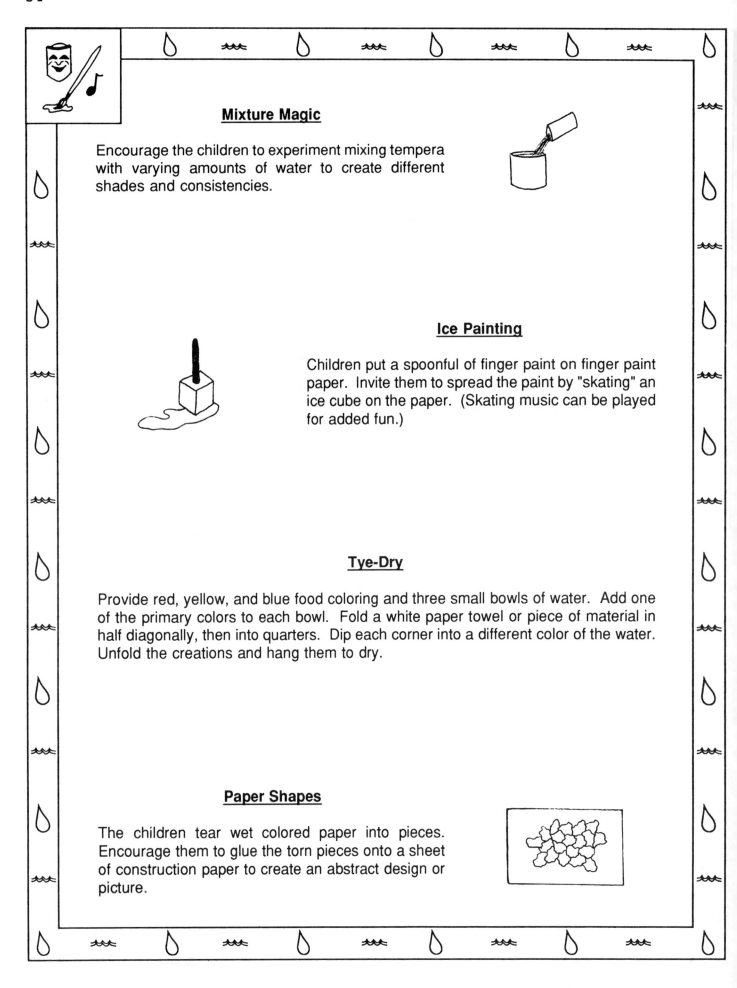

Mixture Magic

Encourage the children to experiment mixing tempera with varying amounts of water to create different shades and consistencies.

Ice Painting

Children put a spoonful of finger paint on finger paint paper. Invite them to spread the paint by "skating" an ice cube on the paper. (Skating music can be played for added fun.)

Tye-Dry

Provide red, yellow, and blue food coloring and three small bowls of water. Add one of the primary colors to each bowl. Fold a white paper towel or piece of material in half diagonally, then into quarters. Dip each corner into a different color of the water. Unfold the creations and hang them to dry.

Paper Shapes

The children tear wet colored paper into pieces. Encourage them to glue the torn pieces onto a sheet of construction paper to create an abstract design or picture.

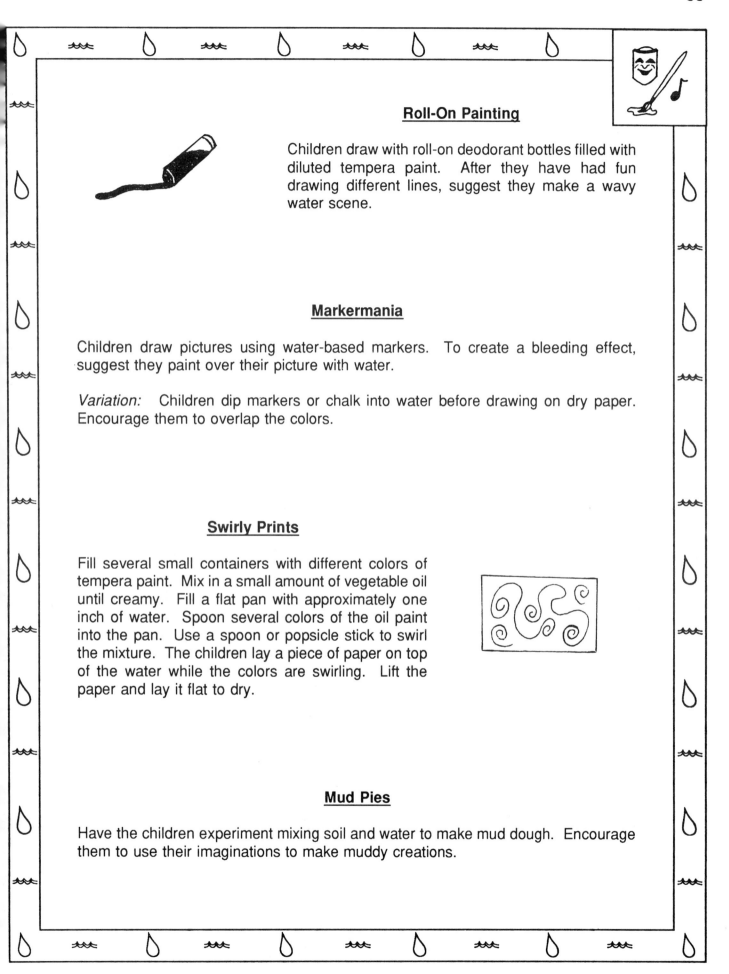

Roll-On Painting

Children draw with roll-on deodorant bottles filled with diluted tempera paint. After they have had fun drawing different lines, suggest they make a wavy water scene.

Markermania

Children draw pictures using water-based markers. To create a bleeding effect, suggest they paint over their picture with water.

Variation: Children dip markers or chalk into water before drawing on dry paper. Encourage them to overlap the colors.

Swirly Prints

Fill several small containers with different colors of tempera paint. Mix in a small amount of vegetable oil until creamy. Fill a flat pan with approximately one inch of water. Spoon several colors of the oil paint into the pan. Use a spoon or popsicle stick to swirl the mixture. The children lay a piece of paper on top of the water while the colors are swirling. Lift the paper and lay it flat to dry.

Mud Pies

Have the children experiment mixing soil and water to make mud dough. Encourage them to use their imaginations to make muddy creations.

Stencil Mist

Provide a variety of stencils and spray bottles filled with diluted tempera paint. The children place a stencil on construction paper and spatter a fine mist of paint over the entire paper. When dry, remove the stencil.

Paint the Town Wet

Invite the children to fill pails, empty paint cans, or similar containers with water. The children use brushes to "paint" chalkboards, floors, doors, tables, or chairs. Outdoors, they can paint sidewalks, slides, trees, fences, or walls.

Variation: Encourage the children to make designs on a chalkboard, sidewalk, etc., with squeeze or squirt bottles.

DRAMA

What's My Job?

Children take turns pantomiming the activities of a plumber, lifeguard, firefighter, street cleaner, window washer, gardener, sea captain, cook, or fisherman for their classmates to guess the occupation.

Water Action

Children dramatize the actions of water-related sources such as a dishwasher, shower, or sprinkler.

Example: "Somebody is opening my door and starting to load me with clothes. Boy, those clothes sure are dirty! Now they're pouring in the soap. O-o-o, it's running down my sides and tickling me. Hey, who closed my lid and turned on my dial? Water is coming in. It feels so warm. The water is rising and the soap is beginning to bubble. I'm swishing the soapy water around so that I get the clothes clean. Now the dirty water is being pumped out of my drain pipe. My insides are spinning around and I'm getting dizzy. Whew, that's hard work! I need to rest a minute. Uh-oh, here comes some more nice warm water to rinse the clothes. Whoosh, whoosh, this part's fun! A little more spinning and pumping and I'll be done. The clothes smell fresh and clean. Oh good, someone is opening my lid. The fresh air feels great. Now they're taking all of the clean clothes out of me. I'm glad because all of those clothes were very heavy. I'm really tired but happy my job is finally done!"

Soaking Wet

Invite the children to pretend to be wet pieces of fabric. Suggest actions for them to dramatize.

Example: Move your body as if you are filled with water. Show how you would get the water out. Pretend you are being shaken, spun, squeezed and wrung. Show how you feel now that you're all dry.

WELL-KNOWN RECORDINGS

Hap Palmer

"Safe Way." Learning Basic Skills Through Music, Volume 3.

"Tug a Tug." Learning Basic Skills Through Music, Volume 5.

"How Are We Going?" Learning Basic Skills Through Music, Vocabulary.

"Fishing Trip." Creative Movement and Rhythmic Exploration.

"Nature's Sweet Endless Song." Easy Does It.

"Muddy Water Puddle." Sally and the Swinging Snake.

Raffi

"Six Little Ducks." More Singable Songs.

"Five Little Frogs." Singable Songs for the Very Young.

"Row, Row, Row Your Boat." Rise and Shine.

Wee Sing

"Jack and Jill." Wee Sing Nursery Rhymes and Lullabies and Wee Sing.

"I'm a Little Teapot." Wee Sing.

"Jack, Jack." Wee Sing and Play.

"Miss Lucy Had a Baby." Wee Sing and Play.

"A Sailor Went to Sea." Wee Sing and Play.

"London Bridge." Wee Sing and Play.

"She Waded in the Water." Wee Sing Silly Songs.

"There's a Hole in the Bucket." Wee Sing Silly Songs.

"The Mulberry Bush." Wee Sing.

"Polly, Put the Kettle On." Wee Sing Nursery Rhymes and Lullabies.

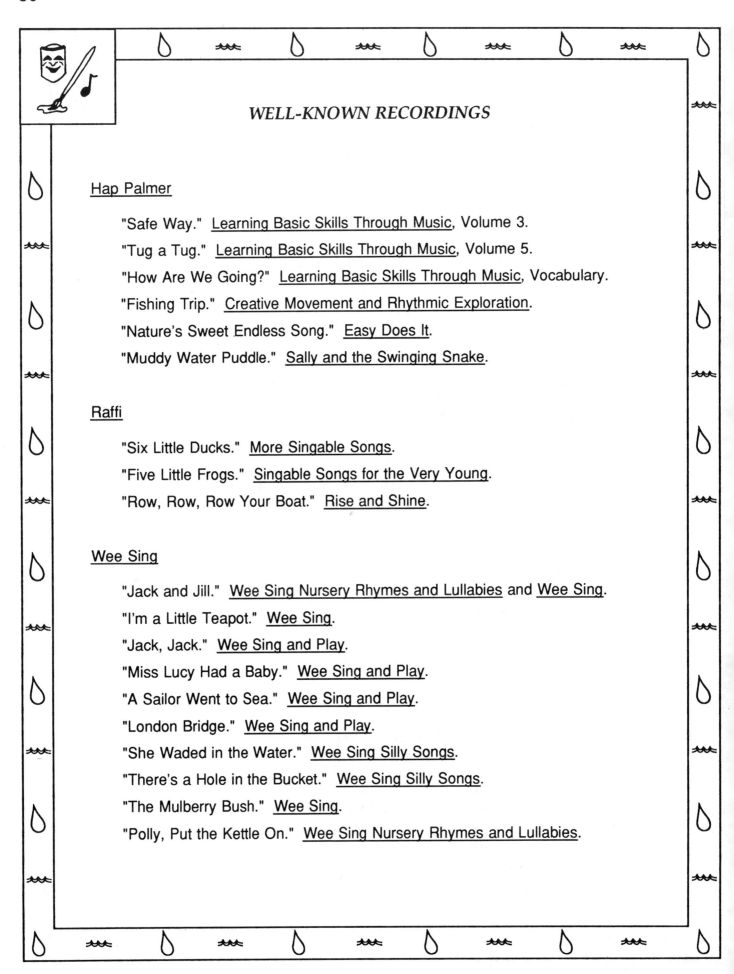

Greg Scelsa and Steve Millang

"Freeze." We All Live Together, Volume 2.

"Dancin' Machine." We All Live Together, Volume 3.

"Rock 'Round the Mulberry Bush." We All Live Together, Volume 3.

"Just Like Me." We All Live Together, Volume 4. (mirror images)

"Across the Bridge." We All Live Together, Volume 4.

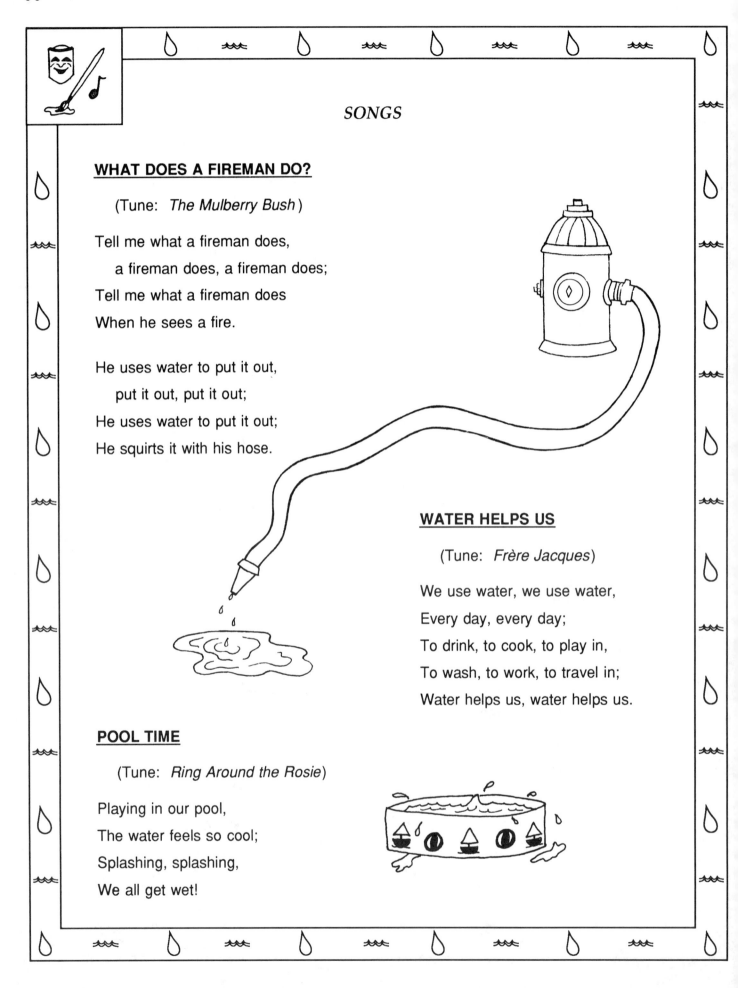

SONGS

WHAT DOES A FIREMAN DO?

(Tune: *The Mulberry Bush*)

Tell me what a fireman does,
   a fireman does, a fireman does;
Tell me what a fireman does
When he sees a fire.

He uses water to put it out,
   put it out, put it out;
He uses water to put it out;
He squirts it with his hose.

WATER HELPS US

(Tune: *Frère Jacques*)

We use water, we use water,
Every day, every day;
To drink, to cook, to play in,
To wash, to work, to travel in;
Water helps us, water helps us.

POOL TIME

(Tune: *Ring Around the Rosie*)

Playing in our pool,
The water feels so cool;
Splashing, splashing,
We all get wet!

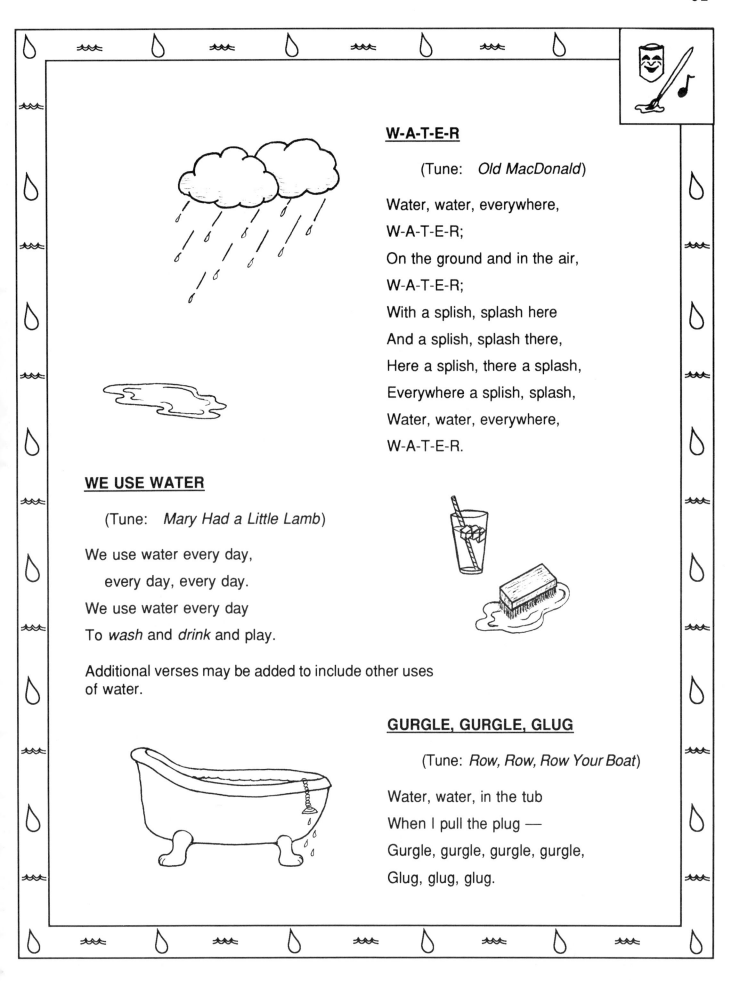

W-A-T-E-R

(Tune: *Old MacDonald*)

Water, water, everywhere,

W-A-T-E-R;

On the ground and in the air,

W-A-T-E-R;

With a splish, splash here

And a splish, splash there,

Here a splish, there a splash,

Everywhere a splish, splash,

Water, water, everywhere,

W-A-T-E-R.

WE USE WATER

(Tune: *Mary Had a Little Lamb*)

We use water every day,

   every day, every day.

We use water every day

To *wash* and *drink* and play.

Additional verses may be added to include other uses
of water.

GURGLE, GURGLE, GLUG

(Tune: *Row, Row, Row Your Boat*)

Water, water, in the tub

When I pull the plug —

Gurgle, gurgle, gurgle, gurgle,

Glug, glug, glug.

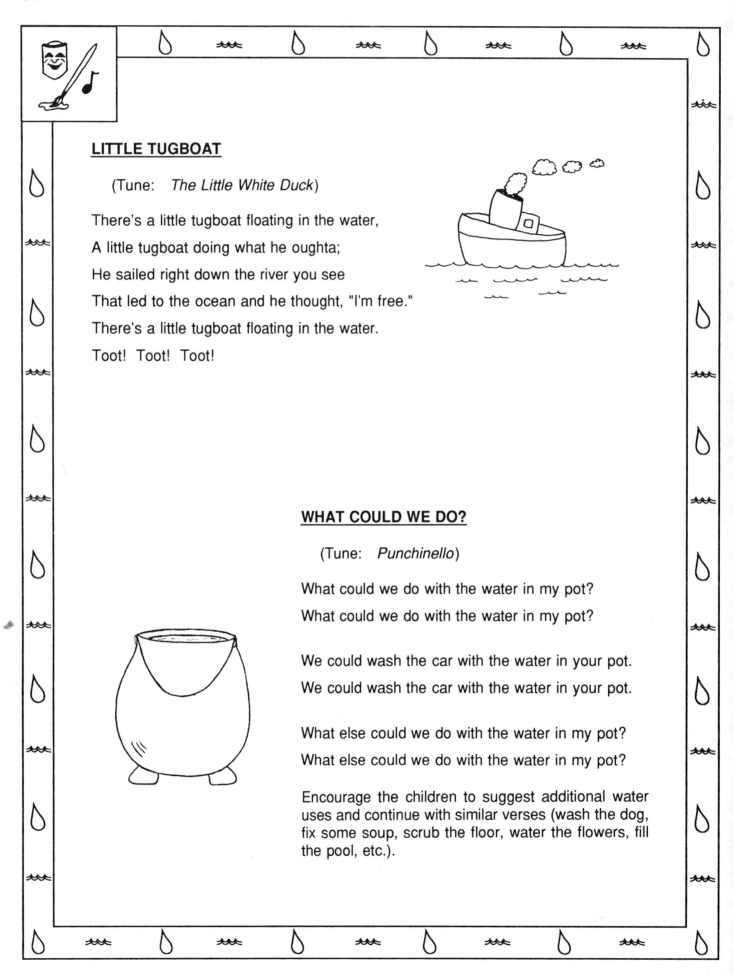

LITTLE TUGBOAT

(Tune: *The Little White Duck*)

There's a little tugboat floating in the water,

A little tugboat doing what he oughta;

He sailed right down the river you see

That led to the ocean and he thought, "I'm free."

There's a little tugboat floating in the water.

Toot! Toot! Toot!

WHAT COULD WE DO?

(Tune: *Punchinello*)

What could we do with the water in my pot?

What could we do with the water in my pot?

We could wash the car with the water in your pot.

We could wash the car with the water in your pot.

What else could we do with the water in my pot?

What else could we do with the water in my pot?

Encourage the children to suggest additional water uses and continue with similar verses (wash the dog, fix some soup, scrub the floor, water the flowers, fill the pool, etc.).

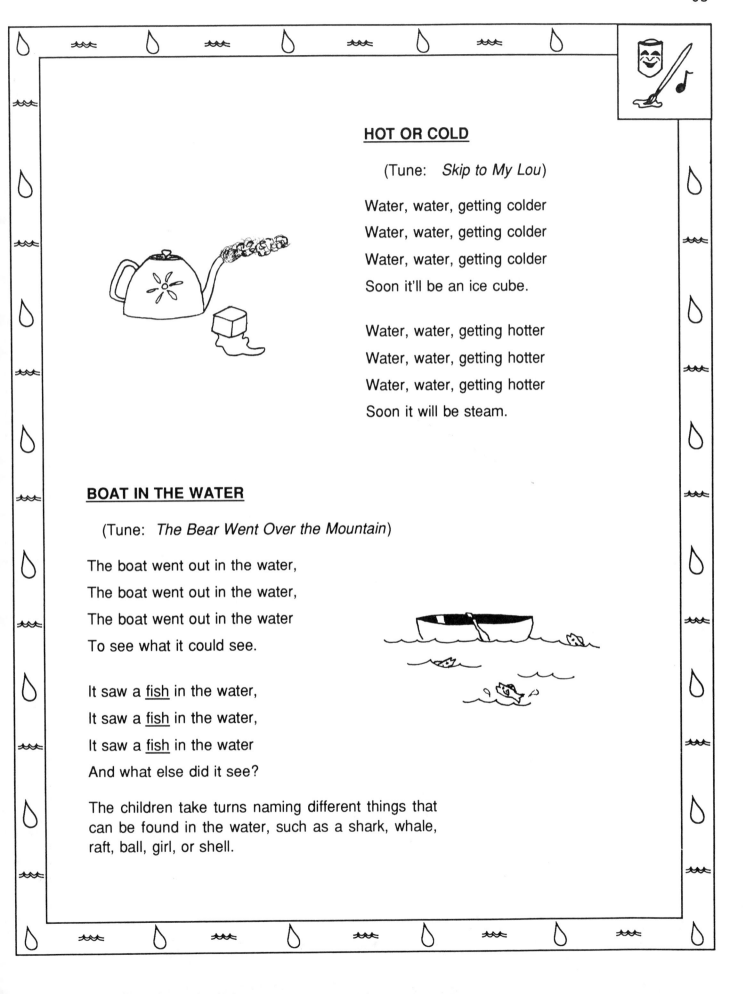

HOT OR COLD

(Tune: *Skip to My Lou*)

Water, water, getting colder
Water, water, getting colder
Water, water, getting colder
Soon it'll be an ice cube.

Water, water, getting hotter
Water, water, getting hotter
Water, water, getting hotter
Soon it will be steam.

BOAT IN THE WATER

(Tune: *The Bear Went Over the Mountain*)

The boat went out in the water,
The boat went out in the water,
The boat went out in the water
To see what it could see.

It saw a <u>fish</u> in the water,
It saw a <u>fish</u> in the water,
It saw a <u>fish</u> in the water
And what else did it see?

The children take turns naming different things that
can be found in the water, such as a shark, whale,
raft, ball, girl, or shell.

64

WATER CAN CHANGE

(Tune: *London Bridge*)

Water can change the way it looks,
   way it looks, way it looks;
Water can change the way it looks —
Liquid, solid, or gas.

As a liquid, it will flow,
   it will flow, it will flow;
As a liquid, it will flow —
It pours from glass to glass.

As a solid, it is hard,
   it is hard, it is hard;
As a solid, it is hard —
It is now called ice.

As a gas, it's hard to see,
hard to see, hard to see;
As a gas, it's hard to see —
It is now called steam.

Water can change the way it looks,
way it looks, way it looks;
Water can change the way it looks —
Liquid, solid, or gas.

POEMS AND ACTION RHYMES

TEN BRAVE FIREMEN*

Ten brave firemen sleeping in a row,   (Fingers curled to make
                                            sleeping men)

Ding, dong, goes the bell,   (Pull down on the bell cord)

And down the pole they go.   (With fists together make
                                  hands slide down pole)

Off on the engine, oh, oh, oh.   (Steer engine with hands)

Using the big hose, so, so, so.   (Imitate holding hose)

When all the fire's out, home so-o-slo.   (Steer engine with hands)

Back to bed, all in a row.   (Curl all fingers again for sleeping men)

FIVE LITTLE POLAR BEARS*

Five little polar bears,   (Hold up one hand)
Playing on the shore;
One fell in the water,
And then there were four.   (Put down one finger as you say each verse)

Four little polar bears,
Swimming out to sea;
One got lost,
And then there were three.

Three little polar bears said
"What shall we do?"
One climbed an iceberg,
Then there were two.

Two little polar bears
Playing in the sun;
One went for food,
Then there was one.

One little polar bear,
Didn't want to stay;
He said, "I'm lonesome,"
And swam far away.

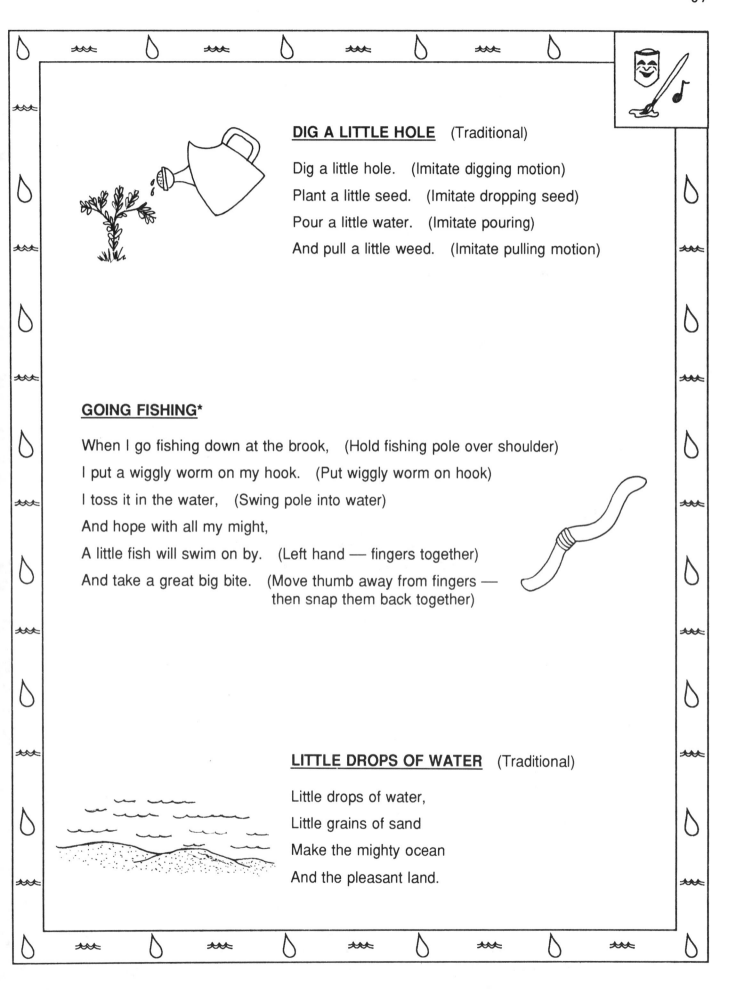

DIG A LITTLE HOLE (Traditional)

Dig a little hole.   (Imitate digging motion)

Plant a little seed.   (Imitate dropping seed)

Pour a little water.   (Imitate pouring)

And pull a little weed.   (Imitate pulling motion)

GOING FISHING*

When I go fishing down at the brook,   (Hold fishing pole over shoulder)

I put a wiggly worm on my hook.   (Put wiggly worm on hook)

I toss it in the water,   (Swing pole into water)

And hope with all my might,

A little fish will swim on by.   (Left hand — fingers together)

And take a great big bite.   (Move thumb away from fingers —
then snap them back together)

LITTLE DROPS OF WATER (Traditional)

Little drops of water,

Little grains of sand

Make the mighty ocean

And the pleasant land.

WASHING MYSELF*

When I was very little and had to wash my face,

I didn't use much water or soap — well, hardly a trace.

I'd fill the bowl with water and dab some on my face.

Here, and here, and here, and here,   (Use pointer finger, touch forehead, tip of nose, right cheek, left cheek)

And, one other place.   (Touch chin)

I'd go to show my mother. She'd check my face and then,

Because I wasn't clean enough, she'd say, "Go wash again."

STORY BOOKS

Happy Birthday, Dear Duck by Eve Bunting

Duck receives many wonderful, water-related birthday gifts from his animal friends but finds he is unable to use them until the final present arrives.

Little Toot by Hardie Gramatky

A little tugboat feels unwanted until he finds a way to help an ocean liner in trouble.

The Duck Who Loved Puddles by Michael J. Pellowski

A little duck, who thinks water is only for splashing, is fascinated to learn of its many other uses.

Scuffy the Tugboat by Gertrude Crampton

When a toy tugboat longs for bigger things in life and finds them, he decides the simple life is best after all.

Tom and Pippo and the Washing Machine by Helen Oxenbury

After playing in the mud with Tom, Pippo the toy monkey gets cleaned in the washing machine.

Wombat Stew by Marcia K. Vaughan

After a dingo cleverly catches a wombat and plans to cook him in the stew, he finds himself tricked into adding mud, feathers, flies, slugs, bugs, creepy crawlies, and gumnuts instead of the wombat.

D. W. All Wet by Marc Brown

Although Arthur the aardvark's little sister is determined not to have a good time at the beach, she soon finds herself discovering the joys of playing in the water.

Firemouse by Nina Barbaresi

A little mouse gets his chance to become a real firefighter when he and his mice friends put out the fire that has been started by the firehouse cat.

Let's Go Swimming by Shigeo Watanabe

After his love of water turns to uncertainty at the thought of learning to swim, a little bear finally agrees to try and finds it to be an enjoyable experience.

Bear's Adventure by Benedict Blathway

A teddy bear discovers the wonders on the ocean floor when he is washed out to sea.

The Seal and the Slick by Don Freeman

The story of a seal pup who struggles to stay alive in water polluted by oil.

The Marvelous Mud Washing Machine by Patty Wolcott;

A young boy with a great affinity for mud also has a unique way of washing for dinner.

Vera in the Washtub by Marjolein Bastin

A little mouse and her friends take a bath and do the laundry before going to sleep in the laundry basket.

Smokey the Fireman by Richard Scarry

Smokey the Fireman uses water to put out fires at work and play.

Last One In Is a Rotten Egg by Leonard Kessler

To avoid being called the rotten egg, Freddy learns to swim with the help of Tom, the lifeguard.

CONCEPT BOOKS

Why Does It Float? by Chris Arvetis and Carole Palmer; *Just Ask* series

Christopher Mouse listens as his friend Turtle explains and demonstrates buoyancy.

What Is an Iceberg? by Chris Arvetis and Carole Palmer; *Just Ask* series

The beauty and danger of icebergs are explained to Christopher Mouse by the animals of the North and South Poles.

What Is an Ocean? by Chris Arvetis and Carole Palmer; *Just Ask* series

Christopher Mouse learns how an ocean differs from rivers and lakes.

Water by Alfred Leutscher

Many aspects of water, such as its different forms, powers, and importance, are presented in this well-illustrated, informative book.

Water Is Wet by Sally Cartwright

This easy-to-read book portrays various qualities of water through suggested observations and activities.

Do You Know About Water? by Mae Blacker Freeman

Depicted in this book are many uses of water and the common places where water can be found.

Water, Water Everywhere by Joanne Barkan; *First Facts* series

Through simplistic wording and colorful illustrations, this book allows children to investigate where water comes from as well as how it is used.

Floating and Sinking by Franklyn M. Branley; *Let's-Read-and-Find-Out Science* series

The concepts of floating and sinking are explored through simple activities.

<u>Water</u> by David Bennett; *Bear Facts* series

Bear presents facts about the characteristics of water and its many uses.

<u>Let's-Try-It-Out . . . Wet and Dry</u> by Seymour Simon

Challenging situations are presented that encourage exploration of the effects of water on a variety of items.

<u>Reflections</u> by Ann Jonas

This cleverly designed book offers a unique look at reflections as it is read, right side up and upside down.

<u>Water Wonders</u> by Better Homes and Gardens

Water is explored through many easy-to-make projects and recipes.

<u>Easy-to-Make Water Toys That Really Work</u> by Mary Blocksma and Dewey Blocksma

Instructions are presented that show how to use household materials to make a variety of water toys.

<u>Fire! Fire!</u> by Gail Gibbons

This informative book includes many helpful fire prevention tips and safety rules as well as a look at how fires are battled in many situations.

NOTES

NOTES

STORY O'MIMUS

asks

What is

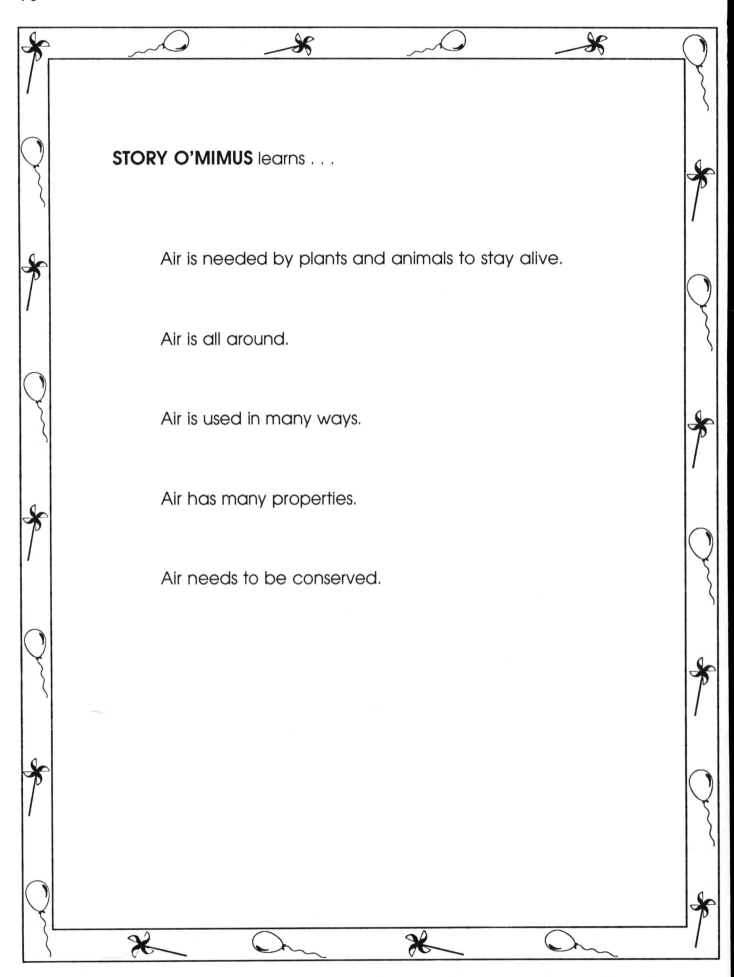

STORY O'MIMUS learns . . .

Air is needed by plants and animals to stay alive.

Air is all around.

Air is used in many ways.

Air has many properties.

Air needs to be conserved.

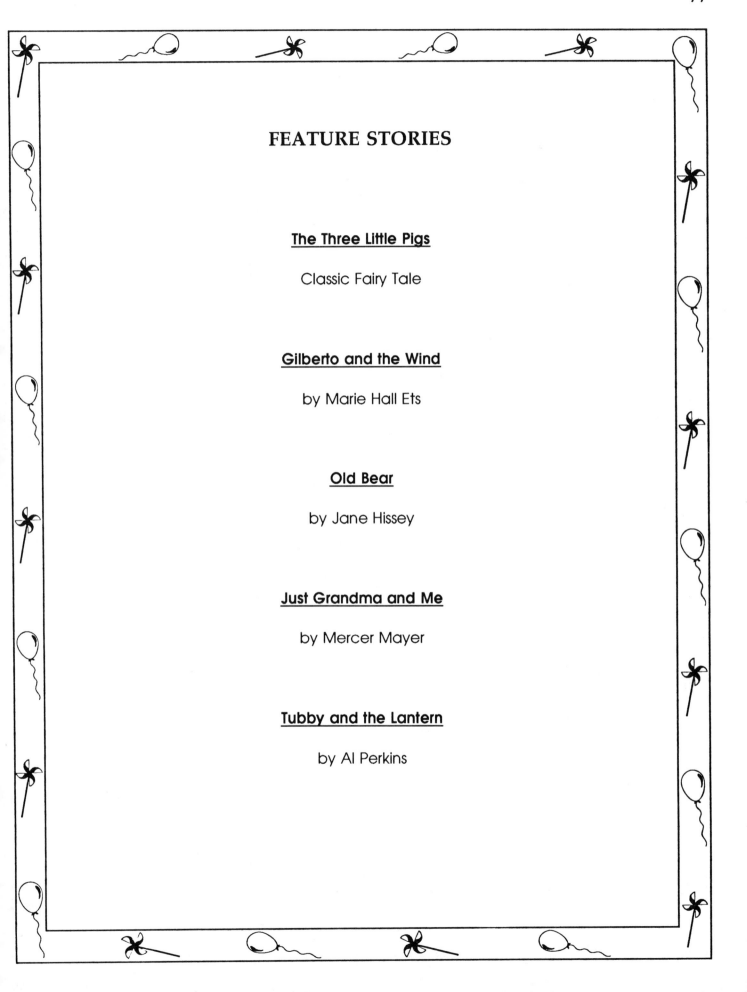

FEATURE STORIES

The Three Little Pigs

Classic Fairy Tale

Gilberto and the Wind

by Marie Hall Ets

Old Bear

by Jane Hissey

Just Grandma and Me

by Mercer Mayer

Tubby and the Lantern

by Al Perkins

PLANNING GUIDE

Feature Stories

THREE LITTLE PIGS	Language Arts	Math	Science, Health, Social Studies	Motor
Blow a Tune			○	●
Chinny-Chin-Chin	●			○
Wonderful Wands		●		○
Puff a Goal		○		●
Blow a "B" – Puff a "P"	●	○		
Blow Me Down	●			○
Pig Hunt	○	●		
Squeeze Squirts		●		○
Under Control	○	○		●
Blow the House Up			●	○
Which Word?	●			
How Many Huffs and Puffs?	○	●		
Out of Breath			●	○
Breathing Patterns		●		○
The Big "Good" Wolf			●	
Bulging Bags	○		●	
Huff and Puff a Word	●			
Sound Off			●	

GILBERTO AND THE WIND	Language Arts	Math	Science, Health, Social Studies	Motor
Bubbles Galore	○	○		●
Awesome Air Windsock	○	○	○	●
Sail to Sea			○	●
Don't Be Fooled by the Wind	●			
Take One	●			
Balloon Pop	●	○		
Blow It Away		●	○	
Mischievous Wind	●			
Scattered Leaves		●		
Gilberto's Games	○	●		○
Wind Parade			○	●
Run, Gilberto, Run	○			●
Bursting Bubbles				●

Instructional Focus: ● Primary   ○ Secondary

(Continued)

GILBERTO AND THE WIND (Con't)	Language Arts	Math	Science, Health, Social Studies	Motor
Balloon Bop		●		○
For Safety's Sake			●	○
Who's Whispering at My Door?	●			
Balloon Factory		●		○
Breezy Bubbles			●	○

OLD BEAR	Language Arts	Math	Science, Health, Social Studies	Motor
Lift the Plane			●	○
Get Set Jet		○	●	
Geronimo			●	
The Flying Solution	●			○
Glider Rescue		○		●
Too High	●			
Amazing Air Pressure			●	
Tall Toppling Towers		●		○
Parade of Parachutes			●	○
Parachute Shake				●
Parachute Bubble			○	●
Merry-Go-Round the Parachute	○			●
Going Up		○		●
Friends to the Rescue	○			●

JUST GRANDMA AND ME	Language Arts	Math	Science, Health, Social Studies	Motor
Grandma's Bag			●	○
Bop It Back		○		●
Sand Writing	○	○		●
Air-Filled Riddles	●			
The Good Times	●			
Tangled Strings	●	○		
Floating Fun			●	
Picture Quest	●			
I Tried, But . . .	●			○
Puff-n-Pass			○	●
Sand Measure		●		
Pump It Up		●		
Kite's Tail	●			

TUBBY AND THE LANTERN	Language Arts	Math	Science, Health, Social Studies	Motor
Paper Lanterns	○			●
Enormous Mural		●		○
Hot Hurts			●	
Lights Out!			●	
The Enormous Candle		○	○	●
Warm Bed			●	
It's My Birthday		●		○
Going Up, Coming Down			●	
The Pirates Are Coming				●
Better Late Than Never	●			
Load 'Em Up		●		
Floating Adventures	●			○
Woodworking Wish				●
Make It Enormous				●

MISCELLANEOUS	Language Arts	Math	Science, Health, Social Studies	Motor
Wind Be Still				●
Airy Meringues	○	●		○
Empty or Not?			●	
Catch the Wind			○	●
Air Is Where?			●	
Flowing Streamers				●
Are Two Straws Better Than One?			●	
Playful Air	●			
Air Escape			●	
Edible Pinwheels	○	●		○
Sow Your Seeds			●	
Growing Clean Air			●	

THREE LITTLE PIGS

Classic Fairy Tale

well-loved version, Walt Disney's *Three Little Pigs*

adapted by Milt Banta and Al Dempster

Western Publishing Company, Inc. (Golden Book)

ISBN 0-307-01028-7

Summary:

This well-known classic tells the story of three little pigs and a hungry wolf. The first and second pigs are "huffed and puffed" out of their homes by the sly wolf. They find refuge with their brother, who wisely built his house out of bricks. As the wolf attempts to enter the sturdy house, he finds he has been outsmarted by the little pigs.

Blow a Tune

Cover one end of a cardboard cylinder with a small piece of waxed paper and secure it with a rubber band. Encourage the children to experiment blowing sounds into the opposite end of the tube to produce musical tunes.

Variation: Ask the children to bring an object from home that will produce a musical sound when air is blown into it, such as a plastic bottle, shell, or gum box. The children can play their musical instruments together to form a homemade band.

Chinny-Chin-Chin

Challenge the children to touch their chin to their knee. Continue to give directions that include the chin with other body parts. If the children cannot touch the named part with their chin, they shout, "Not by the hair of my chinny-chin-chin!"

Wonderful Wands

Provide a variety of objects for use as bubble wands. Large buttons, beads, slotted serving spoons, funnels, bottomless paper cups, strawberry baskets, and bent pipe cleaners are some of the many interesting objects that make great wands.

Ask the children to predict which objects will produce small bubbles and which will produce large ones. Encourage them to try many "wands" to test their predictions. (A recipe for bubble solution is provided on page 333.)

Puff a Goal

Tape a container to each end of a table. The children stand at opposite ends of the table and try to "huff and puff" a ping pong ball into the opponent's container. Score can be kept with tally marks or numeral cards.

Blow a "B" – Puff a "P"

Place an alphabet strip on the floor. The children take turns blowing a ping pong ball down the strip. Encourage them to move the ball down the strip as far as possible in just one blow, naming the letter that the ball last touches.

Variation: Use a number line for numeral recognition.

Blow Me Down

Children recall the characters in the story. Provide materials for them to make a puppet or mask of their favorite character. These can be used to reenact the story. (Patterns are provided on pages 327–328.)

Variation: Children use their bodies to form "the pigs' houses" and actually fall down when the "wolf" huffs and puffs.

Pig Hunt

Cut the bottoms off three small milk cartons. Cover the cartons to represent the pigs' houses. Ask the children to place the houses in the correct sequence. While they cover their eyes, hide a small plastic pig or wolf under one of the cartons. The children guess where the animal is hiding by responding with the ordinals—first, second, or third.

Squeeze Squirts

Ask the children to estimate the number of squirts of air needed to move an object from one designated point to another. Provide squirt bottles and lightweight objects, such as styrofoam packing material or cotton balls, for the children to test their guesses.

Variation: Children experiment with smaller, controlled squirts of air to move an object along a pathway or obstacle course. (A mat is provided on page 329.)

Under Control

Draw large shapes, numerals, or letters on the floor. With the air inside of them, the children blow ping pong balls on the figures, trying to keep the balls on course. Ask them which lines were easier to follow.

Blow the House Up

Instruct the children to insert a straw into the open end of a gallon-size storage bag. Tape the bag closed and lay it on a flat surface. Invite the children to be one of the "little pigs" and build a block house on their bag.

After construction is complete, the children become a "big bad wolf" and blow into the straw, trying to knock the house down.

Variation: Challenge a child to try to sit on a large plastic trash bag as air is pumped into it.

Which Word?

Read a sentence from the story. Ask the children to repeat the sentence. Reread the sentence, omitting a word each time. The children identify the missing word. Continue to reread the same sentence many times, omitting different words for the children to identify.

Examples: The big bad wolf huffed and puffed and blew the _____ in.

The big _____ wolf huffed and puffed and blew the house in.

How Many Huffs and Puffs?

Recall what the wolf said when the pigs refused to let him in. Ask the children to listen to a recording of "The Three Little Pigs" and count the number of times they hear the wolf say, "I'll huff and I'll puff and I'll blow your house in!"

Out of Breath

Encourage the children to observe their normal breathing pattern as they sit quietly. Instruct them to jog swiftly in place. After they stop, ask the children to describe how the increased activity affected their breathing.

Breathing Patterns

Children take turns creating a variety of breathing patterns for the others to repeat. Have the children use manipulatives and/or physical actions to visually recreate the breathing patterns.

Examples: haa - haa - hoo, haa - haa - hoo, . . .

hoo - hee - hee, hoo - hee - hee, . . .

sss - hee - sss, sss - hee - sss, . . .

The Big "Good" Wolf

Brainstorm ways the wolf could have used his huffing and puffing constructively (to inflate balloons, toys, balls, tires, etc.). Help each child attach a straw to a sandwich bag using tape or a twist tie. Instruct them to blow into the straw and watch their bag inflate. Invite the children to attach a second bag to the other end of the straw and squeeze the bags, moving air from one bag to the other.

Bulging Bags

Instruct a child to hide an object in a small paper bag. Ask the child to describe the hidden object. The child who guesses correctly is next to fill the bag. After many children have had a turn, fill the bag with only air and challenge the children to guess the contents.

Huff and Puff a Word

Choose a child to be the wolf. The remaining children represent pigs. Provide an alphabet letter for each child. Call out a three-letter word. The children that have letters needed to spell the word, arrange themselves in the correct sequence. When the wolf blows, the "pigs" make their letter sounds in order from left to right. (Mask patterns are provided on pages 327–328.)

Sound Off

Show the children a variety of wind instruments such as a kazoo, horn, harmonica, or flute. After the instruments have been identified, ask the children to describe their similarities. If possible, let the children try to blow air into the instruments to produce sounds. (Wipe the mouthpieces with antiseptic after each use.)

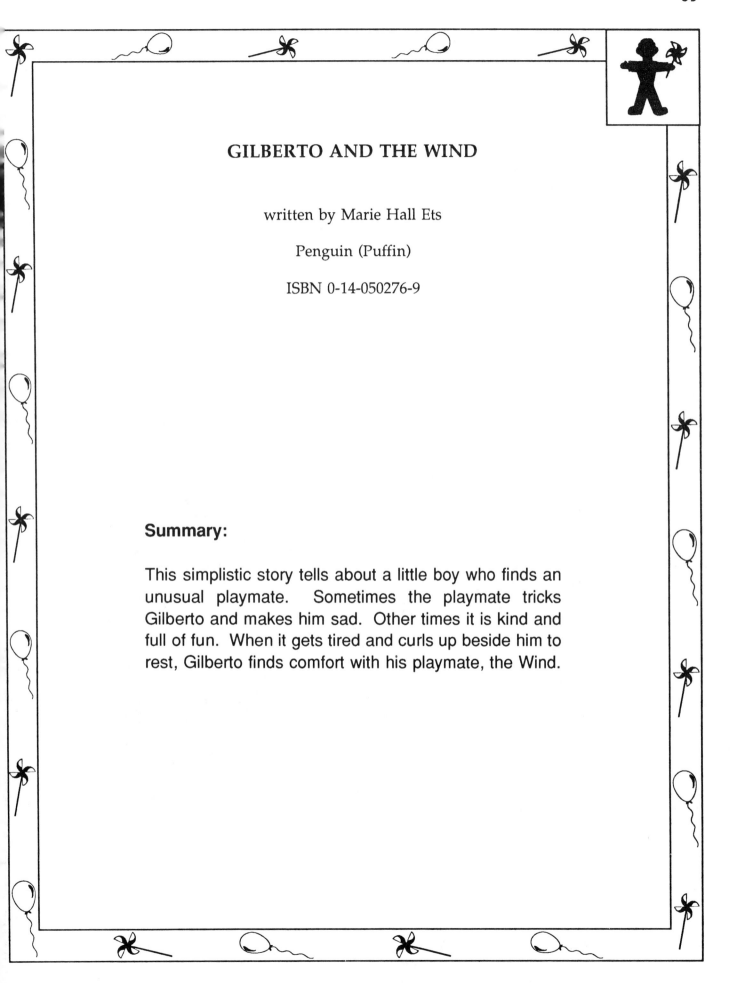

GILBERTO AND THE WIND

written by Marie Hall Ets

Penguin (Puffin)

ISBN 0-14-050276-9

Summary:

This simplistic story tells about a little boy who finds an unusual playmate. Sometimes the playmate tricks Gilberto and makes him sad. Other times it is kind and full of fun. When it gets tired and curls up beside him to rest, Gilberto finds comfort with his playmate, the Wind.

Bubbles Galore

Print each child's name on a sheet of paper. Ask the children to draw bubbles to trace their names. They can add various-sized circles around their names to create bubbles galore.

Awesome Air Windsock

Recall the many uses of air in the story. Have each child illustrate a use of air on a 12" x 18" sheet of construction paper. Tape the ends together to form a cylinder. Add crepe paper streamers to the bottom of the cylinder. Punch three holes at the top and attach strings. Hang the windsocks outdoors for the children to observe the direction the wind is blowing.

Sail to Sea

Provide materials such as wood scraps, milk cartons, styrofoam meat trays, straws, craft sticks, and cloth for the children to design sailboats. Invite them to float their boats in water and act as the wind, blowing them "out to sea."

Don't Be Fooled by the Wind

Hang several articles of clothing on a clothesline. Choose a child to act as the wind. The remaining children cover their eyes. The "wind" removes an article of clothing from the line. The children guess which article is missing. (Clothing patterns are provided on pages 330–331.)

Variation: The "wind" changes the order of the clothing. The children place the clothing in its original order.

Take One

Encourage the children to act out the many ways Gilberto played with the Wind. Provide several props related to the story, such as a balloon, kite, sailboat, pinwheel, broom, an umbrella, or bubbles.

Balloon Pop

Draw balloons on a chalkboard. Write a word on each balloon. The children "pop" the balloons by erasing the words they identify.

Variation: Write letters, numerals, or shapes on the balloons for the children to identify.

Blow It Away

Invite the children to feel the wind created by an electric fan. Provide items such as a milk jug, block, sheet of paper, or an inflated balloon. Ask the children to predict which object will be blown the farthest when placed in front of the fan. Test their predictions. The children can order the items according to the distance blown.

Variation: Experiment outside on a windy day to test the wind's strength.

Mischievous Wind

Recall the ways that the Wind annoyed Gilberto. Ask the children to take turns completing the following sentence:

"If I were the wind, I'd _____."
(blow the clothes off the line, tangle up
the kite string, etc.)

Scattered Leaves

Ask the children what the Wind did with Gilberto's pile of leaves. Scatter an assortment of leaves for the children to sort by size, shape, color, or variety.

Gilberto's Games

Recall some of the activities Gilberto liked to do with the Wind. Ask the children to choose their favorite windy day activity and illustrate it. Construct a graph using the pictures.

Wind Parade

Ask each child to make a hat out of tagboard. Glue a piece of cork on the inside near the top. After the glue has dried, attach a pinwheel to the front of the hat by pushing its pin into the cork. Invite the children to wear their hats and parade in the wind. (A pattern and directions for making a pinwheel are provided on page 332.)

Run, Gilberto, Run

Instruct the children to form a circle and hold hands. Choose one child, "Gilberto," to stand in the center. Choose a second child, "the Wind," to stand outside of the circle. The remaining children chant,

> "Gilberto, Gilberto, you'd better *run*.
> It looks like the Wind's going to have some *fun*."

Each time the word *run* is chanted, the children raise their arms to form arches. They lower them when they hear the word *fun*. "The Wind" tries to catch "Gilberto" as they run into and out of the circle.

Bursting Bubbles

Provide a hula hoop to represent a bubble wand. Choose one child to be Gilberto. The remaining children scatter around the playing area and wait for Gilberto. As he places the "wand" over the children, they turn into floating bubbles. If the "bubbles" bump into anything, including each other, they "burst" to the floor and wait for "Gilberto." Challenge "Gilberto" to try to get all of his "bubbles" floating at one time.

Balloon Bop

Give a child an inflated balloon. Ask the child to tap the balloon in the air as the remaining children count. To encourage accurate counting, tell the children to count only when the child's hand taps the balloon.

Variation: Have the children choose partners. Designate a "tapper" and a "counter" in each pair. Show a numeral card to the "tappers." The "counters" try to determine the numeral that was shown by counting the number of times their partner taps the balloon.

For Safety's Sake

Ask the children how Gilberto could have kept the Wind from blowing away his balloon. Discuss the dangers of balloons, not only to people but to the environment. Encourage the children to make safety posters illustrating the dangers of balloons.

Mommy says balloons are dangerous for babies. They can choke me.

When balloons pop, the noise scares me and can hurt my ears.

When salt water takes the color out of balloons, they look like jellyfish to me. They may look good enough to eat, but they can kill me if I do.

Who's Whispering at My Door?

Choose a child to be Gilberto. He sits in a chair with his back to the class. Point to one of the remaining children to mimic the sound of the wind by saying,

"Gilberto, come and play with me."

"Gilberto" listens and tries to identify "the voice of the wind."

Balloon Factory

Provide sandwich bags and many deflated balloons. The children pretend to be workers in a balloon factory, counting and packaging bags of nine balloons. The "workers" print a *9* on each bag while chanting,

"A balloon with a line looks like a nine."

Variation: Children package balloons in groups of 10 for use in place value activities.

Breezy Bubbles

Ask the children to blow on their hands creating different wind strengths. After feeling the differences, encourage them to experiment blowing soap bubbles. (A recipe for bubble solution is provided on page 333.)

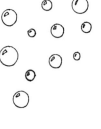

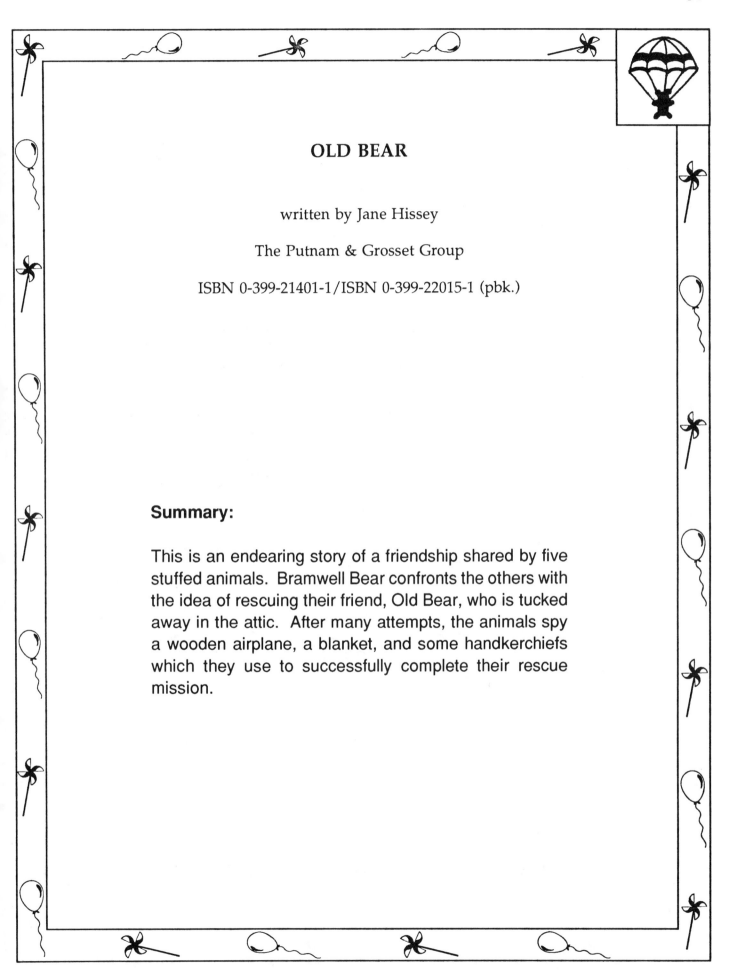

OLD BEAR

written by Jane Hissey

The Putnam & Grosset Group

ISBN 0-399-21401-1/ISBN 0-399-22015-1 (pbk.)

Summary:

This is an endearing story of a friendship shared by five stuffed animals. Bramwell Bear confronts the others with the idea of rescuing their friend, Old Bear, who is tucked away in the attic. After many attempts, the animals spy a wooden airplane, a blanket, and some handkerchiefs which they use to successfully complete their rescue mission.

Lift the Plane

Ask the children to draw an airplane on a lightweight piece of paper, about 5" x 8". Instruct them to hold one end of the paper against their chin and blow. As they blow, their plane will lift. Relate this activity to the way a plane takes off.

Get Set Jet

Inflate a balloon and tightly hold the opening closed. Slowly let the air out of the balloon for the children to feel the jet of air. Choose a child to act as Bramwell. Blow the balloon up again. "Bramwell" counts down and lets go of the balloon as the children watch it move in the opposite direction of the escaping air. Relate this activity to the way a jet plane moves.

Geronimo

Ask the children why Rabbit and Little Bear tied a handkerchief to Old Bear. Give each child two identical pieces of paper. Crumple one piece into a ball. Ask the children to predict which paper will reach the floor first if they are dropped together from the same height. Have them drop the papers to test their prediction.

The Flying Solution

Ask the children how Rabbit and Little Bear got up to the attic to rescue their friend. Encourage them to think of other things that fly, which the animals could have used to aid in the rescue, such as balloons, kites, bubbles, birds, butterflies, or helicopters. Have the children pantomime the solutions.

Variation: Children make things that fly, using a variety of materials. (A pattern and directions for making a "helicopter" are provided on page 333.)

Glider Rescue

Invite the children to make and decorate paper gliders. Suspend a hoop from the ceiling to represent a trap door. The children aim their glider toward the hoop, pretending to be one of Old Bear's friends trying to rescue him.

Variation: Children fly gliders as far as possible and measure the distance flown.

Too High

Recall the ways Old Bear's friends tried to rescue him. Discuss the reasons why some of their ideas did not work. Ask the children to share an experience they have had trying to reach something.

Amazing Air Pressure

Fill a glass with water. Hold an index card firmly in place on the rim of the glass. Quickly turn the glass upside down. Ask the children to predict what will happen when you take your hand away. Remove your hand from the card to test their predictions.

Tall Toppling Towers

Recall what happened when Old Bear's friends tried to build a tower of blocks. Challenge the children to build a tall tower, counting the number of blocks they can stack before their tower topples.

Parade of Parachutes

Recall what the animals used to get Old Bear down from the attic. Provide a square of brightly colored tissue paper for each child to make a parachute. Instruct them to tape a 12" piece of string to each corner of the tissue. Ask them to draw a picture of Old Bear on a 1" x 2" piece of cardboard and attach it to the other end of the strings. Invite the children to throw their parachute high into the air and watch it float to the ground.

Variation: A class parachute can be made with a handkerchief tied to an item that is heavier than the fabric, such as a small plastic animal, spool, or clothespin.

Parachute Shake

Children stand in a circle around a parachute grasping the edge overhand. Place many balls on top of the parachute. Instruct the children to shake the balls off by rapidly bending and straightening their arms at the elbows.

Parachute Bubble

Children grasp the edge of a parachute overhand. Have them stretch their arms overhead to raise the parachute. Instruct the children to quickly pull the edge down to the ground, trapping air inside.

Variation: Children inflate a parachute, release their hands, and step in toward the center. As the parachute floats to the ground, they kneel down, remaining inside until it deflates.

Merry-Go-Round the Parachute

Children grasp the edge of a parachute with one hand. Instruct them to follow directions such as circle forward, circle backward, move into the center and back out, hop, or jump.

Going Up

Recall Rabbit's exciting dream about bouncing as high as an airplane. Make horizontal lines going up a wall using different colored tape or paper strips. Ask the children to stand next to the wall and touch the highest line they can reach. Challenge them to jump and reach a higher line. Encourage the children to jump higher each time.

Friends to the Rescue

Ask the children to recall the names of the characters who tried to rescue Old Bear. Have the children grasp a parachute overhand. Going around the circle, assign each child one of the four characters' names (Duck, Rabbit, Little Bear, or Bramwell). Place some teddy bears on the ground under the parachute. Instruct the children to quickly extend their arms, raising the parachute overhead. Call out one of the four characters' names.

The children with that name run under, try to "rescue" a bear, and return to the circle before the parachute drops. The remaining children keep their arms extended overhead until all of the "characters" have returned.

JUST GRANDMA AND ME

written by Mercer Mayer

Western Publishing Company, Inc. (Golden Book)

ISBN 0-307-11893-2/ISBN 0-307-61893-5 (lib. bdg.)

Summary:

This lovable story depicts a special relationship between Little Critter and his grandmother. When spending a day together at the beach, they experience frustration caused by moving air. It moves their beach umbrella toward the sea and blows their kite on top of a sunbather's head. Little Critter soon discovers, however, that air can be helpful when it fills his swim ring and keeps him afloat.

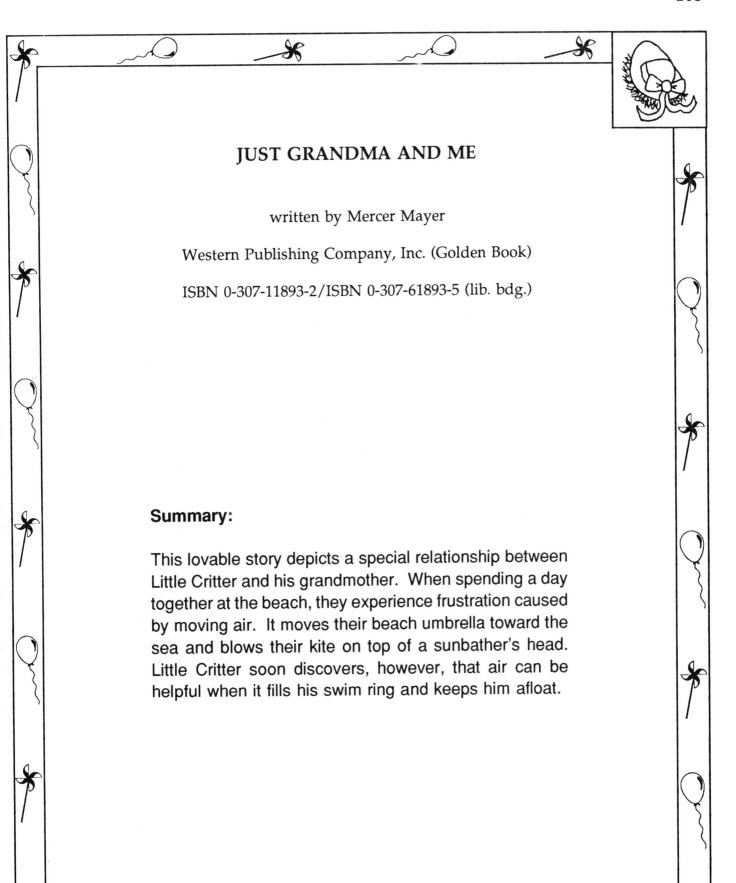

104

Grandma's Bag

Ask the children why Little Critter did not inflate his swim ring before going to the beach. Provide a large tote bag and two beach balls—one deflated, the other inflated. Ask the children which ball they think will be easier to put into the bag and why. Invite the children to try placing each ball into the bag. Brainstorm fun things that can be done with an air-filled ball, such as kicking, throwing, or bouncing. Provide several air-filled balls for the children's use.

Bop It Back

Blow air into a beach ball. Have two children stand facing one another. The children volley the ball back and forth over a net or table. Encourage them to count the number of times they consecutively volley the ball.

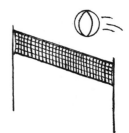

Variation: Children play catch, counting the number of times they consecutively catch the ball.

Sand Writing

Provide models of numerals or letters. Encourage the children to copy them with their fingers in trays of sand.

Air-Filled Riddles

Ask the children to recall how air helped Little Critter have a good time at the beach. Challenge them to answer the following riddles:

1. It's bouncy and round
   And can roll on the ground.   (ball)

2. You hold the string tight
   As it makes its flight.   (kite)

3. A short curved hose is for you and me
   To breathe air in under the sea.   (snorkel)

4. Its cloth triangles are tied to its mast,
   Through the waves, it travels oh so fast.   (sailboat)

5. Under your arms and around your chest,
   To stay afloat, this is the best.   (swim ring)

6. When you blow air through it, it sounds like a bird,
   Making a noise that everyone's heard.   (whistle)

7. It's shaped like a doughnut with a hole in the middle,
   Being part of a tire is the key to this riddle.   (inner tube)

8. In your glass and between your lips,
   By sucking this, you get some sips.   (straw)

The Good Times

Ask the children why they think Little Critter had a good time at the beach. Give them an opportunity to share a good time they have had with someone special.

Tangled Strings

Provide colored kites and corresponding color word cards. Attach the kites to the top of a chalkboard. Shuffle the word cards and randomly place them at the bottom of the chalkboard. The children use chalk to draw a string from each kite to its corresponding word card. (An open-ended reproducible sheet is provided on page 334.)

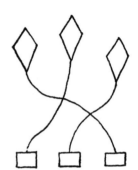

Variation: Match uppercase to lowercase letters or numerals to sets.

Floating Fun

Place several heavy objects onto a small deflated raft floating in a wading pool. Have the children observe. Ask them how to make the objects float. Inflate the raft and replace the objects. Relate this to how air helped Little Critter float.

Picture Quest

Ask a child to describe a favorite page in the story. A classmate tries to find that page, then describes another page.

I Tried, But . . .

Recall some of the things Little Critter tried to do, but found that he could not. Ask the children to share a similar experience they have had. Make and illustrate a class book using an "I_____, but _____" pattern.

Example: I <u>tried to tie my shoe</u>, but <u>my shoelace broke</u>.

Puff-n-Pass

Blow air into a swim ring. Ask the children to pass the ring from one to another using only their chin. Challenge them to find other ways to pass the ring without using their hands.

Variation: Ask the children to predict if the ring will be easier to pass filled with more or less air. Test their predictions by varying the amount of air in the ring.

Sand Measure

Provide a container to act as a standard of measurement, a variety of other containers, and sand. Ask the children to predict which of the containers will hold the same amount of sand as the standard. As they test their predictions, have the children sort the containers into three groups—those that hold more than, less than, or the same amount as the standard.

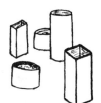

Pump It Up

Provide an air pump and a deflated beach ball. Ask the children to predict the number of pumps needed to inflate the ball. The children count as the ball is filled.

Kite's Tail

Children sit in a circle and tell a group "add-on" story. Choose a child to hold a kite with a ball of string attached. To begin the story, recite the lines,

> "My mother sent me out to play,
> On a kite's tail, I flew away.
> When I looked down, I saw (a house)."

As the kite is passed from one child to the next, ask the children to pretend they are hanging onto its tail, flying high in the sky. Challenge them to repeat the previous "add-ons" and name something else that can be seen from the sky. Continue passing the kite around the circle until all of the children are holding onto the string. As it unravels, so will the story.

TUBBY AND THE LANTERN

written by Al Perkins

illustrated by Rowland B. Wilson

BEGINNER BOOKS (Division of Random House, Inc.)

Book Club Edition

ISBN 0-394-82297-8/ISBN 0-394-92297-2 (lib. ed.)

Summary:

This story is about an enormous paper lantern that a little elephant, Tubby, makes his friend for his birthday. The birthday surprise creates too much hot air and takes Tubby and Ah Mee on an incredible journey in the sky. When the candle goes out and the lantern begins to fall, they are threatened by a ship of pirates. Using the lantern and hot air from a ship's smokestack, they outwit the pirates and float home for a birthday celebration.

Paper Lanterns

Recall the way Ah Mee carried his lanterns to market. Ask the children why they think he put them on a stick. Discuss other ways Ah Mee could have carried the lanterns. Suggest the children make their own paper lanterns. (A pattern and directions are provided on page 335.)

Enormous Mural

Ask the children what Tubby made Ah Mee for his birthday. Brainstorm things that are *enormous*. Ask the children to decide which item is the most *enormous*. Cover a wall with an *enormous* piece of paper. Encourage the children to make *enormous* things on the *enormous* piece of paper.

Hot Hurts

Ask the children why Tubby had to be careful when he was making Ah Mee's enormous lantern. Ask them to share experiences they have had with hot objects. Discuss safety tips, stressing adult supervision when near fire or heat.

Lights Out!

Provide a small birthday candle and a transparent jar. Drip wax on the inside of the lid. Hold the candle in the wax until secure. Light the candle and sing "Happy Birthday" to Ah Mee and Tubby. Ask the children to blow out the candle flame and observe the smoke rise. Encourage them to brainstorm other ways to extinguish the candle. Relight the candle. Place the jar over the candle as the children observe. Discuss the results.

The Enormous Candle

Ask the children how Tubby made the big candle. Place two coffee cans in the holes of a concrete block to prevent tipping. Partially fill one can with cold water and the other with melted wax. Provide each child with a 12" piece of candle wick tied around the middle of an unsharpened pencil. Have the children hold the pencil by both ends to avoid being burned. Instruct them to lower the candle wick into the wax, setting the pencil on the rim of the can.

Next, have the children raise the wick out of the wax and lower it into the water. The children alternate dipping the wick into the hot wax and the cold water. Continue the procedure, watching the little candles get *bigger* and *bigger*.

Warm Bed

Recall the birthday gift Ah Mee made for Tubby. Ask the children which bunk they think was the warmest and why. Place a thermometer near the floor and another close to the ceiling. After a short time, read the thermometers to compare the temperatures.

It's My Birthday!

Ask the children how Ah Mee and Tubby celebrated their birthdays. Encourage them to draw a picture of something they would like to do on their next birthday. Label a birthday graph with the months of the year. Ask the children to state their birth date as they add their picture to the graph.

Going Up, Coming Down

Provide a balloon, bottle and two containers—one partially filled with hot water, the other with icy, cold water. Attach the balloon over the neck of the bottle. Put the bottle in the hot water and encourage the children to watch the balloon inflate. Next, move the bottle to the cold water as the children observe. Discuss the reason why the balloon changed.

Relate this to the way the lantern began to rise when it was filled with hot air. Ask the children what made it come back down.

The Pirates Are Coming

Recall the way Ah Mee and Tubby cooperated with the sailors to escape from the pirates. Choose a small group of children to sit on a lightweight mat, representing sailors on a ship. One child, designated the lookout, guards the "ship." When the "lookout" shouts, "The pirates are coming," the "sailors" quickly crawl under the mat. They work together on their hands and knees to move the "ship" toward a designated point.

Better Late Than Never

Ask the children why Ah Mee was late for his own birthday. Invite them to tell about a time when they were late for something special.

Load 'Em Up

Provide ten paper lanterns and a long stick such as a broom handle. Choose one child to be Ah Mee and another to be his father. As "Ah Mee" holds the stick on his shoulder, "Ah Mee's father" hangs lanterns on the stick. The children count the number of lanterns on the front of "Ah Mee's" stick and the number of lanterns on the back to determine his "load." Have the children state the corresponding addition fact. Continue the activity, creating new "loads" for "Ah Mee."

Variation: To create subtraction problems, the children pretend to be Ah Mee selling his lanterns at the market.

Floating Adventures

Instruct the children to close their eyes and imagine they are floating high in the sky. Ask them where they are and what they see. Encourage the children to illustrate their imaginary adventures.

Woodworking Wish

Invite the children to use a hammer, nails, and soft wood scraps, as Ah Mee did, to construct a miniature bunk bed or other items that can be given as gifts to friends.

Variation: Children use craft sticks and glue to make wooden gifts.

Make It Enormous

Score a picture of an air-related object into equal sized squares. Number the squares on the back and cut the grid apart. Give one of the pieces and a large square sheet of paper to each child. Instruct the children to recreate and enlarge the small picture on their big paper. The children then place their large pictures in order, creating an enormous version of the original air-related picture.

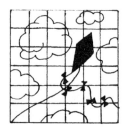

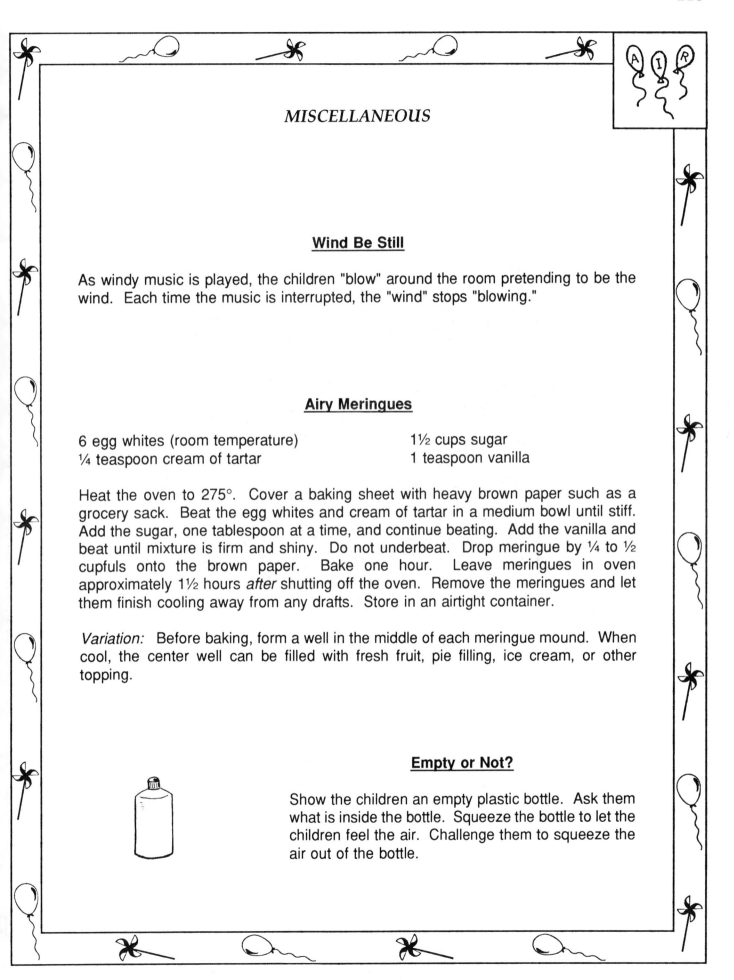

MISCELLANEOUS

Wind Be Still

As windy music is played, the children "blow" around the room pretending to be the wind. Each time the music is interrupted, the "wind" stops "blowing."

Airy Meringues

6 egg whites (room temperature)   1½ cups sugar
¼ teaspoon cream of tartar   1 teaspoon vanilla

Heat the oven to 275°. Cover a baking sheet with heavy brown paper such as a grocery sack. Beat the egg whites and cream of tartar in a medium bowl until stiff. Add the sugar, one tablespoon at a time, and continue beating. Add the vanilla and beat until mixture is firm and shiny. Do not underbeat. Drop meringue by ¼ to ½ cupfuls onto the brown paper. Bake one hour. Leave meringues in oven approximately 1½ hours *after* shutting off the oven. Remove the meringues and let them finish cooling away from any drafts. Store in an airtight container.

Variation: Before baking, form a well in the middle of each meringue mound. When cool, the center well can be filled with fresh fruit, pie filling, ice cream, or other topping.

Empty or Not?

Show the children an empty plastic bottle. Ask them what is inside the bottle. Squeeze the bottle to let the children feel the air. Challenge them to squeeze the air out of the bottle.

Catch the Wind

On a windy day, challenge pairs of children to run and catch the wind in large plastic trash bags. Tie the ends closed and invite the children to sit on the air-filled bags or play catch with them.

Air Is Where?

Provide a brick, cup, soil, and an empty bottle. Ask the children to predict which items contain air. Immerse each item in a tank filled with water to test the predictions. Encourage the children to observe the air bubbles.

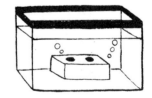

Flowing Streamers

On a breezy day, give the children streamers or ribbons to explore the wind's movement. Music can add to the fun as the children move with the wind.

Are Two Straws Better Than One?

Snack time might be a fun time to try this activity. Provide a cup of juice and two straws for each child. Ask the children to drink their juice using one straw, then two. Next, instruct them to place one of the straws outside the cup and try drinking with both of the straws. Discuss the results.

Playful Air

Add air-related items such as empty plastic bottles, basters, straws, or wire whisks, to the housekeeping center. An air pump, a tire, a raft, or other swim toys might inspire the children to be workers in a bike shop or service station.

Air Escape

Invite the children to take turns pushing a paper cup, bottom down, into a container of water. Next, invert the cup and have them try again. As the children feel the added force, ask them what is causing it. Poke a hole in the bottom of the cup. Then keep it inverted and lower it into the water. Encourage the children to feel the air push through the hole.

Edible Pinwheels

3 large cans of refrigerated crescent rolls
Butter or margarine
Cinnamon sugar

Heat the oven to 375°. Separate the dough into 12 rectangles. Press the perforations firmly together on each rectangle. Cut the rectangles in half, forming 24 squares. Slit the corners of each square almost to the center. Lift the point of one corner and press it into the center of the square. Continue with alternate corners to create a pinwheel effect.

Place each pinwheel on an ungreased cookie sheet. Bake for 11 to 12 minutes or until golden brown. After removing the pinwheels from the oven, butter and sprinkle with cinnamon sugar.

Variation: Fill the centers of plain pinwheels with toppings such as cheese, jelly, or pie filling.

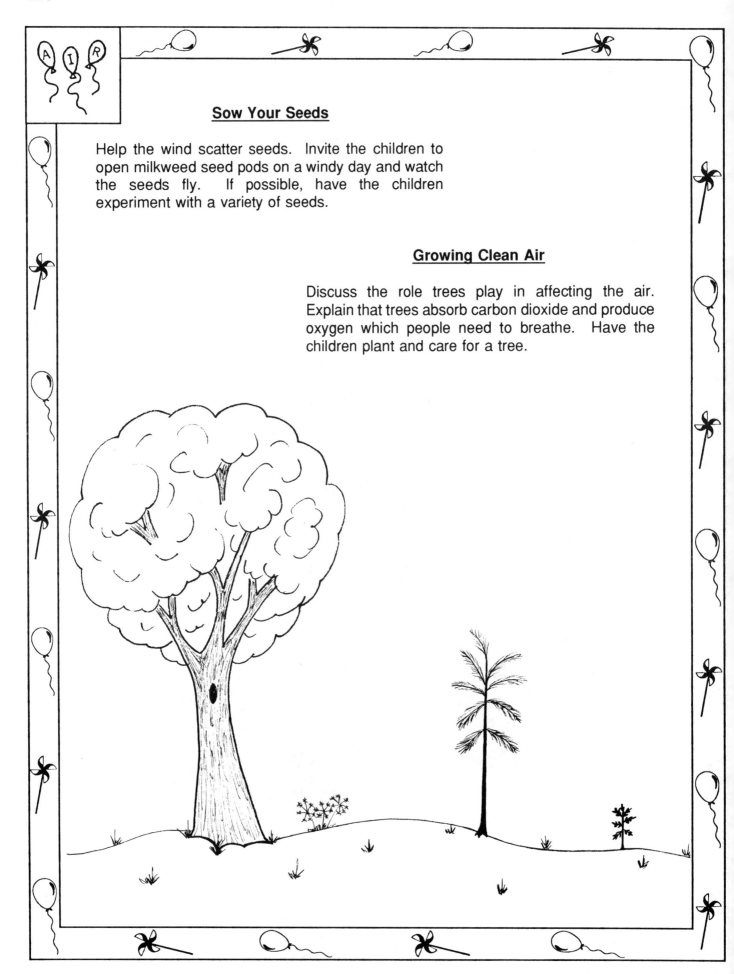

Sow Your Seeds

Help the wind scatter seeds. Invite the children to open milkweed seed pods on a windy day and watch the seeds fly. If possible, have the children experiment with a variety of seeds.

Growing Clean Air

Discuss the role trees play in affecting the air. Explain that trees absorb carbon dioxide and produce oxygen which people need to breathe. Have the children plant and care for a tree.

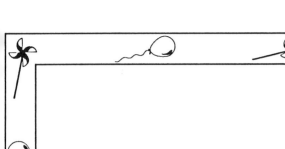

ART

Ping Pong Puff

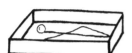

Place a sheet of paper in a shallow box. Fill small containers with different colors of paint. The children use eyedroppers to drip drops of paint onto the paper. Ask the children to place a ping pong ball in the box and blow it back and forth across the paper to create interesting patterns and designs.

Sand Blowing

Ask the children to make a scene or design with glue, on brightly colored construction paper. Then have them blow sand across their paper. Shake off the excess sand.

Variation: Use colored sand on white paper.

Kite String Painting

Instruct the children to fold a piece of paper in half and place it on a flat surface. Dip a kite string, twice the length of the paper, into paint and lay it inside the folded paper. Press down gently on top of the paper with one hand and pull out the string. The children unfold the paper to see the colorful design.

Variation: Use a clothespin to hold one end of a painted string, dip the string in paint and swirl it on paper to make designs.

Fancy Folded Fans

Children create a design or pattern on both sides of a 9" x 12" sheet of construction paper. Help them fold the paper back and forth in accordion pleats. Staple one end to create a fan.

Air Heads

Make tagboard shoes as the base for a balloon creature. Inflate a balloon, tie a knot and attach it to the "shoes." Encourage the children to use their imagination and decorate the balloon with permanent markers and stickers. Every time the balloon creatures are tossed in the air, they land on their feet! (A shoe pattern is provided on page 336.)

Class–E–Ball

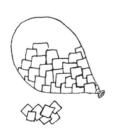

Inflate a round balloon. The children take turns dipping squares of non-bleeding tissue paper into liquid starch and applying the paper squares onto the balloon until the surface is covered. Dry overnight.

Additional layers can be applied until all of the children have participated. After drying thoroughly, pop the balloon and listen for air to escape. Children can play with their handmade paper ball.

Huff and Puff a Picture

Children spoon thinned tempera onto paper. They blow air through halved straws to spread the paint. The children can experiment blowing different directions and speeds.

Variation: After the paint dries, add other details to the picture using construction paper or crayons.

Bubble Prints

Put a small amount of bubble solution in several bowls. Add drops of food coloring or tempera paint and stir. The children put a straw into the mixture and blow until bubbles rise above the rim of the bowl. Lay a piece of finger paint paper on the rim. As the paper is lifted and the bubble pops, a fancy bubble print will remain. Move the paper from bowl to bowl creating colorful designs.

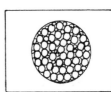

Windy Whip

In a large mixing bowl, add ½ cup water to 2 cups of Ivory Snow®. Using a wire whisk or a hand beater, children whip air into the mixture until it is thick and creamy. Invite them to finger paint with the soap mixture on colored paper while listening to "windy" music.

Variation: Finger paint a design on a smooth, flat surface. Press a paper on the design and lift the print.

Air Pressure Art

Fill paint containers with thinned tempera. Ask the children to lower one end of a straw into the paint. Have them cover the open end with their finger as they raise the straw out of the paint. Instruct them to remove their finger and release the paint onto a paper towel. Encourage the children to drop different colors of paint onto their towel, watching the colors explode!

Kite String Design

Provide a board about 1" thick, a ¾" flat head screw, kite string, and colored chalk. Fasten the screw 1" from the top center edge. Leave a ⅛" gap between the board and the head of the screw. Tie a piece of string around the screw and rub it with chalk.

Cut paper into large air-related shapes such as kites or balloons. The children place a shape under the string, pull it taut with one hand, and snap it against the paper with the other. Move the paper in different positions to make criss-cross patterns. Spray the shape with fixative.

Dirty Air

Suggest the children draw a picture of our beautiful world using colored chalk or crayons. Paint with black tempera on the entire surface of a large tray. While the paint is wet, have the children place their drawing face down on the painted tray. The children lift the paper to discover the effect of "dirty air."

DRAMA

Piloting a Plane

Read the following script as the children pilot an imaginary plane.

"Let's go into the cockpit. Watch your head, the door is low. Now buckle your seat belt and turn the key in the ignition. The propeller is spinning and the engine is R O A R I N G! 'Pilot to tower, pilot to tower, come in please.' All is clear for takeoff. Push the throttle forward — ZOOM, ZOOM! We're picking up speed. Oh no, it's starting to rain. Turn on your windshield wipers. BUMP, BUMP! Those are big clouds. Finally, high above the clouds, flying smoothly. Right on course. Look down at the airport . . . there it is on your left. Don't miss it. Pull your throttle back and slow down. Down, down we go toward the runway. THUMP, THUMP! Your wheels are down. Foot on the brake — S C R E E C H! Taxi down the runway and pull into your parking space. Unbuckle your seat belt. That was a long trip . . . better stretch. Ah-h-h, down the stairs—here at last!"

The Invisible Visitor

Read the following story in a quiet voice. The story becomes more eerie with each line. The last line is a sudden shout. Ask the children to listen and determine the identity of the visitor.

There was an old lady who sat in her house,
Waiting for a visitor—even a mouse.
She sat and she sat and she moaned the same song;
Sat rocking and moaning all the day long.
Suddenly she heard him—her gate how it cre-e-eaked.
When up walked the visitor; her porch boards they sque-e-eaked.
She looked and she looked, but no one was there,
Not even a mouse coming up the front stair.
Her eyes were quite bad; she must have them fixed;
Or could it just be her ears playing tricks?
He tugged at her dress and rattled her keys,
Blew dust in her nose and caused her to sneeze.
"Co-o-ome, Co-o-ome," said the visitor as he twirled around,
"Co-o-ome, follow me—more mischief I've found."

"Ha-ha, hoo-hoo," he laughed as he tousled her hair,
Whirled through her house without even a care.
She looked and she looked and she strained her eyes,
But still saw no visitor; was he in disguise?
He tangled her curtains and blew out her light,
Shook the whole house and gave her a fright.
"What is it you want—I can't see you, you know.
You're ruining my house; I wish you would go."
"Oh-h-h-h?" said the visitor with a sad little sigh.
She was feeling quite certain he was ready to cry.
He whirled and he whirled around the dark room
And finally came to rest aside of her broom.
"Forgi-i-ive me-e-e," said the visitor, "I mean you no harm.
I just came to show you a bit of my charm."
He came right up beside her and tickled her knee,
Swished out to her clothesline and dried her laundry.
He returned to her house and stirred up her fire
For he did not want her to think him a liar.
"E-e-e-excu-u-use me-e-e, ma-a-am, your house I did not mean to upset.
I can be very friendly; please do not fret."
And just as she was feeling so calm without fear,
He gave a great **PUFF AND BLEW HER OUT OF HER CHAIR**!

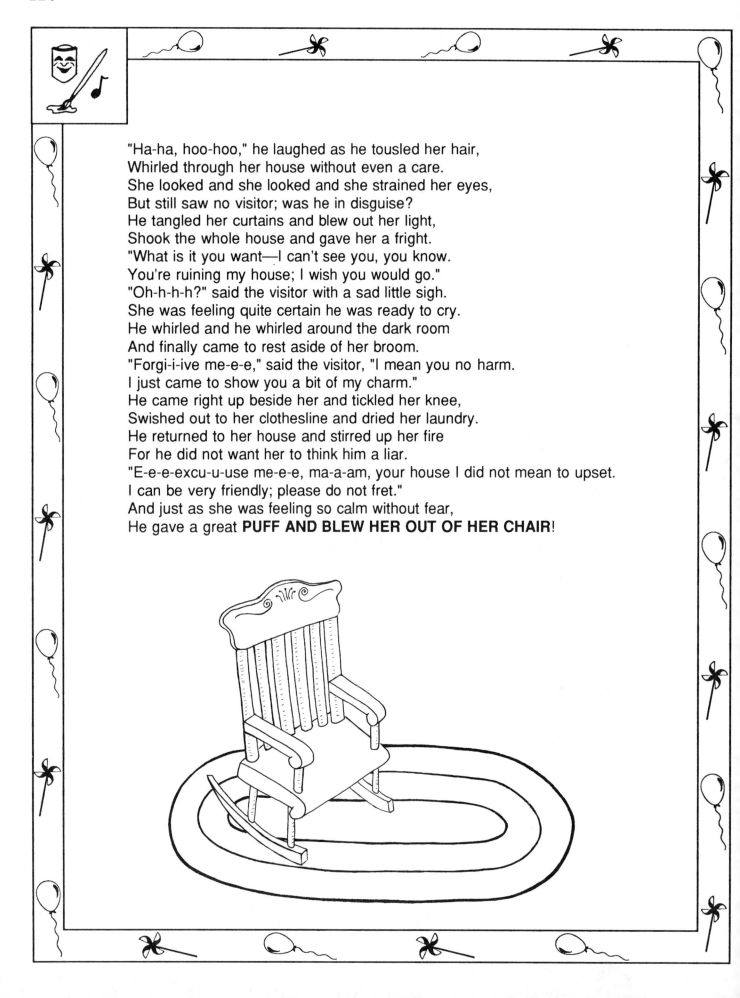

WELL-KNOWN RECORDINGS

Hap Palmer

"Tree Fell Down." Easy Does It.

"Smoke Drifts to the Sky." Easy Does It.

"How Are We Going?" Learning Basic Skills Through Music, Vocabulary.

"High and Low." Learning Basic Skills Through Music, Vocabulary.

Greg Scelsa and Steve Millang

"What If." We All Live Together, Volume 4.

Ella Jenkins

"Harmonica Happiness." Play Your Instruments and Make a Pretty Sound.

"Let's Listen to the Band." Play Your Instruments and Make a Pretty Sound.

Wee Sing

"Little Boy Blue." Wee Sing Nursery Rhymes and Lullabies.

"Rock-A-Bye, Baby." Wee Sing Nursery Rhymes and Lullabies.

"Bubble Gum." Wee Sing and Play.

"Roll That Ball." Wee Sing and Play.

SONGS

FLYIN' THE PLANE

(Tune: *Ballin' the Jack*)

First you put your two wings out to the side,
Start up your engine and you glide, glide, glide.
You steer to the left, then you steer to the right,
You pull the throttle down with all your might.
Spin your propeller 'round and 'round,
It helps to lift you off the ground.
You steer down the runway in the right lane,
And that's what we call flyin' the plane.

You dip and you turn and you fly up high,
Now you are soarin' in the sky, sky, sky.
You fly up above the deep blue sea,
Where a big whale looks as small as a pea.
You glide down swiftly though the air,
Then you put your brakes on with lots of care.
You steer down the runway in the right lane,
And that's what we call flyin' the plane . . .
And that's what we call flyin' the plane.

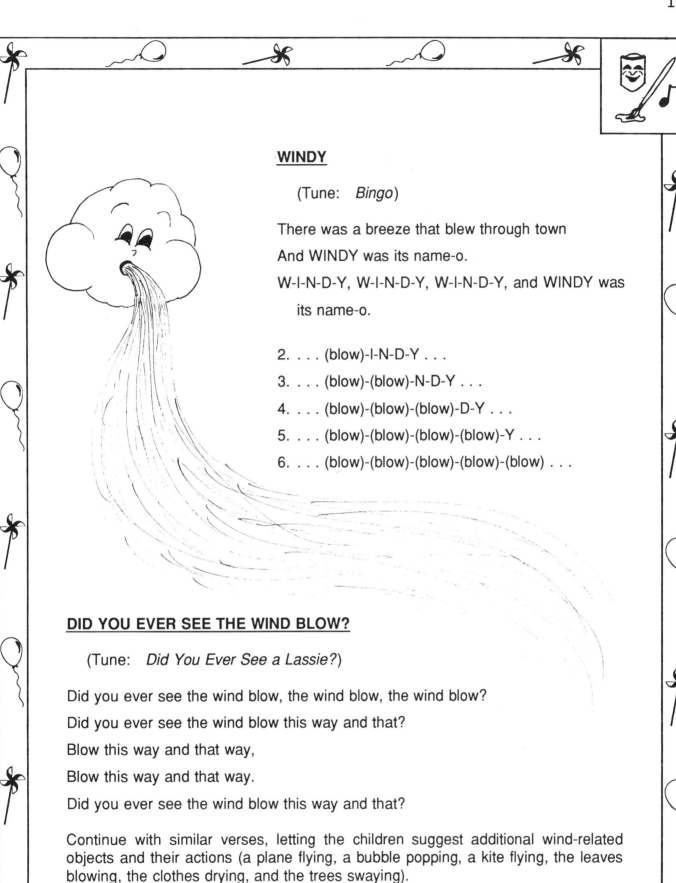

WINDY

(Tune: *Bingo*)

There was a breeze that blew through town
And WINDY was its name-o.
W-I-N-D-Y, W-I-N-D-Y, W-I-N-D-Y, and WINDY was
   its name-o.

2. . . . (blow)-I-N-D-Y . . .
3. . . . (blow)-(blow)-N-D-Y . . .
4. . . . (blow)-(blow)-(blow)-D-Y . . .
5. . . . (blow)-(blow)-(blow)-(blow)-Y . . .
6. . . . (blow)-(blow)-(blow)-(blow)-(blow) . . .

DID YOU EVER SEE THE WIND BLOW?

(Tune: *Did You Ever See a Lassie?*)

Did you ever see the wind blow, the wind blow, the wind blow?

Did you ever see the wind blow this way and that?

Blow this way and that way,

Blow this way and that way.

Did you ever see the wind blow this way and that?

Continue with similar verses, letting the children suggest additional wind-related objects and their actions (a plane flying, a bubble popping, a kite flying, the leaves blowing, the clothes drying, and the trees swaying).

BUBBLE BLOWIN'

   (Tune: *She'll Be Comin' 'Round the Mountain When She Comes*)

Oh, I'm blowing *tiny* bubbles; watch me blow! (Blow, blow)

Oh, I'm blowing *tiny* bubbles; watch me blow! (Blow, blow)

Oh, I'm blowing *tiny* bubbles,

Oh, I'm blowing *tiny* bubbles,

Oh, I'm blowing *tiny* bubbles; watch me blow! (Blow, blow)

Verse 2:   Substitute *big* for *tiny* and blow harder.

Verse 3:   Substitute *giant* for *tiny* and blow even harder.

INHALE, EXHALE

   (Tune: *This Old Man*)

Inhale in, exhale out,

That's what breathing's all about—

With a huff and a puff,

Just fill your lungs with air;

Slowly let it out with care.

WHAT DO WE BREATHE?

   (Tune: *Billy Boy*)

Do you know what we breathe in our lungs, in our lungs?

Do you know what we breathe in our lungs?

It is air that we need;

It's important, yes indeed.

It is air that we breathe in our lungs.

WINDY DAY PLAY

(Tune: *One Little Elephant Went Out to Play*)

One little kite went out to play,

Up in the sky on a windy day.

It had such enormous fun

That it called for the *second* little kite to come.

Two little kites went out to play,

Up in the sky on a windy day.

They had such enormous fun

That they called for the *third* little kite to come.

Continue adding verses. Other air-related items may be substituted for kites, such as balloons, planes, or leaves.

A-I-R

(Tune: *Are You Sleeping?*)

A-I-R,

A-I-R,

That spells air.

That spells air.

See it when a kite blows;

Feel it on your wet toes.

We know it's there.

We know it's there.

POP! POP!

(Tune: *Little Green Frog*)

Pop, pop, went the little balloon one day.

Pop, pop, went the little balloon.

Pop, pop, went the little balloon one day

As it grew and grew and grew. POP! (Clap hands)

HISS! HISS!

(Tune: *Boom, Boom, Ain't It Great to Be Crazy?*)

Hiss, hiss, goes the <u>tire</u> when air comes out.

Hiss, hiss, goes the <u>tire</u> when air comes out.

Gently squeeze it or push it all out.

Hiss, hiss, goes the <u>tire</u> when air comes out.

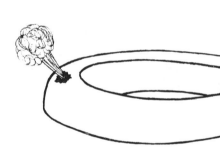

Additional verses may be added with children naming different items that hold air, such as a raft, float, balloon, or various types of balls.

WINDMILL, WINDMILL

(Tune: *Twinkle, Twinkle, Little Star*)

Windmill, windmill, spin so slow

As the gentle breezes blow.

Watch your vanes turn very fast

When the stronger winds blow past.

Windmill, windmill, help us see

What the wind is going to be.

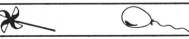

POEMS AND ACTION RHYMES

MY BALLOON

When I was small, I could not blow
The air inside and make it grow.

But now I'm big and know the way
To blow air in and make it stay.

I blow and blow and blow and blow
And watch my balloon just grow and grow.

But one thing yet I can't decide—
What do I do with the air inside?

I try to tie it in a knot
But my fingers still get caught.

Just when I think I've got it right
My balloon takes off and goes in flight.

And then it looks as it did before
Though now I laugh 'cause it flew out the door.

WARM HANDS*

Warm hands warm.   (Rub palms together)
Do you know how?
If you want to warm your hands
Blow your hands now.

THE WIND*

The wind is a friend when it's at rest,   (Clasp hands over stomach)
But sometimes we find the wind is a pest.   (Shake head)

When the air is hot, wind cools me off,   (Fan face, smile)
But when it's cold, it makes me cough.   (Cough)

It turns windmills to give us power,   (Make circular motion with arm)
But makes a storm of a summer shower.   (Drum fingers on desk,
                                            make thunder noises)

It pushes our sailboats and kites and things,   (Blow at moving, cupped hand)
But also throws sand at us, which stings.   (Grasp arm as if hurt)

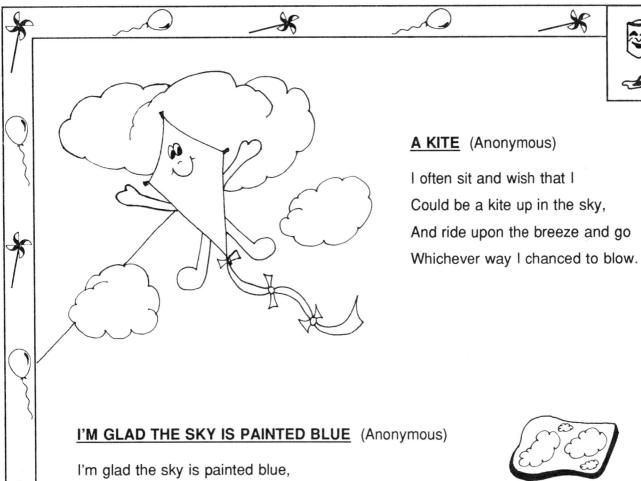

A KITE (Anonymous)

I often sit and wish that I
Could be a kite up in the sky,
And ride upon the breeze and go
Whichever way I chanced to blow.

I'M GLAD THE SKY IS PAINTED BLUE (Anonymous)

I'm glad the sky is painted blue,
And the earth is painted green,
With such a lot of nice fresh air
All sandwiched in between.

LEAVES ARE FLOATING DOWN*

Leaves are floating softly down;   (Flutter fingers)
They make a carpet on the ground
Then swish! The wind comes swirling by   (Bring hand around rapidly)
And sends them dancing to the sky.   (Flutter fingers upward)

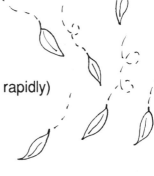

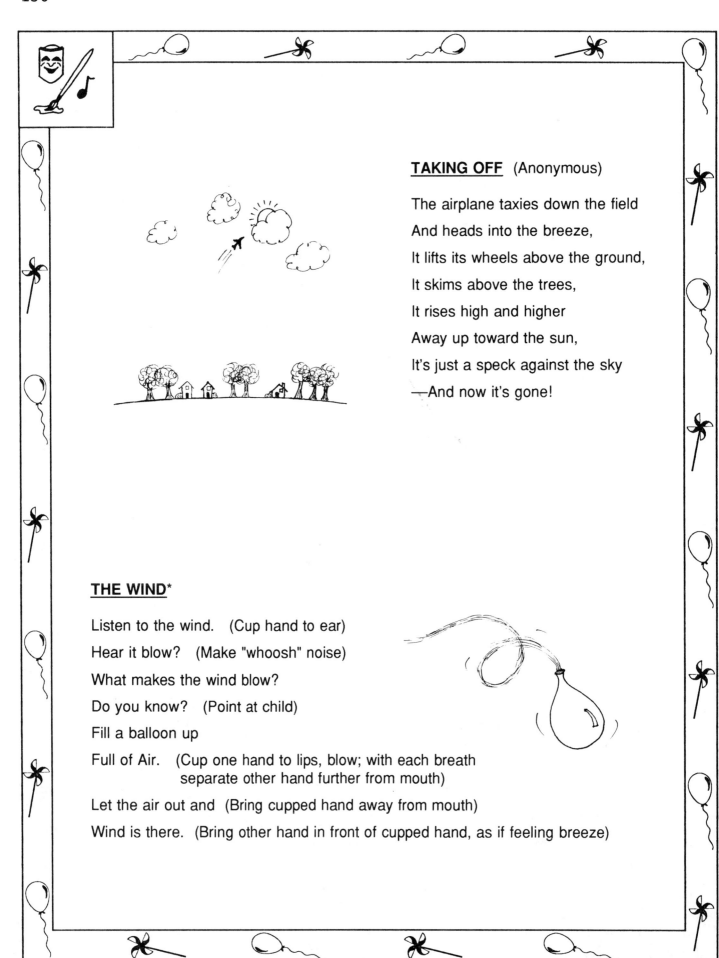

TAKING OFF (Anonymous)

The airplane taxies down the field
And heads into the breeze,
It lifts its wheels above the ground,
It skims above the trees,
It rises high and higher
Away up toward the sun,
It's just a speck against the sky
—And now it's gone!

THE WIND*

Listen to the wind.   (Cup hand to ear)

Hear it blow?   (Make "whoosh" noise)

What makes the wind blow?

Do you know?   (Point at child)

Fill a balloon up

Full of Air.   (Cup one hand to lips, blow; with each breath
                      separate other hand further from mouth)

Let the air out and (Bring cupped hand away from mouth)

Wind is there. (Bring other hand in front of cupped hand, as if feeling breeze)

STORY BOOKS

Hot-Air Henry by Mary Calhoun

After stowing away in a hot-air balloon, a Siamese cat takes a suspenseful flight across the country.

Who Took the Farmer's Hat? by Joan L. Nodset

When searching for his hat, a farmer discovers that the wind has found someone else who can put the hat to good use.

Whistle for Willie by Ezra Jack Keats

A little boy spends many long hours trying to whistle and then delights in his accomplishment.

Basil Brush Goes Flying by Peter Firmin

A fox, yearning to fly, observes how other things fly and then tries for himself.

The Wind and Me by Beverly Butler

A clever verse that portrays a child's perception of the wind.

The Wind Blew by Pat Hutchins

The mischievous wind takes away many belongings from people, only to return them in the end.

The True Story of the Three Little Pigs by Jon Scieszka

A humorous look at the other side of the story as told from the wolf's point of view.

Three in a Balloon by Sarah Wilson

This poetic book tells the true story of a sheep, duck, and rooster on their flight in the world's first hot-air balloon.

138

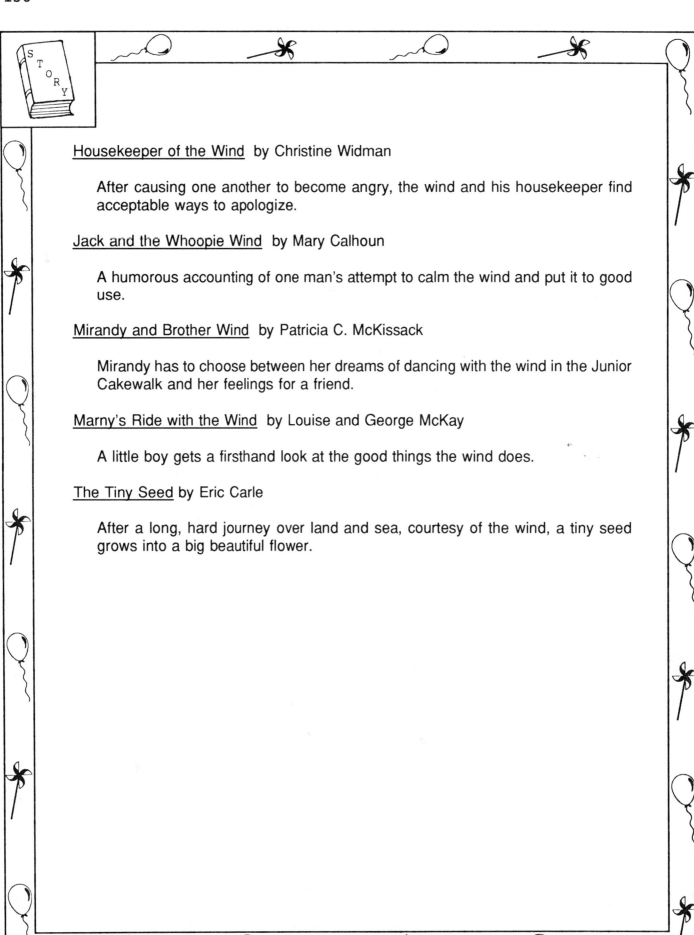

Housekeeper of the Wind by Christine Widman

After causing one another to become angry, the wind and his housekeeper find acceptable ways to apologize.

Jack and the Whoopie Wind by Mary Calhoun

A humorous accounting of one man's attempt to calm the wind and put it to good use.

Mirandy and Brother Wind by Patricia C. McKissack

Mirandy has to choose between her dreams of dancing with the wind in the Junior Cakewalk and her feelings for a friend.

Marny's Ride with the Wind by Louise and George McKay

A little boy gets a firsthand look at the good things the wind does.

The Tiny Seed by Eric Carle

After a long, hard journey over land and sea, courtesy of the wind, a tiny seed grows into a big beautiful flower.

CONCEPT BOOKS

<u>Why Does It Fly?</u> by Chris Arvetis and Carole Palmer; *Just Ask* series

Christopher Mouse learns how air lifts an airplane, helping it to fly.

<u>Catch the Wind! All About Kites</u> by Gail Gibbons

Two children learn about kites and how to make one of their own.

<u>Air, Air All Around</u> by Joanne Barkan; *First Facts* series

Through simplistic wording and colorful illustrations, this book helps children investigate the many properties and uses of air and the reasons it is so important to life.

<u>Air</u> by David Bennett; *Bear Facts* series

Bear presents a simplistic look at air and explains the reasons it is one of life's necessities.

<u>Wind Is to Feel</u> by Shirley Cook Hatch

Wind concepts are explored through observations and simple activities.

<u>My Balloon</u> by Fiona Pragoff, Kay Davies, and Wendy Oldfield; *Simple Science* series

Brightly colored photographs depict children exploring basic air concepts through easy activities.

<u>Air</u> by David Lloyd

This well-illustrated, informative book covers many aspects of air, including its strength and uses.

<u>Soap Bubbles</u> by Seymour Simon

Children are encouraged to experiment and discover as they play with bubbles.

<u>Air is All Around You</u> by Franklyn M. Branley; *Let's-Read-and Find-Out Science* series

This informative book presents a look at where air can be found even though it is not seen or heard.

<u>Oxygen Keeps You Alive</u> by Franklyn M. Branley; *Let's-Read-and-Find-Out Science* series

The importance of oxygen in the air and the many ways it affects life are explained in simplistic terms.

<u>Planes</u> by Anne Rockwell

All kinds of vehicles that fly are presented in this easy-to-read book.

<u>Air</u> by Maria Ruis and J. M. Parramon; *The Four Elements* series

Air is explained in easy-to-understand terms.

NOTES

142

NOTES

STORY O'MIMUS

asks

What is

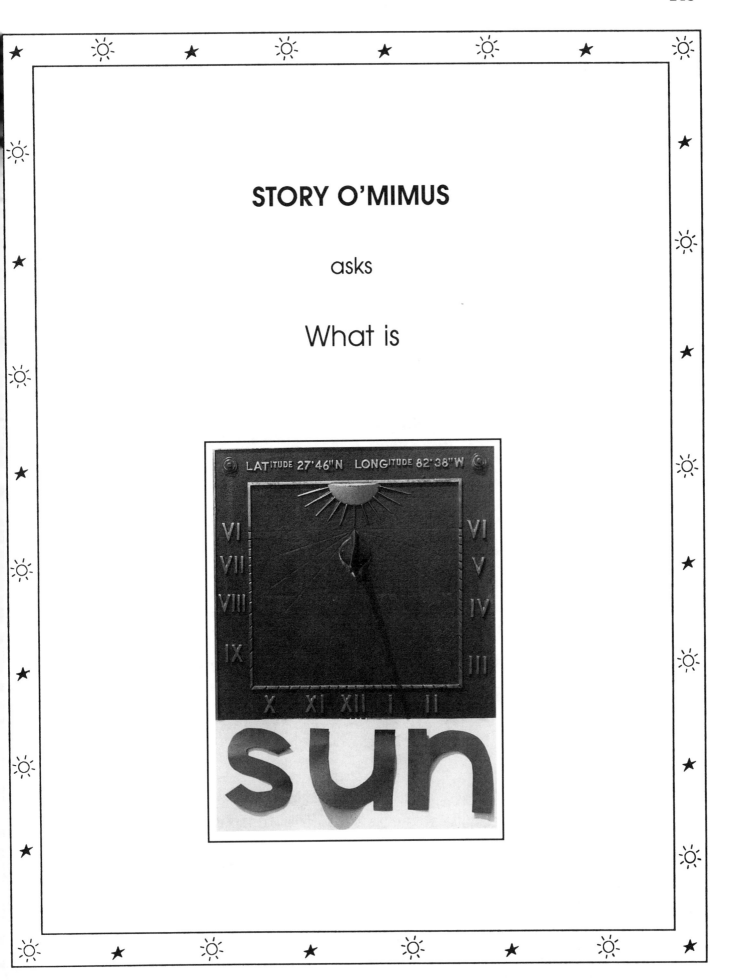

144

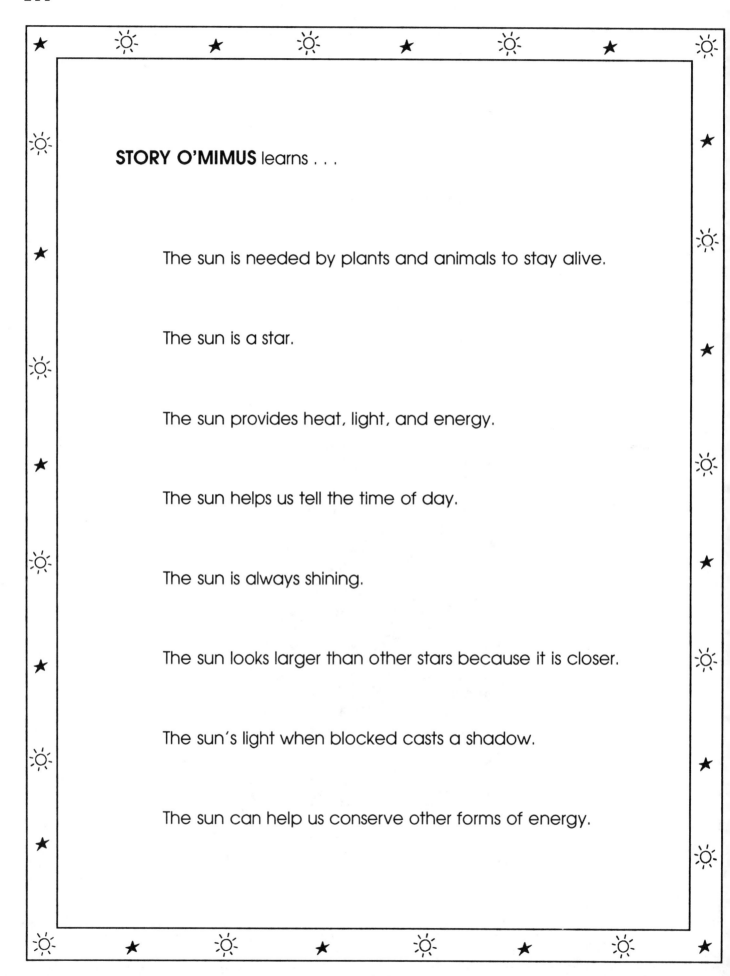

STORY O'MIMUS learns . . .

The sun is needed by plants and animals to stay alive.

The sun is a star.

The sun provides heat, light, and energy.

The sun helps us tell the time of day.

The sun is always shining.

The sun looks larger than other stars because it is closer.

The sun's light when blocked casts a shadow.

The sun can help us conserve other forms of energy.

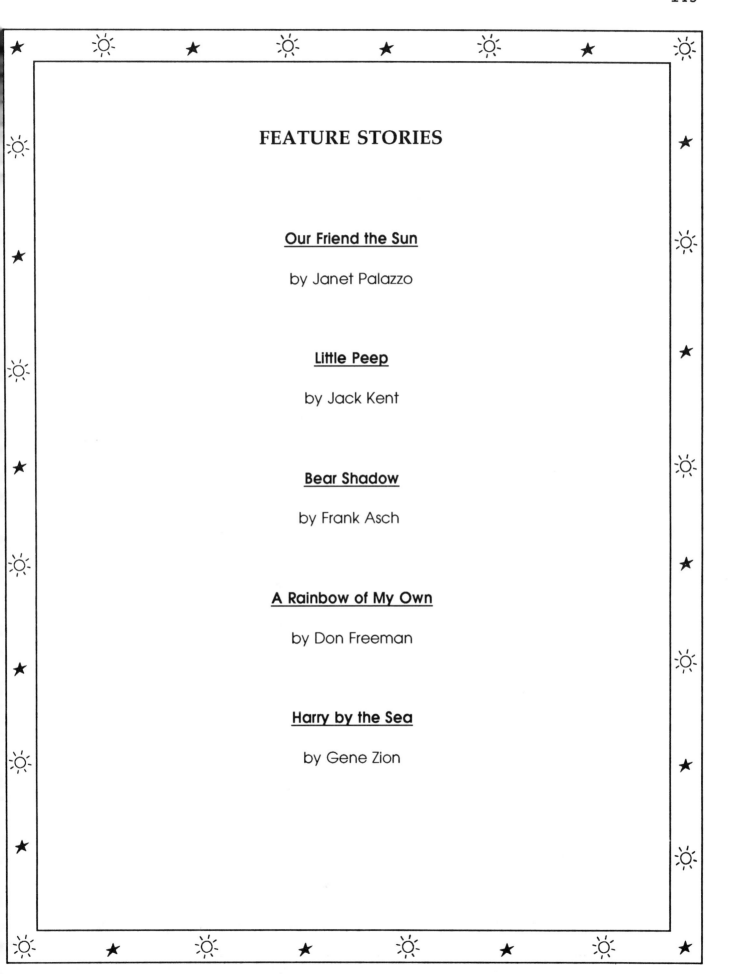

FEATURE STORIES

Our Friend the Sun

by Janet Palazzo

Little Peep

by Jack Kent

Bear Shadow

by Frank Asch

A Rainbow of My Own

by Don Freeman

Harry by the Sea

by Gene Zion

PLANNING GUIDE

Feature Stories

OUR FRIEND THE SUN	Language Arts	Math	Science, Health, Social Studies	Motor
Our Sunny Friend	●		○	
Sunflowers			●	
Spheres of All Sizes		●	○	
One World, One Sun			●	
Far Star		○	●	
Is It a Question?	●			
Out of Order	●	○		
Warm It Up			●	
Hot's Where It's At			○	●
Sunny Hours		●	○	
Model Mover			●	
Beam Me Out			○	●
Just One		●		○
Lacking Light			●	
Why Can't I See?			●	

LITTLE PEEP	Language Arts	Math	Science, Health, Social Studies	Motor
Sun Up Fun				●
Peeping Puppets	●			○
Never, Never, Never			●	○
Cock-a-Peeple-Cock	●			
Re-Peep	●			
Mo-o-ove Over			●	○
Peep Peep Clock		●		
Make My Day		●		○
Day, Night, Day, Night		●		
Speed It Up	●			○
Moo, Oink, Moo	○	●		
Time's Up				●
Sun Dance			●	○
Midnight Breakfast		○	○	●
Rotate and Revolve	○		●	○

Instructional Focus: ● Primary   ○ Secondary

BEAR SHADOW	Language Arts	Math	Science, Health, Social Studies	Motor
Where's Bear?	●	○		
Bear Shadow Tag			○	●
Let's Make a Deal			●	
Gummy Worms		●		
Coming Through			●	
Hide-n-Seek Shadows			●	
Trace a Bear			●	○
Me and My Shadow				●
Catch of the Day	○	○		●
Under Obstruction	○			●
Bear on the Move	●		○	○
Nail It Down	○		○	●
Will You Be My Shadow?				●

A RAINBOW OF MY OWN	Language Arts	Math	Science, Health, Social Studies	Motor
Rainbow Up				●
Seven, Seven, Seven		●		
Roll a Rainbow	●			
Huge Symmetrical Rainbow		○		●
Rainbow Sorting		●		○
Rainbow Relay			○	●
Twice as Nice	●			
Concealed Color	●			
Catch a Rainbow				●
Rainbow Transformations	●			○
Rainbow Dancing			●	
Burple Purple	●			
Bubbly Rainbows			●	○
As Orange As An Orange	●			
Pair a Word	●			○

HARRY BY THE SEA	Language Arts	Math	Science, Health, Social Studies	Motor
How Many Sunbeams?		●		○
Hurry, Harry!	●			
Only You Can Prevent Sunburn			●	
Creative Castles				●
Hot Spot			●	
Beanbag Sun Hats				●
The Unusual Umbrella	○			●
A Crowd in the Shade		●	○	
More or Less Protection		●	○	
Bead Up, Don't Burn Up			●	
Solar Cookin'			●	
Bushy-Backed Sea Slug	○			●
Cool Hats			●	○
Be Cool			●	
What Place?	●			○
Repeating Stripes		●		
Lemonade for Sale		●		
Hot Dog	●			○

MISCELLANEOUS	Language Arts	Math	Science, Health, Social Studies	Motor
Reach for the Sun			●	
Size It Up		●		
Sunny Time Rhymes	●			○
Sun Visors			○	●
Sunny Spies			●	
Fading Fast	●		○	
Sun-Dried Treats			●	
What Makes the Moon Shine?			●	
Sun's Too Bright			●	
"Go" Power			●	
Sentimental Silhouettes			●	
If the Sun Could Talk . . .	●			○
Sun's Playtime	○	○	●	○
Tea Party			●	

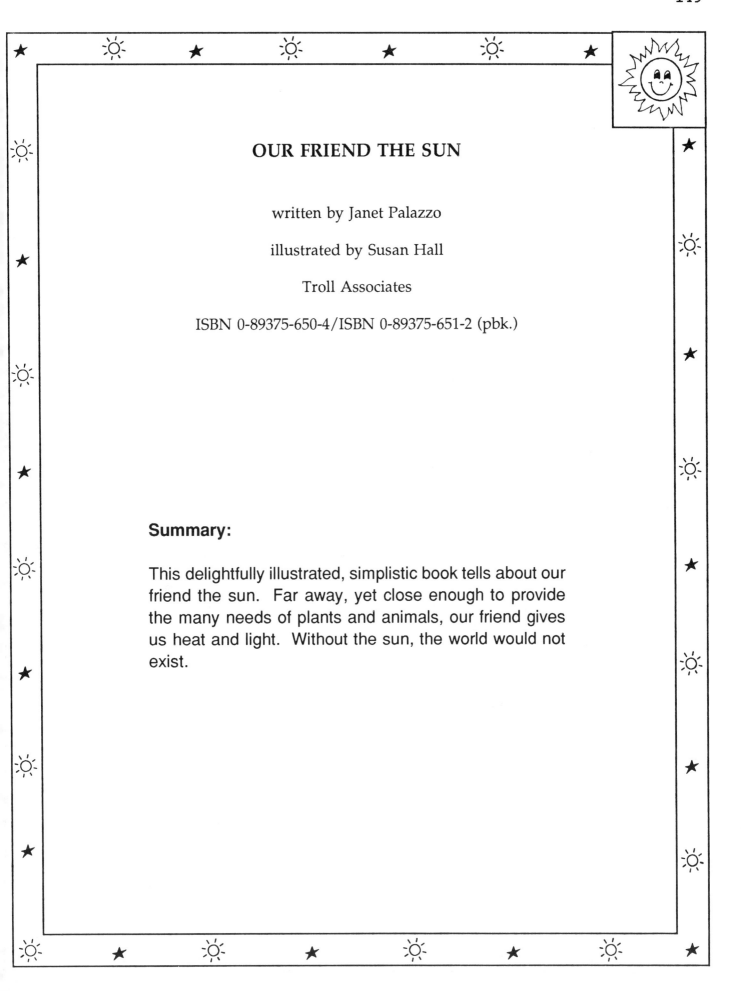

OUR FRIEND THE SUN

written by Janet Palazzo

illustrated by Susan Hall

Troll Associates

ISBN 0-89375-650-4/ISBN 0-89375-651-2 (pbk.)

Summary:

This delightfully illustrated, simplistic book tells about our friend the sun. Far away, yet close enough to provide the many needs of plants and animals, our friend gives us heat and light. Without the sun, the world would not exist.

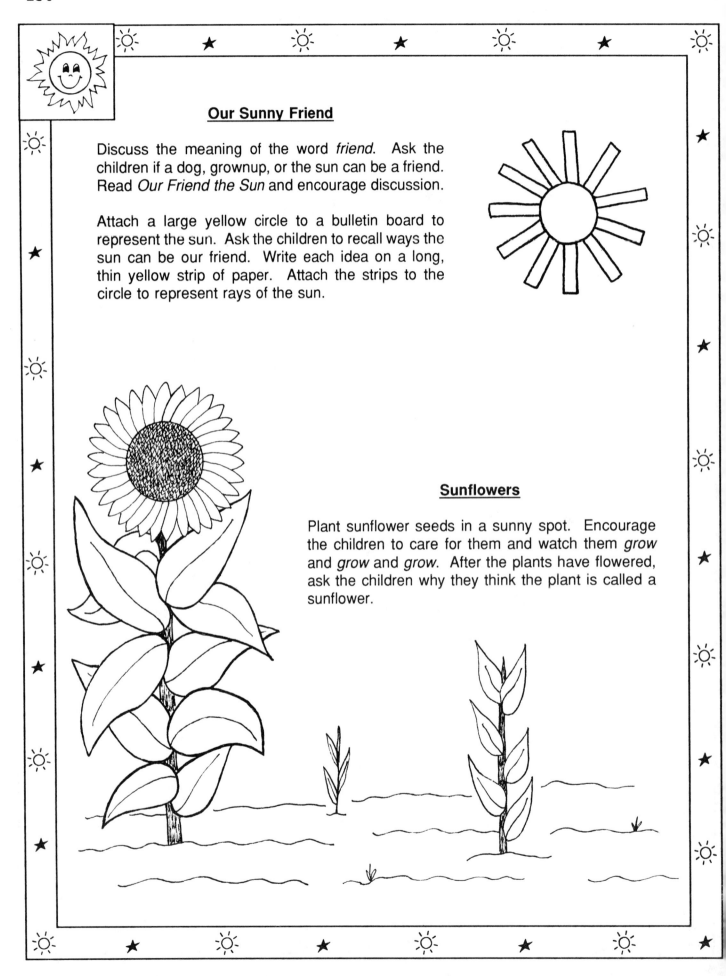

Our Sunny Friend

Discuss the meaning of the word *friend*. Ask the children if a dog, grownup, or the sun can be a friend. Read *Our Friend the Sun* and encourage discussion.

Attach a large yellow circle to a bulletin board to represent the sun. Ask the children to recall ways the sun can be our friend. Write each idea on a long, thin yellow strip of paper. Attach the strips to the circle to represent rays of the sun.

Sunflowers

Plant sunflower seeds in a sunny spot. Encourage the children to care for them and watch them *grow* and *grow* and *grow*. After the plants have flowered, ask the children why they think the plant is called a sunflower.

Spheres of All Sizes

Ask the children to tell the shape of the sun. If it is identified as a circle, use a ball and a record to show the difference between a circle and a sphere. Define the ball's roundness as a sphere and explain that the sun and earth are spheres. Encourage the children to locate spheres in the classroom. Brainstorm other sphere-shaped objects. Invite the children to manipulate classroom spheres to feel their roundness.

Variation: Children form their own spheres with clay. A large yellow sphere can represent the sun; a smaller blue one, the earth.

One World, One Sun

Sing or play a recording of "It's A Small World" and discuss the song's meaning. Ask the children to think of things people all over the world share, such as air, water, love, and the sun.

Far Star

Provide two identical playground balls and ask if they are the same size. Instruct one child to carry a ball to the opposite end of the playground. Ask the children why that ball looks smaller than the other. Instruct the child to return. Ask the children to describe the size of the ball as it gets closer and closer.

During this activity, if you are lucky, a plane might even fly overhead. If so, ask the children why planes look so small when they are in the sky. Discuss the reason why the sun and other stars look smaller than they really are.

Is It a Question?

Give each child three punctuation cards—a period, question mark, and exclamation mark. Reread the story to the children. Stop reading after each sentence. Ask the children to punctuate the sentence by holding up one of their cards. The children can pose questions and statements for their classmates to punctuate.

Out of Order

Recall the way the sun helps us order our day. Name three items or activities out of sequence. Instruct the children to restate them in order. Continue the activity using other sequences.

Examples: yesterday, tomorrow, today
evening, morning, noon
juice, drink, cup

Warm It Up

Provide two dishes, each containing an ice cube. Place one dish in the sun, the other in the shade. Ask the children which ice cube they think will be the first to melt. Have them check the ice cubes periodically to compare. After the cubes have melted completely, have the children watch to see which dish of water evaporates first.

Hot's Where It's At

One child leaves the room while an object, representing the sun, is hidden. The child returns and tries to find the "sun." The remaining children call out, "Hotter," as the child gets closer to the object. When the child moves farther away, the children call out, "Colder." Play continues until the object is found.

Sunny Hours

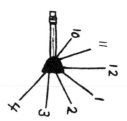

Locate a sunny area outside. Put a small mound of clay on the ground and push a pencil into it. Each hour mark a line on the ground where the shadow of the pencil falls. Indicate the hour. On the following day, ask the children to tell time using the sundial.

Variation: Daily activity times can be indicated instead of hour markings.

Model Mover

Display a toy car, toy dinosaur, and globe of the earth for the children to view. Focus their attention on the toy car and ask questions such as "What is it?" or "Is it a real car or a model of a car?" Repeat the questioning process with the dinosaur and the globe. If possible, use an orbiter gear-driven planetarium to demonstrate the earth revolving around the sun while rotating on its axis.

Beam Me Out

Choose one child, the "shiner," to sit in a chair, holding a flashlight. Darken the room. The remaining children crawl around the room trying to avoid being "beamed out" by the "shiner." When the children are still, they are safe; when moving, they become targets.

Just One

Ask the children how many suns we have in our world. Have them focus on *"one*-ness" by brainstorming other things there are just *one* of, such as *one* you and *one* me. Have each child color *one* sun on *one* piece of paper and rub it with *one* cotton ball. The effect of rubbing will make the "sun shine."

Lacking Light

Provide two healthy plants. Place one in a sunny spot and the other in a dark closet. Give each plant the same amount of water. After several days, have the children observe and compare the plants.

Variation: Cover an area of grass with a large container. After several days, remove the container and ask the children to describe the grass.

Why Can't I See?

Place objects in a lidded box. Poke a hole at one end of the box. Have the children use their sense of sight to look through the hole and try to identify the objects. Ask them why the objects are difficult to see. Poke a hole at the other end of the box and let the children look again. They will discover that they need light as well as their eyesight to see.

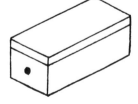

LITTLE PEEP

written by Jack Kent

Simon and Schuster Inc.

ISBN 0-671-67051-4/ISBN 0-671-67052-2 (pbk.)

Summary:

This humorous story tells about some barnyard animals who credit the rooster with waking the sun each day. Commotion begins when a newly hatched chick tries to take over the cock's important job. As Little Peep and the cock argue through the night, the sun comes up on its own. The barnyard animals are surprised as they realize the truth about the sun's daily ritual.

Sun Up Fun

Choose one child to represent the sun. The remaining children sit in a circle. The "sun" moves around the outside of the circle as the children chant,

"Rooster, rooster on the farm,

Wake the sun with your alarm."

As the chant ends, the "sun" taps the closest child who becomes the rooster. The "rooster" chases the "sun" around the circle and crows, "Cock-a-doodle-doo, cock-a-doodle-doo!" The "sun" tries to return to the "rooster's" spot without being caught. If successful, the "sun" may rest and the "rooster" becomes the new "sun." If the "rooster" catches the "sun," the "sun" goes to the center of the circle.

Peeping Puppets

Ask the children to recall the setting and characters in the story. Discuss the words and actions the author used to depict the behavior of the characters. Provide materials for the children to make puppets of the story's characters. These can be used to reenact the story. Props, such as a flashlight or pail, might add to the fun. (Puppet patterns are provided on pages 349–353.)

Never, Never, Never

Ask the children why the animals told Little Peep he must *never* annoy the cock. Brainstorm things people should *never* do. If the following *nevers* are not included by the children, add them to the discussion:

Never, never, never look at the sun.

Never, never, never stay in the sun without protecting your skin.

The children can make *Never, Never, Never* safety posters.

Cock-a-Peeple-Cock

Divide the class into groups. Ask each group to sit in a circle in a different part of the room. Whisper a silly animal sound combination, such as "Oink-a-moodle-oink," to one player in each group. The sound combination is whispered from one child to the next until the last child in each group "crows" out what was heard. The children will have fun listening to the end result.

Re-Peep

Recall the difficulty Little Peep had when he tried to repeat what the cock said. Recite tongue twisters for the children to "re-peep." Encourage the children to say them as quickly as they can. Sometimes they might not come out just right, but the secret is—to keep on practicing.

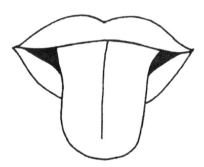

Examples: Silly Shelly sips shakes at the sunny seashore.

The blazing sun burned blisters on Billy Blair's back.

Mo-o-ove Over

Ask the children why the cock did not deserve the animals' respect. Encourage them to talk about a time when they have been bossed. The children take turns being the boss, repeating the following chant:

"Bossy, bossy is my name.
You must stop and play my game."

The boss gives a command for the others to follow, such as "Put your nose on your toes."

Peep Peep Clock

Encourage the children to help Little Peep tell time using a standard clock, preferably one that is gear-driven. Instruct the children to "peep" the number of times indicated by the short hand each time the long hand points to the **12**.

Make My Day

Ask the children to name activities they do during daylight hours. Provide white construction paper and markers for the children to illustrate an activity. Have them sort the illustrations into time periods of the day—morning, noon, or afternoon.

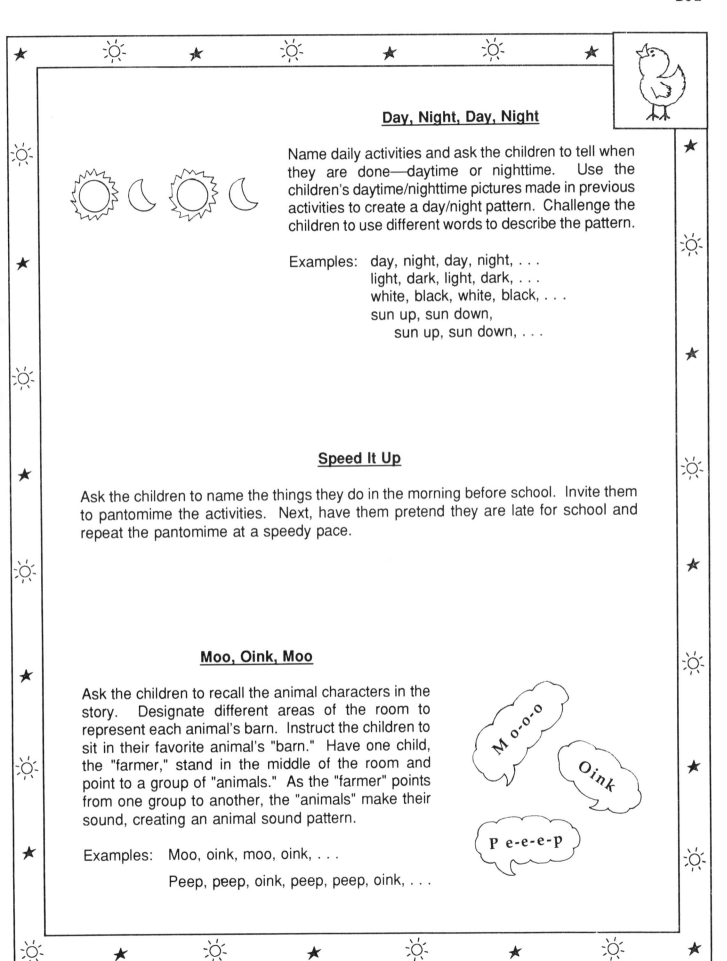

Day, Night, Day, Night

Name daily activities and ask the children to tell when they are done—daytime or nighttime. Use the children's daytime/nighttime pictures made in previous activities to create a day/night pattern. Challenge the children to use different words to describe the pattern.

Examples: day, night, day, night, . . .
light, dark, light, dark, . . .
white, black, white, black, . . .
sun up, sun down,
    sun up, sun down, . . .

Speed It Up

Ask the children to name the things they do in the morning before school. Invite them to pantomime the activities. Next, have them pretend they are late for school and repeat the pantomime at a speedy pace.

Moo, Oink, Moo

Ask the children to recall the animal characters in the story. Designate different areas of the room to represent each animal's barn. Instruct the children to sit in their favorite animal's "barn." Have one child, the "farmer," stand in the middle of the room and point to a group of "animals." As the "farmer" points from one group to another, the "animals" make their sound, creating an animal sound pattern.

Examples: Moo, oink, moo, oink, . . .

Peep, peep, oink, peep, peep, oink, . . .

162

Time's Up

Ask the children to sit in a circle. Pass a timer around the circle as the children sing the following song. The child caught holding the timer when it goes off must go to the center of the circle. Reset the timer and continue play.

(Tune: *The Farmer in the Dell*)

A'cock-a-doodle-doo!
A'cock-a-doodle-doo!
The rooster tries to wake the sun,
A'cock-a-doodle-doo!

A'peep-a-deedle-peep!
A'peep-a-deedle-peep!
The chick tries to wake the sun,
A'peep-a-deedle-peep!

A'moo-ka-doodle-moo!
A'moo-ka-doodle-moo!
The cow tries to wake the sun,
A'moo-ka-doodle-moo!

An oink-a-diddle-oink!
An oink-a-diddle-oink!
The pig tries to wake the sun,
An oink-a-diddle-oink!

Additional verses can be added using other farm animals.

Sun Dance

Choose two children—one to be the farmer, the other his wife. The remaining children sit in a circle. The "farmer" and his "wife" skip around the outside of the circle as the children sing the following song:

(Tune: *He's Got the Whole World in His Hands*)

> The farmer and his wife need the sun.
>
> The farmer and his wife need the sun.
>
> The farmer and his wife need the sun.
>
> The whole world needs the sun.

At the end of the verse, the "farmer" and his "wife" each choose another child who must name something else that needs the sun. The four children skip around the circle singing a new verse, such as "The dog and the cat need the sun . . ." Play continues until all of the children have been chosen. At that time, everyone joins hands and dances around the circle singing the following verse:

> The whole wide world needs the sun.
>
> The whole wide world needs the sun.
>
> The whole wide world needs the sun.
>
> The whole world needs the sun.

Midnight Breakfast

Ask the children why the animals started looking for their breakfast during the night. Brainstorm activities that are really done at night. Provide chalk dipped in liquid starch, which will serve as a fixative, for the children to illustrate a nighttime activity on black construction paper.

Rotate and Revolve

Choose one child to represent the sun and stand in the center of the room. Choose two others to stand back-to-back, hooking arms at the elbows to represent the earth. The "earth" rotates and revolves around the "sun." When one half of the "earth" faces the "sun," the remaining children call out "Day." When the same half turns away from the sun, the children call out "Night." Let the children take turns being the "sun" and the "earth."

Variation: Children substitute the words for day and night in other languages.

	Day	Night
Spanish	dia (dee-ah)	noche (no-chay)
French	jour (zhoor)	nuit (new-ee)
German	Tag (taak)	Nacht (nahkht)
Italian	giorno (jor-no)	notte (nawt-tay)
Japanese	hiru (he-rue)	yoru (yoe-rue)

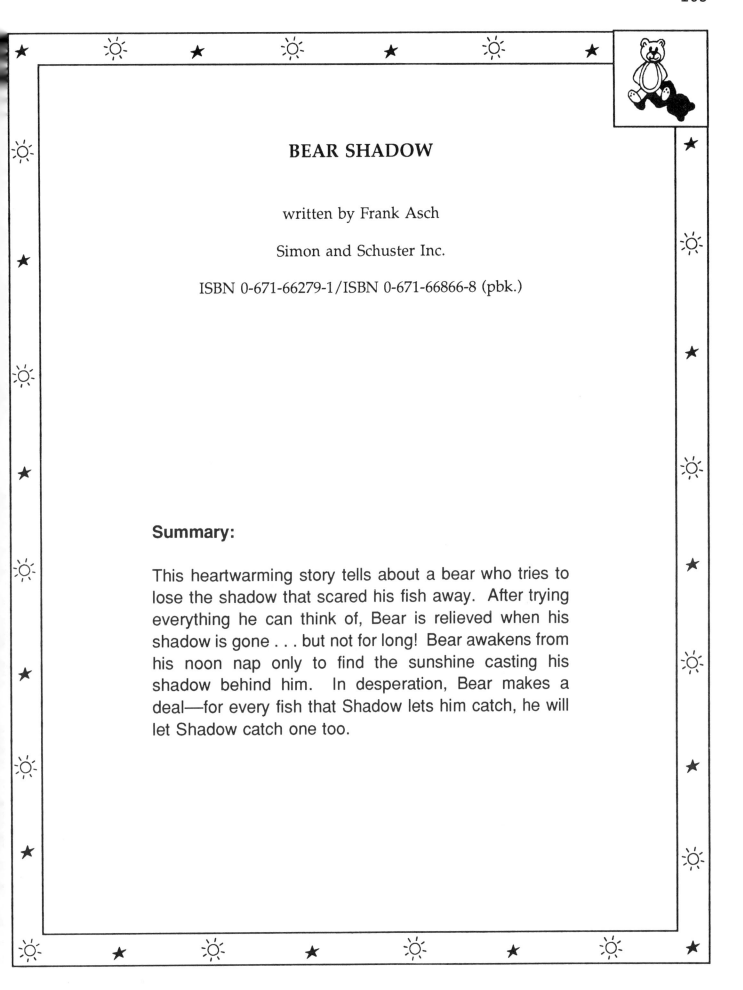

BEAR SHADOW

written by Frank Asch

Simon and Schuster Inc.

ISBN 0-671-66279-1/ISBN 0-671-66866-8 (pbk.)

Summary:

This heartwarming story tells about a bear who tries to lose the shadow that scared his fish away. After trying everything he can think of, Bear is relieved when his shadow is gone . . . but not for long! Bear awakens from his noon nap only to find the sunshine casting his shadow behind him. In desperation, Bear makes a deal—for every fish that Shadow lets him catch, he will let Shadow catch one too.

Where's Bear?

Hide a small bear in the classroom. Give the children clues to the bear's hiding place using positional terms such as *high*, *higher than*, *below*, or *near*.

Bear Shadow Tag

The children choose partners, one pretending to be Bear and the other his shadow. On a signal, "Bear" chases his "shadow" around the playing area. "Bear" captures his "shadow" by stepping on his partner's shadow. Once caught, the partners trade roles and play continues.

Let's Make a Deal

Recall Bear's problem and discuss how he solved it. Encourage the children to share an experience they have had making a deal with someone.

167

Gummy Worms

Recall what Bear put on his hook to catch a fish. Invite the children to view a clear container filled with edible worms. Ask them to estimate the number of worms in the container. After the worms have been counted, the children can pretend to be Bear and "hook" a worm for a chewy treat.

Coming Through

Ask the children why Bear had a shadow. Provide a light source and scraps of aluminum foil, waxed paper, fabric, plastic wrap, cellophane, or newspaper. Instruct the children to hold each in front of the light and observe. Sort the materials into categories—those that completely block the light, those that block some of the light, and those that do not block the light.

Variation: Colanders, strainers, screens, or nets can be used to make interesting designs.

Hide-n-Seek Shadows

Suspend a large white sheet in front of a film projector or other light source. Choose a small group of children to sit between the sheet and the projector. The remaining children sit in front of the sheet. Turn on the projector. Ask one child in the small group to perform an action. The children in front of the sheet try to guess the identity of the child by observing the shadow.

Trace a Bear

Early in the morning ask the children to observe the sun shining through a window. Attach a bear shape to the window and ask the children to find the bear's shadow. Show them how to place a piece of paper on the shadow and draw around its outline with a marking pen. Encourage the children to trace the bear's shadow at different times of the day, noticing the changes.

Me and My Shadow

Take the children outdoors on a sunny day for them to experience moving with their shadows. Incorporate locomotor skills such as skipping, running, walking, or hopping with other directions.

Examples: <u>Walk</u> sideways.   <u>Hop</u> in a zigzag pattern.
           <u>Skip</u> with a partner.   <u>Run</u> backward.

Catch of the Day

Provide a dowel fishing pole with a magnet tied to the end of the string. Cut paper fish of various shapes and sizes and attach a paper clip to each "mouth." Place the fish on aluminum foil representing a pond. The children pretend to be Bear fishing in the pond. Provide challenges for them to accomplish. (Fish patterns are provided on page 356.)

Examples: Catch the longest fish.
            Catch two fish that are the same color.
            Catch two fish that are the same shape.

Under Obstruction

Recall the many ways Bear tried to lose his shadow. Set up a course of obstacles to recreate the story's setting. Invite the children to participate in the design and construction. Challenge them to complete the obstacle course.

Bear on the Move

Provide the materials needed to make jointed bear puppets. (A pattern is provided on page 354.) Encourage the children to explore the positions their bear can make.

Variation: Place a bear puppet on an overhead projector so its shadow is projected onto a screen. Move the arms and legs and add the necessary props to recreate actions in the story. Ask the children to guess what "Bear" is doing. (Patterns are provided on page 354.)

Nail It Down

Relate this activity to Bear nailing down his shadow. Secure a scrap of wood in a vice or clamp so it lies flat. Stand a sturdy stencil to represent the initial of a child's name at the edge of the wood. Shine a light directly at the letter, casting its shadow on the wood. The child hammers nails on the shadow and will delight in seeing the shape of the letter remain after the light is removed.

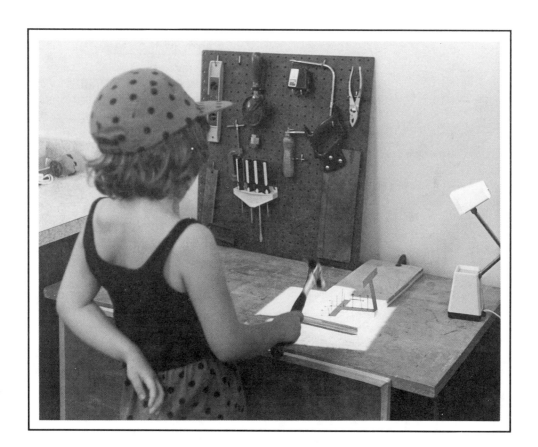

Will You Be My Shadow?

Children choose partners and stand facing each other. One child, pretending to be Bear, slowly performs an action, such as nodding his head, turning around, or jumping up and down. The partner, "Bear's" shadow, mimics the action. After several turns, the children switch roles.

A RAINBOW OF MY OWN

written by Don Freeman

Penguin (Puffin)

ISBN 0-14-050328-5/ISBN 0-670-58928-4 (pbk.)

Summary:

This well-loved story portrays a little boy's wish to catch a rainbow on a rainy day. When he discovers this is impossible, the little boy imagines the many fun things he would do with a rainbow of his own. As the little boy returns home from his imaginary adventure, he discovers the sun has made his dream come true. There, dancing on his bedroom wall, is a rainbow of his very own.

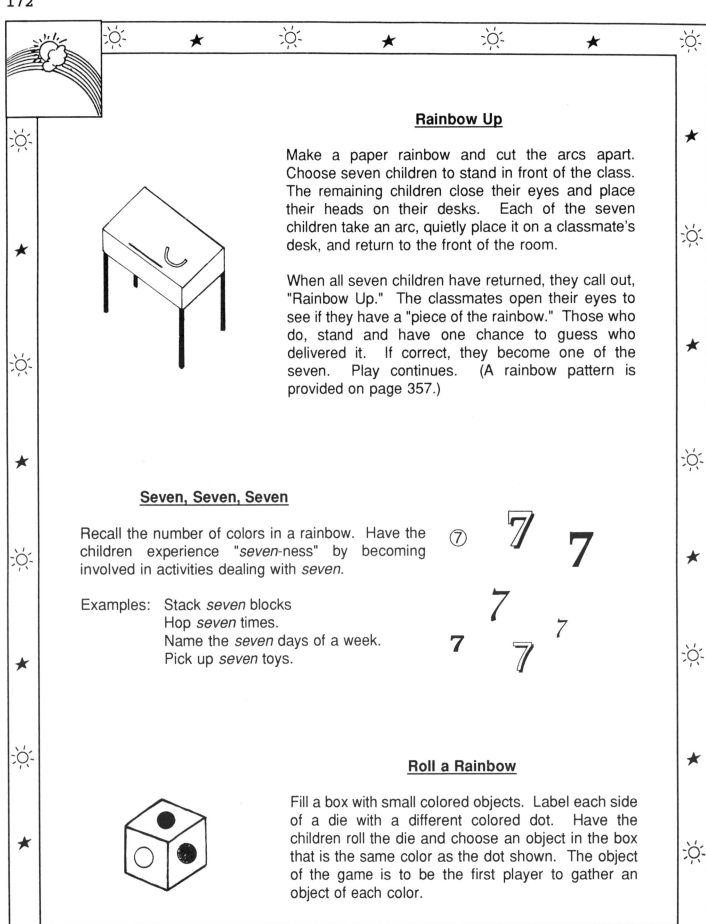

Rainbow Up

Make a paper rainbow and cut the arcs apart. Choose seven children to stand in front of the class. The remaining children close their eyes and place their heads on their desks. Each of the seven children take an arc, quietly place it on a classmate's desk, and return to the front of the room.

When all seven children have returned, they call out, "Rainbow Up." The classmates open their eyes to see if they have a "piece of the rainbow." Those who do, stand and have one chance to guess who delivered it. If correct, they become one of the seven. Play continues. (A rainbow pattern is provided on page 357.)

Seven, Seven, Seven

Recall the number of colors in a rainbow. Have the children experience "*seven*-ness" by becoming involved in activities dealing with *seven*.

Examples: Stack *seven* blocks
Hop *seven* times.
Name the *seven* days of a week.
Pick up *seven* toys.

Roll a Rainbow

Fill a box with small colored objects. Label each side of a die with a different colored dot. Have the children roll the die and choose an object in the box that is the same color as the dot shown. The object of the game is to be the first player to gather an object of each color.

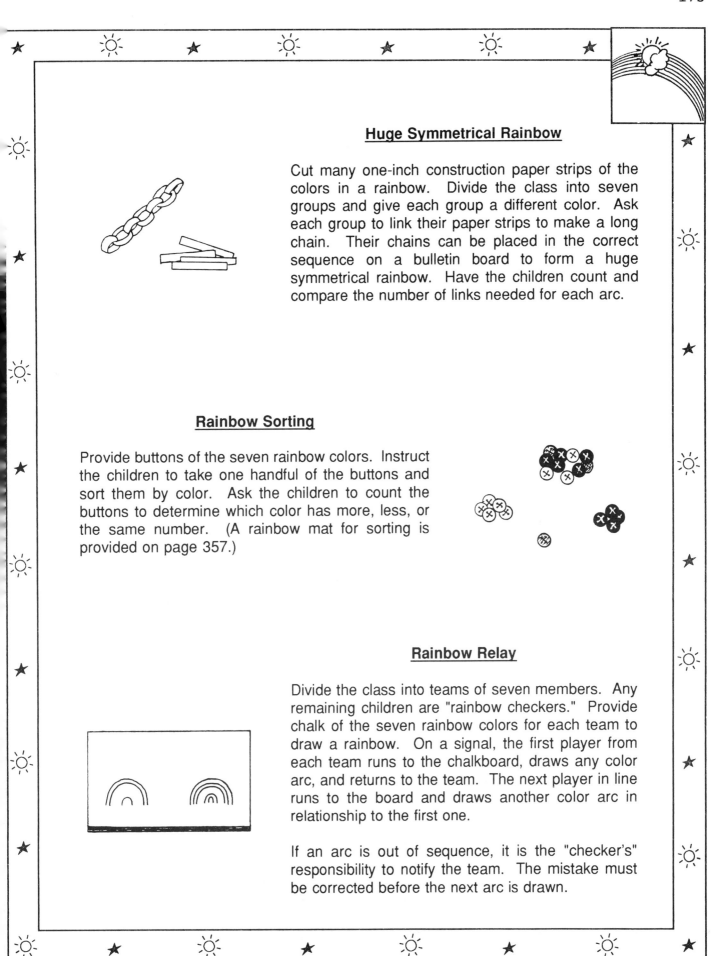

Huge Symmetrical Rainbow

Cut many one-inch construction paper strips of the colors in a rainbow. Divide the class into seven groups and give each group a different color. Ask each group to link their paper strips to make a long chain. Their chains can be placed in the correct sequence on a bulletin board to form a huge symmetrical rainbow. Have the children count and compare the number of links needed for each arc.

Rainbow Sorting

Provide buttons of the seven rainbow colors. Instruct the children to take one handful of the buttons and sort them by color. Ask the children to count the buttons to determine which color has more, less, or the same number. (A rainbow mat for sorting is provided on page 357.)

Rainbow Relay

Divide the class into teams of seven members. Any remaining children are "rainbow checkers." Provide chalk of the seven rainbow colors for each team to draw a rainbow. On a signal, the first player from each team runs to the chalkboard, draws any color arc, and returns to the team. The next player in line runs to the board and draws another color arc in relationship to the first one.

If an arc is out of sequence, it is the "checker's" responsibility to notify the team. The mistake must be corrected before the next arc is drawn.

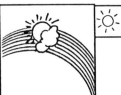

Twice As Nice

Say three or four colors of the rainbow, naming one color twice. Instruct the children to name the color that was repeated.

Examples: red, yellow, red
blue, green, purple, green
indigo, violet, blue, indigo

Variation: Children repeat the entire series in the correct sequence.

Concealed Color

Make a paper rainbow and cut the arcs apart. Place the arcs in order. After asking the children to close their eyes, remove one arc and place it out of sight. Instruct the children to open their eyes and determine what color is missing. Repeat the activity removing different arcs. (A rainbow pattern is provided on page 357.)

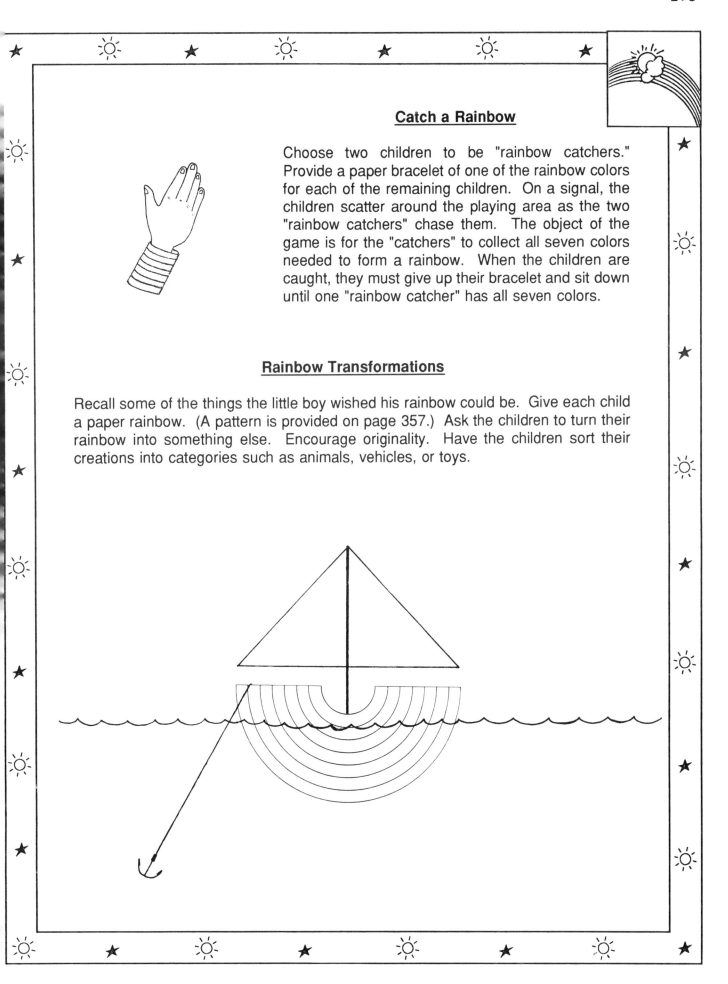

Catch a Rainbow

Choose two children to be "rainbow catchers." Provide a paper bracelet of one of the rainbow colors for each of the remaining children. On a signal, the children scatter around the playing area as the two "rainbow catchers" chase them. The object of the game is for the "catchers" to collect all seven colors needed to form a rainbow. When the children are caught, they must give up their bracelet and sit down until one "rainbow catcher" has all seven colors.

Rainbow Transformations

Recall some of the things the little boy wished his rainbow could be. Give each child a paper rainbow. (A pattern is provided on page 357.) Ask the children to turn their rainbow into something else. Encourage originality. Have the children sort their creations into categories such as animals, vehicles, or toys.

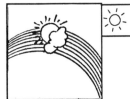

Rainbow Dancing

Ask the children what made the little boy's rainbow at the end of the story. Provide a flashlight and a fishbowl filled with water. Darken the room. Challenge the children to shine the flashlight at the water in the fishbowl to make rainbows "dance" on the wall.

Variation: Children use prisms, mirrors, or other reflective materials to create rainbows.

Burple Purple

Ask the children to complete colorful rhymes, such as "I'm thinking of a color that rhymes with *two*. It is *blue*."

Examples: bed – red
                 fellow – yellow
                 bean – green
                 bindigo – indigo

Bubbly Rainbows

On a sunny day, invite the children to go outside and blow soap bubbles. Encourage them to watch for rainbows in the bubbles as the light shines through. (A recipe for bubble solution is provided on page 333.)

Variation: Children use straws to blow bubbles in soapy water.

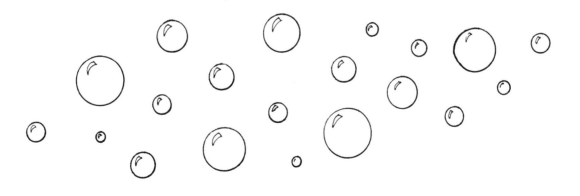

As Orange As An Orange

Children sit in a circle. Ask one child to complete "As orange as a(n)_____." The next child repeats what the first child said and names another orange item. Continue until the children cannot respond with an appropriate item. Repeat the activity, describing other colors.

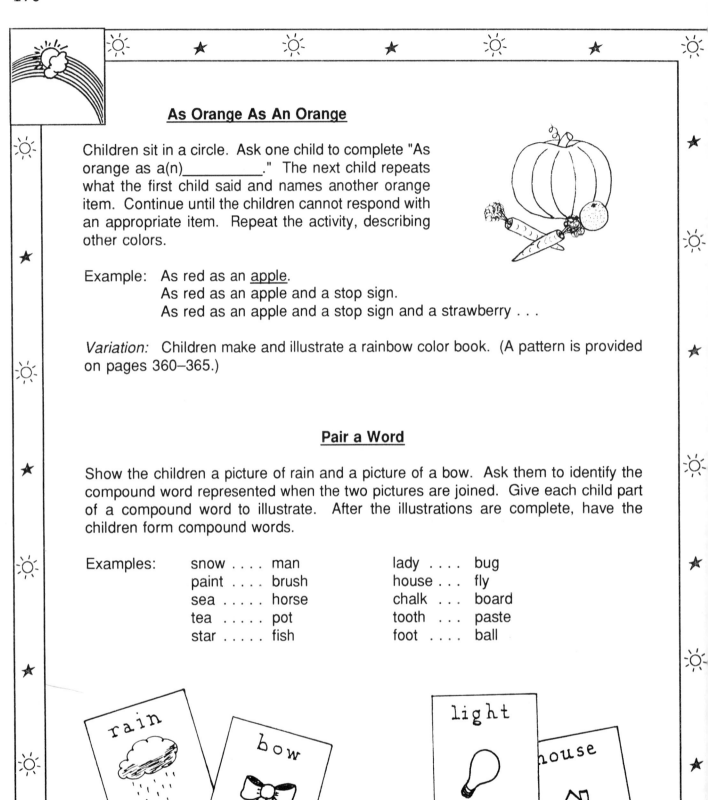

Example: As red as an <u>apple</u>.
  As red as an apple and a stop sign.
  As red as an apple and a stop sign and a strawberry . . .

Variation: Children make and illustrate a rainbow color book. (A pattern is provided on pages 360–365.)

Pair a Word

Show the children a picture of rain and a picture of a bow. Ask them to identify the compound word represented when the two pictures are joined. Give each child part of a compound word to illustrate. After the illustrations are complete, have the children form compound words.

Examples: snow . . . . man   lady . . . . bug
              paint . . . . brush   house . . . fly
              sea . . . . . horse   chalk . . . board
              tea . . . . . pot   tooth . . . paste
              star . . . . . fish   foot . . . . ball

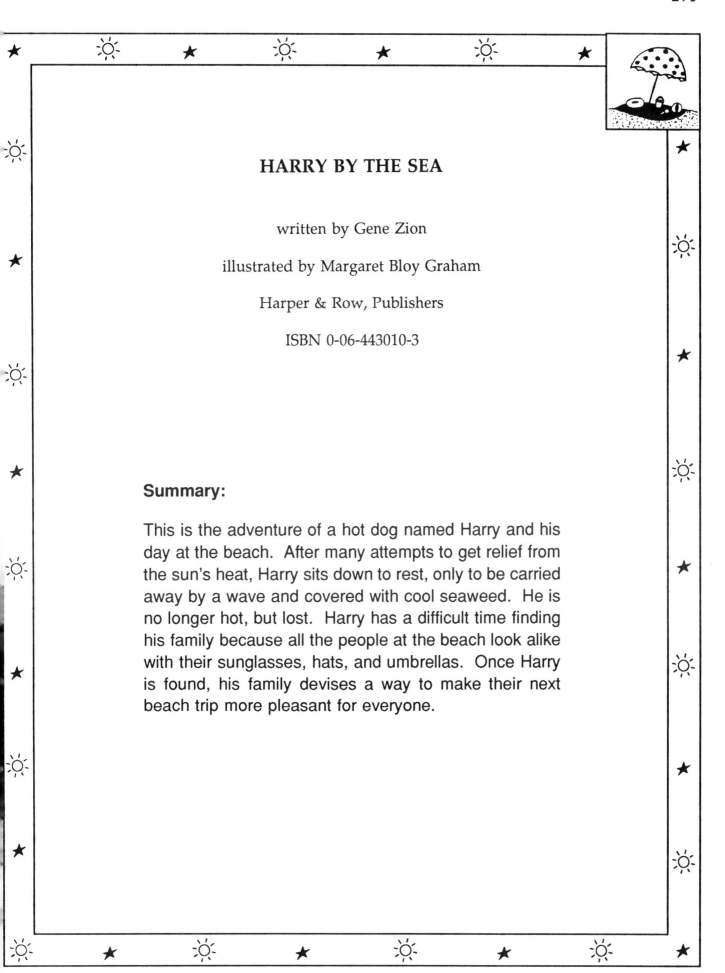

HARRY BY THE SEA

written by Gene Zion

illustrated by Margaret Bloy Graham

Harper & Row, Publishers

ISBN 0-06-443010-3

Summary:

This is the adventure of a hot dog named Harry and his day at the beach. After many attempts to get relief from the sun's heat, Harry sits down to rest, only to be carried away by a wave and covered with cool seaweed. He is no longer hot, but lost. Harry has a difficult time finding his family because all the people at the beach look alike with their sunglasses, hats, and umbrellas. Once Harry is found, his family devises a way to make their next beach trip more pleasant for everyone.

How Many Sunbeams?

Provide 11 yellow or orange paper plates and 55 clothespins. Write a numeral from 0 to 10 on each plate. Ask the children to clip the corresponding number of clothespins on each "sun" to represent sunbeams.

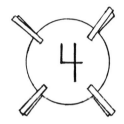

Variation: Number words can be substituted for numerals.

Hurry, Harry!

Ask the children to squat down on all fours and pretend to be Harry. Select one child to represent a vendor. Instruct the "vendor" to call out two words. If the words are the same, such as *Harry, Harry*, the "dogs" jump up one time. If the words are different, such as *Hurry, Harry*, the "dogs" remain still and "bark" once.

Variation: Children listen for beginning sounds, ending sounds, or rhyming words.

Only You Can Prevent Sunburn

Ask the children to recall the many kinds of sun protection used by the people at the beach. Discuss the need for protection when exposed to the sun. Encourage the children to bring different kinds of sun protectors, such as sun hats, sunglasses, or sunscreen lotions to perform a commercial advertising protection from the sun.

Creative Castles

Mix water with sand to provide a good building consistency. Encourage the children to build sand castles. Provide a variety of items such as shells, straws, sticks, or cups for the children to use as creative additions to their castles.

Hot Spot

Prepare two trays, each containing identical metal items, such as keys, coins, or spoons. Place one tray outdoors in a sunny spot. Leave the other tray inside the classroom. After a short period of time, encourage the children to touch the objects on both trays and compare them. Ask the children why the objects outside are warmer. Explain that people are applying this principle to make solar heaters. Discuss how this helps save energy.

Beanbag Sun Hats

Ask the children why the people at the beach were wearing sun hats. Provide each child with a beanbag to use as a sun hat. Tell the children they cannot go out in the sun without their "sun hats." The children walk around the playing area, trying to balance the beanbags on their heads. If a "sun hat" falls off of a child's head, that child must stop and wait for a friend to squat down, pick it up, and put it back in place.

The Unusual Umbrella

Ask the children why Harry had such a difficult time finding his family at the beach. Encourage them to make an original design of a beach umbrella that Harry could easily find. (An umbrella pattern is provided on page 358.)

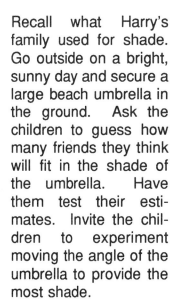

A Crowd in the Shade

Recall what Harry's family used for shade. Go outside on a bright, sunny day and secure a large beach umbrella in the ground. Ask the children to guess how many friends they think will fit in the shade of the umbrella. Have them test their estimates. Invite the children to experiment moving the angle of the umbrella to provide the most shade.

Variation: Provide small paper beverage parasols to represent beach umbrellas. Black-eyed peas can be used to represent little black and white dogs.

More or Less Protection

Collect containers of various strengths of sunscreen lotions. After a discussion of what the *SPF* number means, hold up two of the containers. Ask the children to determine which lotion provides more/less protection. Continue the procedure using different combinations of containers. Have the children order the bottles from the least protection to the most.

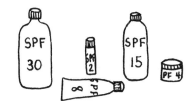

Bead Up, Don't Burn Up

Ask the children to rub waterproof sun lotion on the back of one of their hands and non-waterproof lotion on the back of their other hand. Have them put their hands in a large container filled with water. Encourage them to look at their hands and feel the difference. Ask the children which kind of lotion would offer more protection when swimming.

Solar Cookin'

On a hot, sunny day, let the sun do the cooking. Provide graham crackers, marshmallows, and chocolate morsels or bars. Have the children put a few marshmallows and chocolate pieces on a graham cracker in the hot sun. Observe until the chocolate has melted. Top with a second graham cracker and enjoy the solar-cooked treat.

Bushy-Backed Sea Slug

Choose two children to act as beach attendants. They stand facing each other and hold hands above their heads to form a "basket." The remaining children line up and go under the "beach attendants' basket" as the "attendants" sing the following song:

(Tune: *London Bridge*)

We are going to catch It,

catch It, catch It.

We are going to catch It;

please, stand back!

Take It to the Aquarium,

Aquarium, Aquarium.

Take It to the Aquarium;

please, stand back!

When the words *please, stand back* are sung, the "attendants" bring their arms down around the child under their "basket." As the second verse is sung, the "attendants" take the child caught to a designated spot representing the Aquarium. Play continues until all of the children have been caught and taken to the "Aquarium."

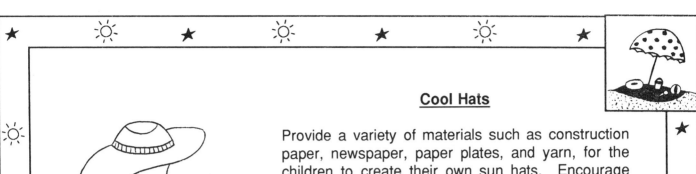

Cool Hats

Provide a variety of materials such as construction paper, newspaper, paper plates, and yarn, for the children to create their own sun hats. Encourage them to design hats that will provide maximum sun protection.

Be Cool

Recall the ways Harry tried to find shade at the beach. Brainstorm other ways to cool off from the sun's heat. After the children have played outside in the sun, suggest they try different ways to cool off, such as sitting still, using a fan, or getting a cool drink. Discuss which ways worked best.

What Place?

Recall the hot *place* where Harry was. Read sentences that include *places* and instruct the children to determine the *place* in each. Ask them to illustrate and dictate a sentence about their favorite *place*.

Examples: Susie went to the *store*.
At *school*, the children learned to read.
The family went to the *lake* for the weekend.

Repeating Stripes

Draw a large umbrella on the chalkboard. Using colored chalk, create a striped pattern similar to those on the beach umbrellas. Give the children colored manipulatives such as color cubes, beads, or stacking blocks. Ask them to use their manipulatives to recreate the color pattern.

Lemonade for Sale

Suggest the children set up their own vending stand and sell ice cold lemonade to help beat the heat. Divide the class into producers and consumers. The producers are responsible for building the stand, making the lemonade, determining the price, advertising, and selling their product. The consumers not only get a cool drink, but also practice money skills, such as coin recognition and values, as they purchase the product. Provide an opportunity for the children to experience both roles.

Hot Dog

Recall what the vendor at the beach was selling. Ask the children why the lady called Harry a hot dog. Explain that some words have more than one meaning. Recall other words in the story that have more than one meaning, such as bark, wave, stand, rest, and cool. Encourage the children to use the words in sentences.

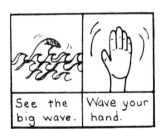

See the big wave. | Wave your hand.

Have the children fold a paper in half and choose one word from the list. Instruct them to illustrate a different meaning on each half. Write a sentence underneath each picture.

MISCELLANEOUS

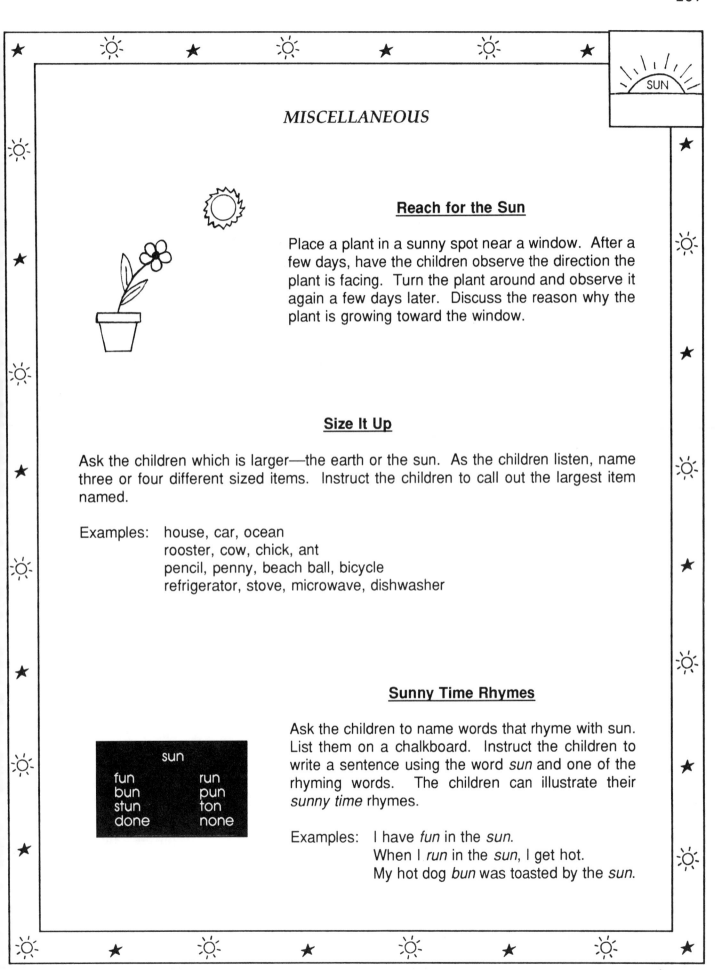

Reach for the Sun

Place a plant in a sunny spot near a window. After a few days, have the children observe the direction the plant is facing. Turn the plant around and observe it again a few days later. Discuss the reason why the plant is growing toward the window.

Size It Up

Ask the children which is larger—the earth or the sun. As the children listen, name three or four different sized items. Instruct the children to call out the largest item named.

Examples: house, car, ocean
rooster, cow, chick, ant
pencil, penny, beach ball, bicycle
refrigerator, stove, microwave, dishwasher

Sunny Time Rhymes

Ask the children to name words that rhyme with sun. List them on a chalkboard. Instruct the children to write a sentence using the word *sun* and one of the rhyming words. The children can illustrate their *sunny time* rhymes.

sun	
fun	run
bun	pun
stun	ton
done	none

Examples: I have *fun* in the *sun.*
When I *run* in the *sun,* I get hot.
My hot dog *bun* was toasted by the *sun.*

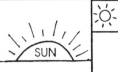

SUN

Sun Visors

Provide visor patterns for the children to place on brightly colored tagboard in a sunny spot. After several hours, have them remove the pattern and cut out the shape left by the sun. They decorate their visor. Attach elastic to both sides so the children can wear them outside on a sunny day. (A visor pattern is provided on page 359.)

Sunny Spies

Take the children for a walk on a sunny day. Encourage them to find things that are affected by the sun, such as paint, metal, or clothes on a line.

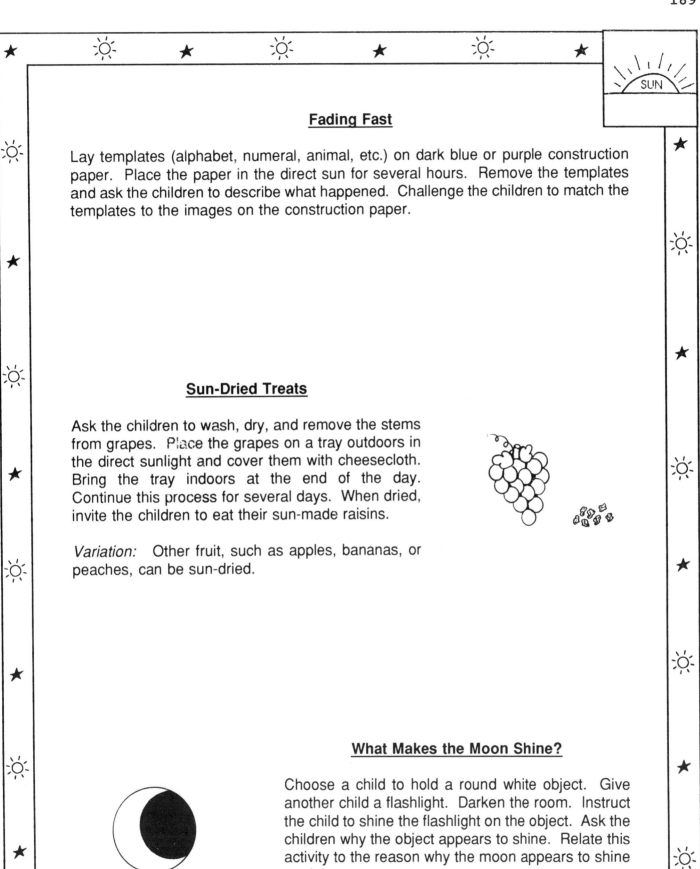

Fading Fast

Lay templates (alphabet, numeral, animal, etc.) on dark blue or purple construction paper. Place the paper in the direct sun for several hours. Remove the templates and ask the children to describe what happened. Challenge the children to match the templates to the images on the construction paper.

Sun-Dried Treats

Ask the children to wash, dry, and remove the stems from grapes. Place the grapes on a tray outdoors in the direct sunlight and cover them with cheesecloth. Bring the tray indoors at the end of the day. Continue this process for several days. When dried, invite the children to eat their sun-made raisins.

Variation: Other fruit, such as apples, bananas, or peaches, can be sun-dried.

What Makes the Moon Shine?

Choose a child to hold a round white object. Give another child a flashlight. Darken the room. Instruct the child to shine the flashlight on the object. Ask the children why the object appears to shine. Relate this activity to the reason why the moon appears to shine at night.

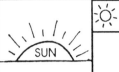

Sun's Too Bright

A special "Sunglasses Day" can be fun and informative. Ask each child to bring a pair of sunglasses from home for this special day. Encourage the children to wear their glasses outdoors. Discuss the importance of protecting our eyes from the sun.

"Go" Power

Ask the children why people put gas in their cars. Discuss the role the sun plays in providing the energy that makes people "go." Make a class mobile. From a sphere, representing the sun, hang several pictures of plants. From the plants, hang pictures of animals, including humans.

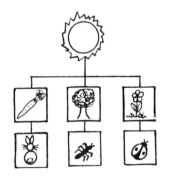

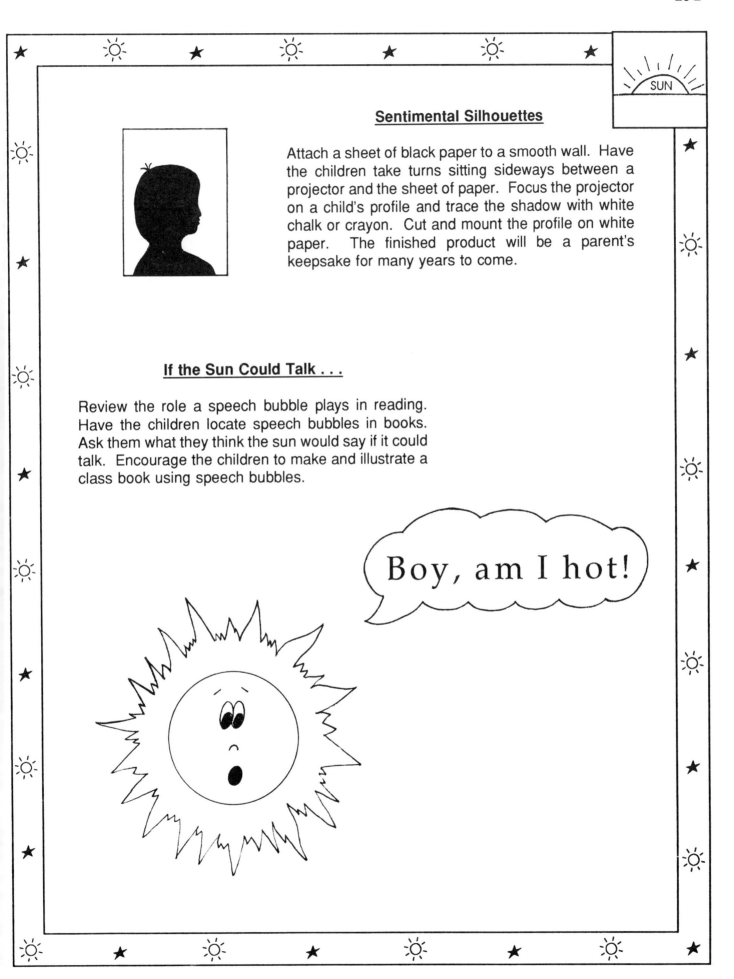

SUN

Sentimental Silhouettes

Attach a sheet of black paper to a smooth wall. Have the children take turns sitting sideways between a projector and the sheet of paper. Focus the projector on a child's profile and trace the shadow with white chalk or crayon. Cut and mount the profile on white paper. The finished product will be a parent's keepsake for many years to come.

If the Sun Could Talk . . .

Review the role a speech bubble plays in reading. Have the children locate speech bubbles in books. Ask them what they think the sun would say if it could talk. Encourage the children to make and illustrate a class book using speech bubbles.

Boy, am I hot!

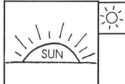

Sun's Playtime

Add sun-related items to classroom centers. Color paddles, prisms, and kaleidoscopes encourage color exploration. Sunglasses, visors, hats, fans, empty sun lotion bottles, and sandals offer the children an opportunity for creative play. Spheres can roll their way into the block center for added fun.

Tea Party

Fill a gallon jar with cold water. Place 6–8 tea bags in the water. Put the lid on the jar and place it in the sun. After several hours, take the jar out of the sun. Add ice and sweetener, if desired. Have a tea party, compliments of the sun.

ART

Darken the Day

Ask the children to draw a daytime scene on white construction paper. Instruct them to press hard with their crayons. To transform the picture into a night-time scene, the children apply a coat of diluted black tempera or watercolor over the paper using a cloth or brush. The paint will be resisted by the crayon and will color only the background of the picture.

Tissue Rainbows

Cut small tissue paper squares of the seven rainbow colors and construction paper arcs. Instruct the children to crumple the squares and glue them on the arc in the color sequence to make a rainbow. (A rainbow pattern is provided on page 357.)

Smudge a Beam

Children draw a circle with yellow chalk at the top of a light blue sheet of construction paper. Have them color the inside of the circle with a heavy coat of chalk and use their index finger to smudge lines outward to represent sunbeams. The children can draw or collage a favorite activity they enjoy doing on a sunny day.

Colorful Recordings

Poke a small hole in the center of a paper plate and place it on a record player. Turn on the record player as a child holds a marker on the plate. Instruct the child to hold the marker still and watch as the record player goes 'round and 'round, making a circular design. The children can experiment using different colored markers.

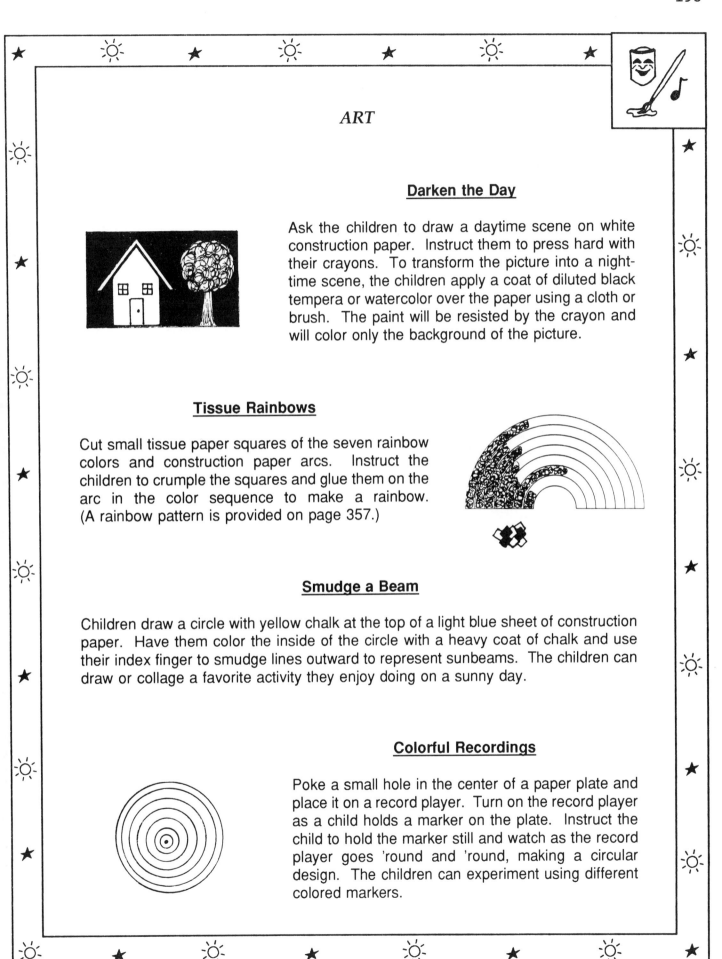

Sunny Stuff

Provide two paper plates for each child. The children paint the bottoms of the plates yellow. When dry, have them glue yellow strips of paper, representing the sun's rays, to the outer edge of one of the plates. Fasten the plates together, leaving an opening for the children to stuff. Close the opening.

Variation: Children create a pattern using yellow and orange "rays" or long and short "rays."

Art in the Dark

To help the children appreciate light, have them experience painting, drawing, or constructing while in a dark room.

Sun Prints

Gather fruits and vegetables such as oranges, carrots, or cucumbers. Cut the fruit and vegetables in half. The children dip them in yellow paint and press them on paper to create "sun" prints. Provide paint, cotton swabs, glue, yarn, or tissue paper for the "sun's" rays.

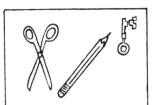

Sunny Patterns

Children arrange objects in a pleasing pattern on a dark colored sheet of construction paper placed in the sun. After several hours, have the children remove the objects and observe their sun-made artwork.

Rainbow Crayons

Make "rainbow" crayons from old crayon pieces. In a double boiler over low heat, melt one color at a time. Partially fill film containers with the melted crayon and allow the crayon to cool until it begins to harden. Add additional layers using different colors of melted crayon. When the "rainbow" crayons have completely hardened, pop them out. Invite the children to use them to make colorful designs.

Sun Texture Scene

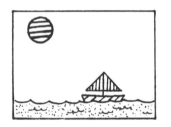

Cut circles of sandpaper or corrugated cardboard. Instruct the children to place newsprint on one of the textured circles. Then, using the side of a yellow or orange crayon, they rub over the circle to create a "sun." Other textured shapes can be added to complete a "sun texture scene."

Colorful Collage

Provide tissue paper or cellophane scraps of the primary colors. Challenge the children to overlap the scraps and glue them on paper to create secondary colors.

Variation: Children can arrange fabric scraps of the rainbow colors to create a colorful collage.

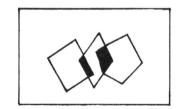

Crayon Melt-a-Ways

Cover a warming tray with foil. Caution the children not to touch the hot tray. Instruct them to draw with crayons on the foil to create a melted masterpiece.

Let It Shine

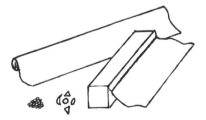

Provide scraps of foil paper, aluminum foil, shiny stickers, sequins, and glitter for the children to create shiny collages. Have them experiment holding their collages in different positions to reflect the sun.

DRAMA

Shall We Go to the Beach?

The leader sings the question (first line). Children answer rhythm (second line). Suit actions to words.

Shall we go to the beach?
   Yes, ma'am!
Shall we take along a peach?
   Yes, ma'am!
Oh, how shall we go?
   Drive our car!
Oh, how shall we go?
   Drive our car!

Shall we walk on the sand?
   Yes, ma'am!
And will you hold my hand?
   Yes, ma'am!
Oh, how shall we walk?
   Hurry, hurry, hurry!
Oh, how shall we walk?
   Hurry, hurry, hurry!

Shall we wear our shades?
   Yes, ma'am!
To block the sun's bright rays?
   Yes, ma'am!
Oh, how shall we wear them?
   Over our eyes!
Oh, how shall we wear them?
   Over our eyes!

Shall we put on lotion?
   Yes, ma'am!
When we're down by the ocean?
   Yes, ma'am!
Oh, how shall we do it?
   Rub, rub, rub!
Oh, how shall we do it?
   Rub, rub, rub!

Shall we swim in the water?
   Yes, ma'am!
Just like a little otter?
   Yes, ma'am!
Oh, how shall we swim?
   Splish, splish, splash!
Oh, how shall we swim?
   Splish, splish, splash!

Will we get sunburned?
   No, ma'am!
After all we've learned?
   No, ma'am!
Oh, why won't it happen?
   We're too smart!
Oh, why won't it happen?
   We're too smart!

Sunny Situations

Invite the children to take turns pantomiming the effects of the sun on people and things, such as a flower growing, an ice cube melting, or paint cracking and peeling.

WELL-KNOWN RECORDINGS

Hap Palmer

"Colors." <u>Learning Basic Skills Through Music</u>, Volume 1.

"Colored Ribbons." <u>Creative Movement and Rhythmic Expression</u>.

"Run Around the Sun." <u>Learning with Circles and Sticks</u>.

"All the Colors of the Rainbow." <u>Learning Basic Skills Through Music</u>, Volume 5.

"Good Morning Merry Sunshine." <u>Patriotic and Morning Time Songs</u>.

"Zipidee Doo Da." <u>Patriotic and Morning Time Songs</u>.

Greg Scelsa and Steve Millang

"It's a Beautiful Day." <u>We All Live Together</u>, Volume 4.

Raffi

"Mr. Sun." <u>Singable Songs for the Very Young</u>.

"One Light, One Sun." <u>One Light, One Sun</u>.

Ella Jenkins

"I Know the Colors of the Rainbow." <u>I Know the Colors of the Rainbow</u>.

"It Won't Rain." <u>I Know the Colors of the Rainbow</u>.

Wee Sing

"Sally Go 'Round the Sun." <u>Wee Sing and Play</u>.

"Twinkle, Twinkle, Little Star." <u>Wee Sing Nursery Rhymes and Lullabies</u>.

SONGS

COLOR A RAINBOW

(Tune: *Twinkle, Twinkle, Little Star*)

Red, orange, yellow, green, and blue,

Indigo, and violet, too.

These are the colors of a bright rainbow.

They're always in order wherever they go.

Red, orange, yellow, green, and blue,

Indigo, and violet, too.

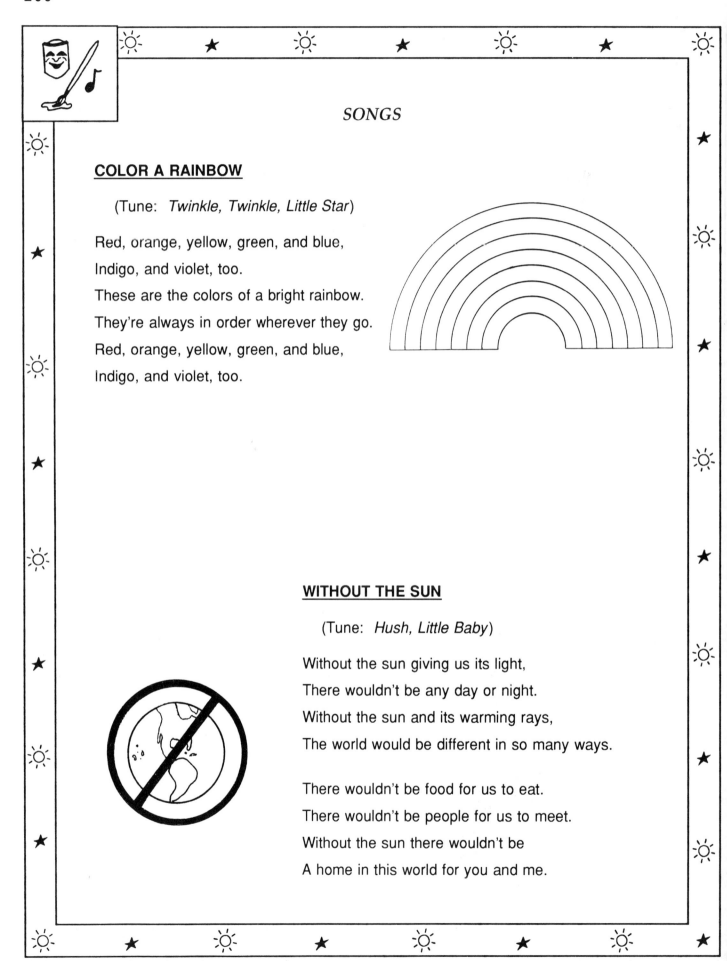

WITHOUT THE SUN

(Tune: *Hush, Little Baby*)

Without the sun giving us its light,

There wouldn't be any day or night.

Without the sun and its warming rays,

The world would be different in so many ways.

There wouldn't be food for us to eat.

There wouldn't be people for us to meet.

Without the sun there wouldn't be

A home in this world for you and me.

A SPECIAL STAR

(Tune: *A Sailor Went to Sea, Sea, Sea*)

The sun's our special star, star, star.

It's up in the sky so far, far, far.

It shines on us each day, day, day

While we're at work and play, play, play.

It gives us light to see, see, see.

It warms both you and me, me, me.

The sun's our friend, you know, know, know.

It helps us all to grow, grow, grow.

THE SUN IS ALWAYS THERE

(Tune: *The Farmer in the Dell*)

The sun is always there.

The sun is always there.

As the world goes 'round and 'round,

The sun is always there.

Verse 2: The sun gives us heat . . .

Verse 3: The sun gives us light . . .

Verse 4: The sun makes day and night . . .

Verse 5: The sun helps us grow . . .

Additional verses can be added.

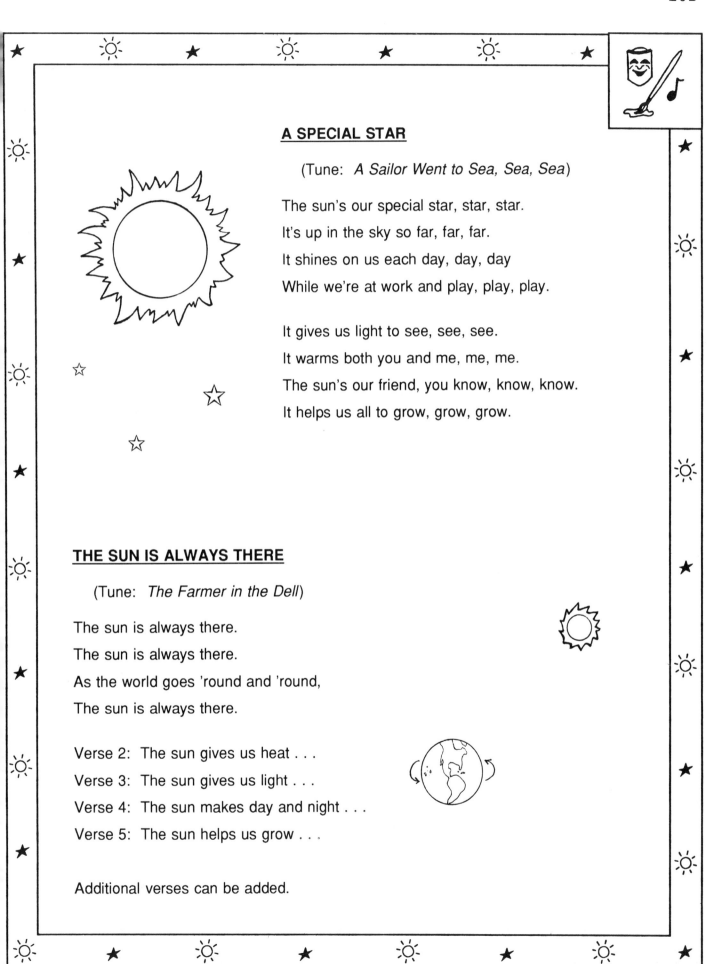

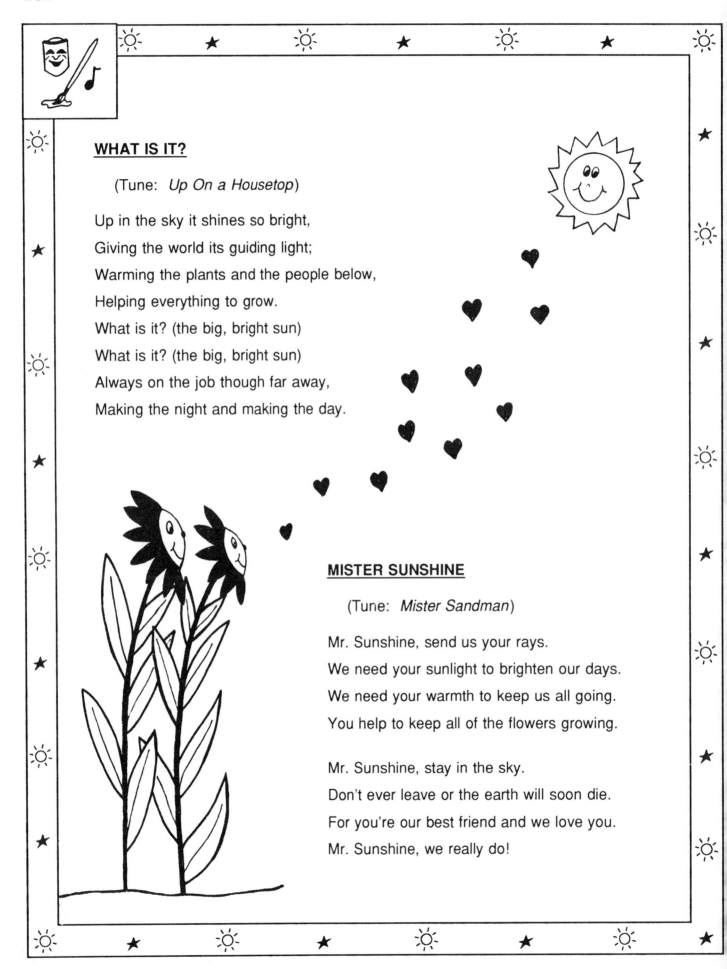

WHAT IS IT?

(Tune: *Up On a Housetop*)

Up in the sky it shines so bright,
Giving the world its guiding light;
Warming the plants and the people below,
Helping everything to grow.
What is it? (the big, bright sun)
What is it? (the big, bright sun)
Always on the job though far away,
Making the night and making the day.

MISTER SUNSHINE

(Tune: *Mister Sandman*)

Mr. Sunshine, send us your rays.
We need your sunlight to brighten our days.
We need your warmth to keep us all going.
You help to keep all of the flowers growing.

Mr. Sunshine, stay in the sky.
Don't ever leave or the earth will soon die.
For you're our best friend and we love you.
Mr. Sunshine, we really do!

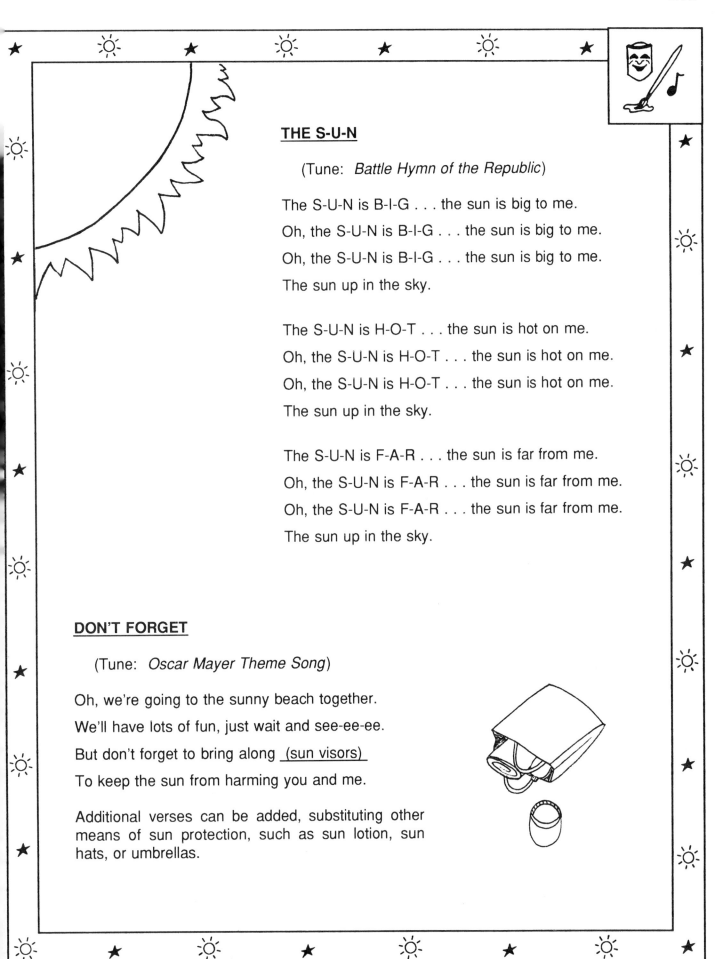

THE S-U-N

(Tune: *Battle Hymn of the Republic*)

The S-U-N is B-I-G . . . the sun is big to me.
Oh, the S-U-N is B-I-G . . . the sun is big to me.
Oh, the S-U-N is B-I-G . . . the sun is big to me.
The sun up in the sky.

The S-U-N is H-O-T . . . the sun is hot on me.
Oh, the S-U-N is H-O-T . . . the sun is hot on me.
Oh, the S-U-N is H-O-T . . . the sun is hot on me.
The sun up in the sky.

The S-U-N is F-A-R . . . the sun is far from me.
Oh, the S-U-N is F-A-R . . . the sun is far from me.
Oh, the S-U-N is F-A-R . . . the sun is far from me.
The sun up in the sky.

DON'T FORGET

(Tune: *Oscar Mayer Theme Song*)

Oh, we're going to the sunny beach together.
We'll have lots of fun, just wait and see-ee-ee.
But don't forget to bring along (sun visors)
To keep the sun from harming you and me.

Additional verses can be added, substituting other means of sun protection, such as sun lotion, sun hats, or umbrellas.

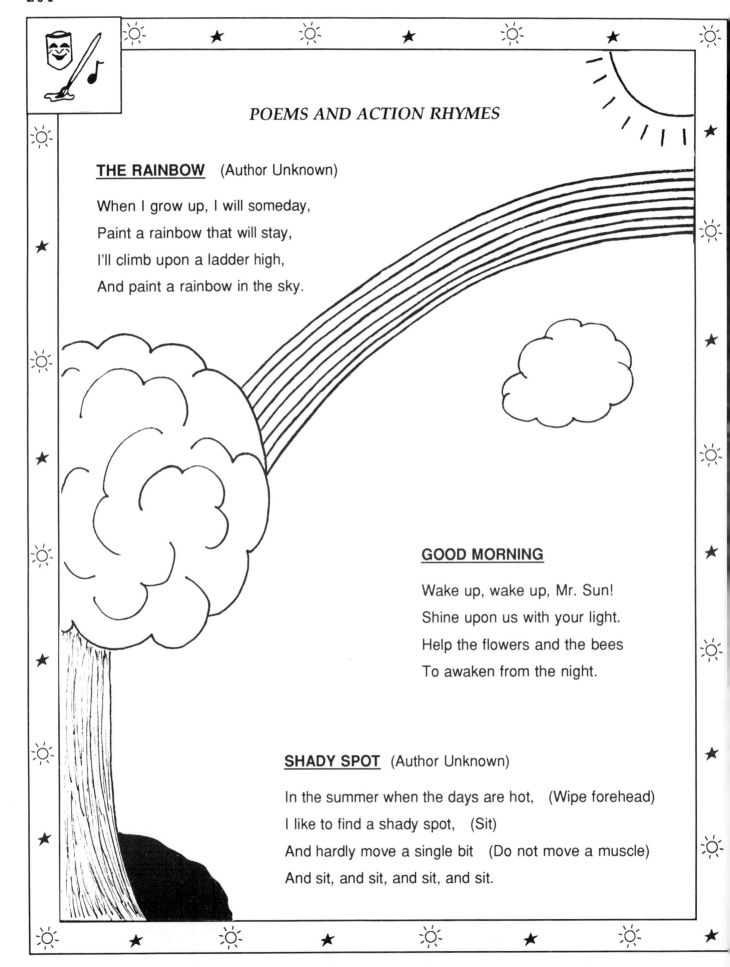

204

POEMS AND ACTION RHYMES

THE RAINBOW (Author Unknown)

When I grow up, I will someday,
Paint a rainbow that will stay,
I'll climb upon a ladder high,
And paint a rainbow in the sky.

GOOD MORNING

Wake up, wake up, Mr. Sun!
Shine upon us with your light.
Help the flowers and the bees
To awaken from the night.

SHADY SPOT (Author Unknown)

In the summer when the days are hot,   (Wipe forehead)
I like to find a shady spot,   (Sit)
And hardly move a single bit   (Do not move a muscle)
And sit, and sit, and sit, and sit.

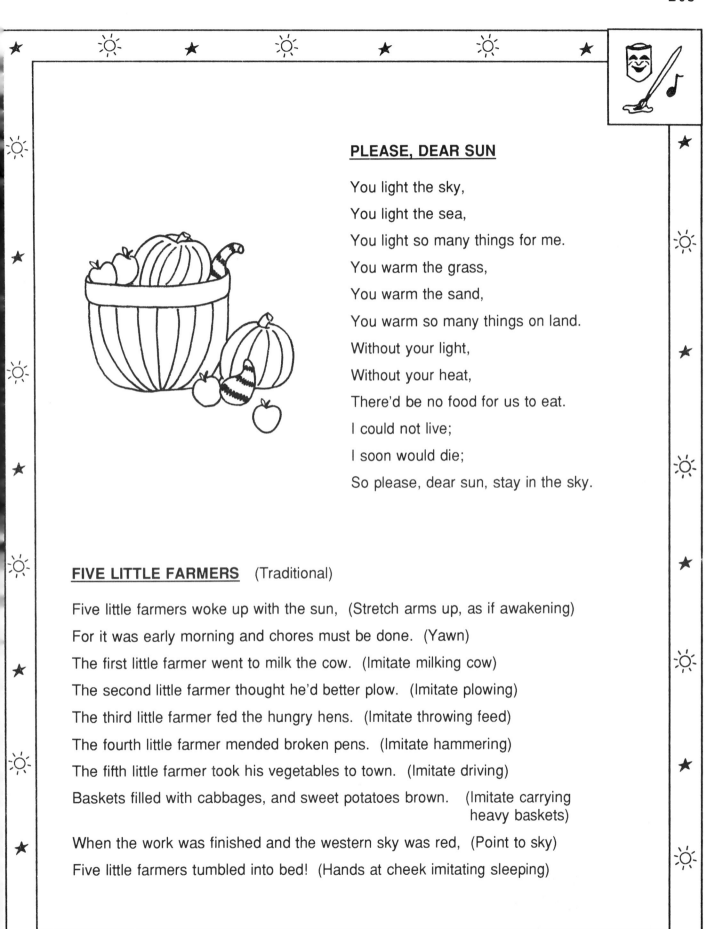

PLEASE, DEAR SUN

You light the sky,

You light the sea,

You light so many things for me.

You warm the grass,

You warm the sand,

You warm so many things on land.

Without your light,

Without your heat,

There'd be no food for us to eat.

I could not live;

I soon would die;

So please, dear sun, stay in the sky.

FIVE LITTLE FARMERS   (Traditional)

Five little farmers woke up with the sun, (Stretch arms up, as if awakening)

For it was early morning and chores must be done. (Yawn)

The first little farmer went to milk the cow. (Imitate milking cow)

The second little farmer thought he'd better plow. (Imitate plowing)

The third little farmer fed the hungry hens. (Imitate throwing feed)

The fourth little farmer mended broken pens. (Imitate hammering)

The fifth little farmer took his vegetables to town. (Imitate driving)

Baskets filled with cabbages, and sweet potatoes brown.   (Imitate carrying
                                                          heavy baskets)

When the work was finished and the western sky was red, (Point to sky)

Five little farmers tumbled into bed! (Hands at cheek imitating sleeping)

THE EVENING IS COMING (Anonymous)

The evening is coming.
The sun sinks to rest.
The birds are all flying
Straight home to their nest.
"Caw, caw," says the crow
As he flies overhead.
It's time little children
Were going to bed.

Here comes the pony.
His work is all done.
Down through the meadow
He takes a good run.
Up go his heels,
And down goes his head.
It's time little children
Were going to bed.

MERRY SUNSHINE (Anonymous)

"Good morning, Merry Sunshine,
    How did you wake so soon,
You've scared the little stars away
    And shined away the moon.
I saw you go to sleep last night
    Before I ceased my playing;
How did you get 'way over there?
And where have you been staying?"

"I never go to sleep, dear child,
    I just go 'round to see
My little children of the East,
    Who rise and watch for me.
I waken all the birds and bees
    And flowers on my way,
And now come back to see the child
    Who stayed out late at play."

STORY BOOKS

The Other Side of the World by Laura Bannon

A unique story about two little boys on opposite sides of the world who share one sun.

The Biggest Shadow in the Zoo by Jack Kent

An elephant has to learn the hard way that sometimes shadows are not visible.

The Day We Saw the Sun Come Up by Alice E. Goudey

After watching the sun rise and set, two children learn many interesting things about the sun from their mother.

Sun's Up by Teryl Euvremer

The sun's day is personified in this wordless picture book.

Wake Up, Jeremiah by Ronald Himler

A little boy finds joy in waking up early to watch the sun rise.

Sun Grumble by Claudia Fregosi

After going on strike because he was tired, the sun realizes how much he is needed when he sees what a mess the earth is in because of his disappearance.

We Want Sunshine in Our Houses retold by Bernice Wells Carlson and Ristiina Wigg

A humorous story of droll folks, who "not using their noodles," build houses without windows and try to figure out ways to let the sun shine in.

Nothing Sticks Like a Shadow by Ann Tompert

When Woodchuck challenges Rabbit to try to escape from his own shadow, both discover that sometimes you can and sometimes you can't.

Someone Is Eating the Sun by Ruth A. Sonneborn

The farm animals, experiencing a solar eclipse, think the sun is being eaten.

Sunshine by Jan Ormerod

In this wordless picture book, the sun plays an important role in beginning the day to set a household in motion.

Under the Sun by Ellen Kandoian

A little girl's curiosity about where the sun goes each night is satisfied when her mother explains how it visits other children of the world while she sleeps.

The Legend of the Indian Paintbrush by Tomie dePaolo

Following his dream, an Indian learns to use his artistic talents to bring the colors of the sunset down to his people.

One Light, One Sun by Raffi

This "singable" book depicts the sun being shared by the different cultures of the world.

Sun and Moon by Marcus Pfister

Each longing for a friend, the Sun and the Moon make the impossible happen and spend time together.

Wake Up, Sun! by David L. Harrison; *Step into Reading Books*

During the middle of the night, the farm animals become worried that the sun won't wake up.

How the Sun Was Brought Back to the Sky by Mirra Ginsburg

After the sun has not shone for three full days, some animals set out to search for it and bring it back.

Who Likes the Sun? by Beatrice Schenk De Regniers

A look at some of the playful things the sun can do.

The Sun's Asleep Behind the Hill by Mirra Ginsburg

As the world grows tired at the end of a day, the sun sets and the moon takes over.

CONCEPT BOOKS

<u>Sunlight</u> by Sally Cartwright

   Sun concepts are explored through observations and simple activities.

<u>Sun Fun</u> by Caroline Arnold

   Many sun projects are presented in this easy-to-read activity book.

<u>Day and Night</u> by David Bennett; *Bear Facts* series

   A simplistic look at day and night and what makes them occur.

<u>What Makes Day and Night</u> by Franklyn M. Branley; *Let's Read and Find Out Science* series

   This book explains the cause of sunrise, sunset, day, and night.

<u>The Sun: Our Nearest Star</u> by Franklyn M. Branley; *Let's Read and Find Out Science* series

   Many of the sun's special characteristics are explored.

<u>Sunshine Makes the Seasons</u> by Franklyn M. Branley; *Let's Read and Find Out Science* series

   An intriguing look at the earth's trip around the sun and how the seasons are made.

<u>What Makes Day and Night?</u> by Chris Arvetis and Carole Palmer; *Just Ask* series

   Christopher Mouse and the other forest animals learn where the sun actually is and why it gets dark at night.

<u>What Is a Rainbow?</u> by Chris Arvetis and Carole Palmer; *Just Ask* series

   Christopher Mouse learns how light bends to form a rainbow.

<u>Look At Rainbow Colors</u> by Rena K. Kirkpatrick

   The colors of the rainbow are found and explored in many different places.

NOTES

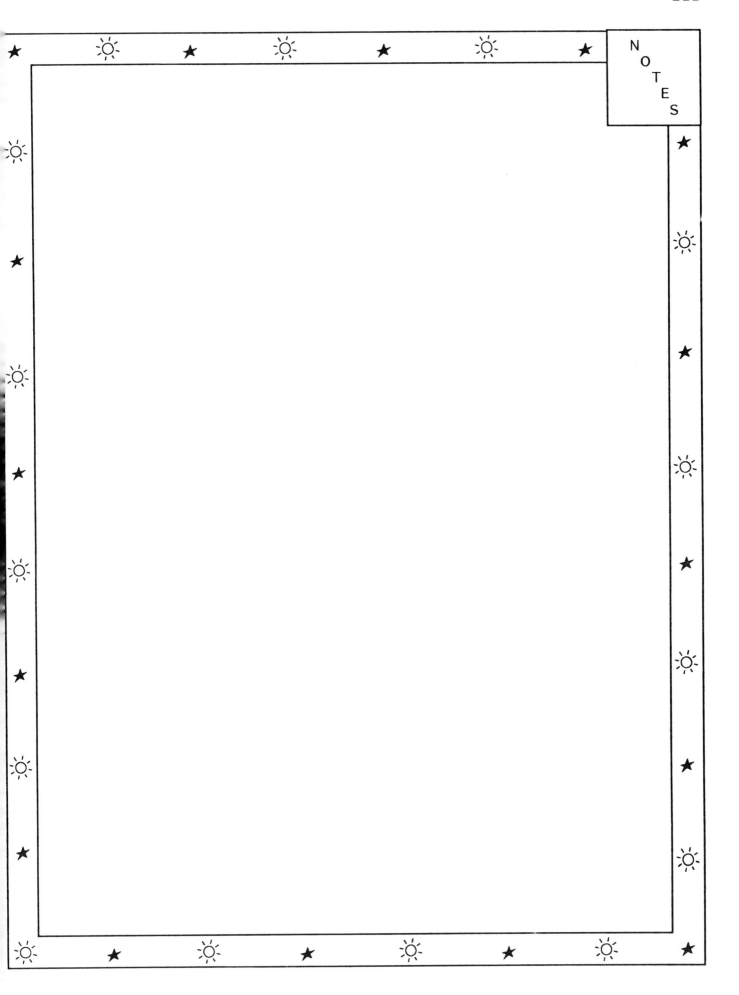

NOTES

212

NOTES

STORY O'MIMUS

asks

What is

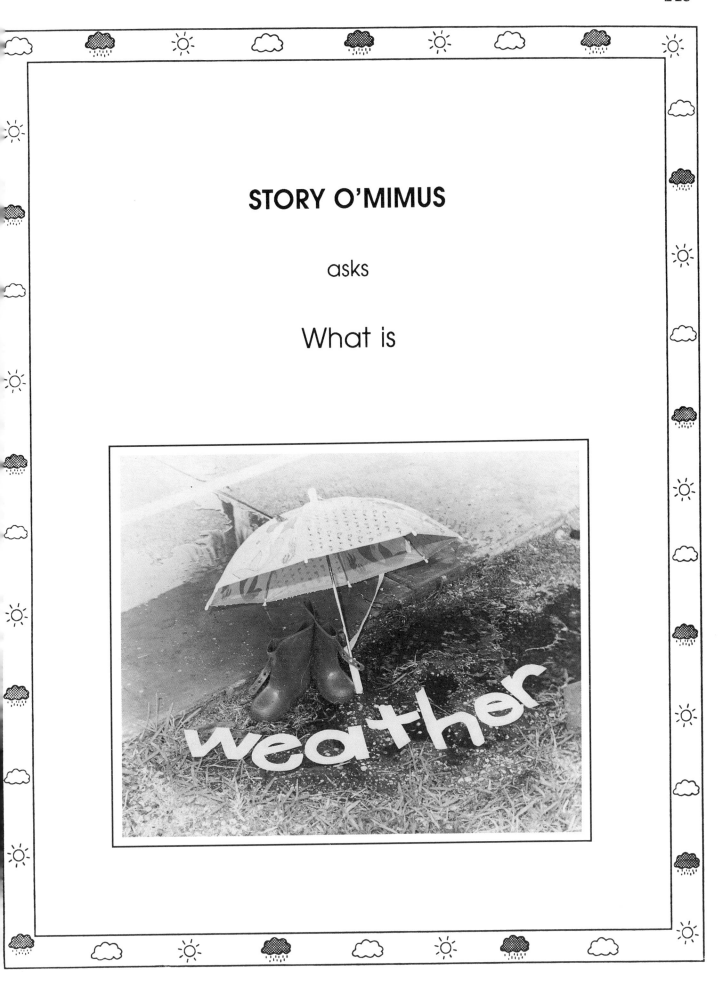

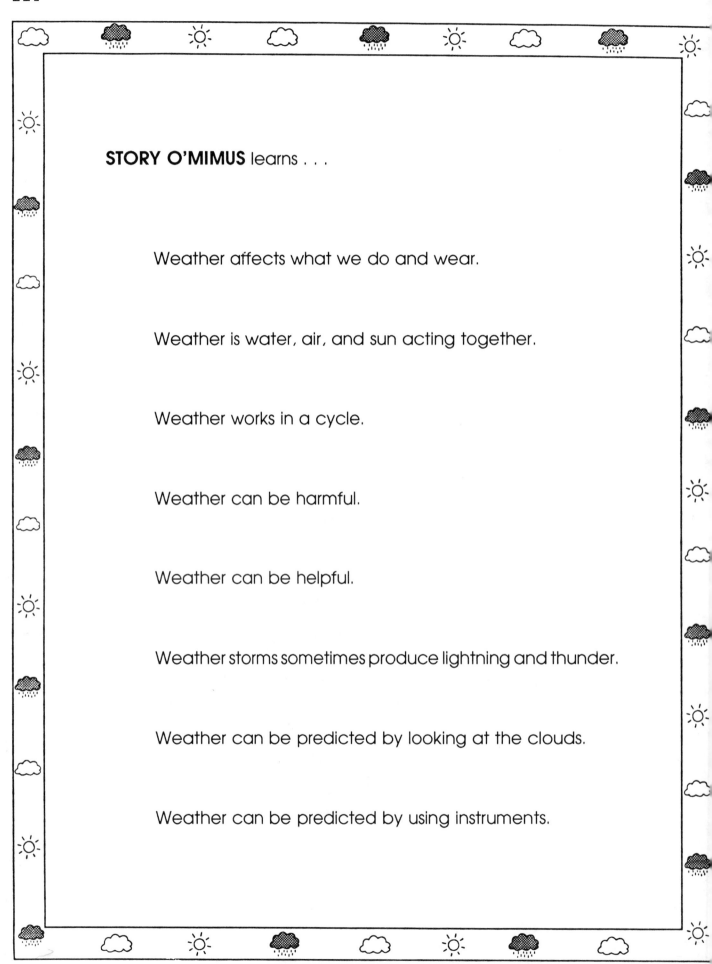

STORY O'MIMUS learns . . .

Weather affects what we do and wear.

Weather is water, air, and sun acting together.

Weather works in a cycle.

Weather can be harmful.

Weather can be helpful.

Weather storms sometimes produce lightning and thunder.

Weather can be predicted by looking at the clouds.

Weather can be predicted by using instruments.

FEATURE STORIES

Snow Lion

by David McPhail

Shingebiss

Indian Folk Tale

Cloudy With a Chance of Meatballs

by Judy Barrett

Umbrella

by Taro Yashima

Stina

by Lena Anderson

PLANNING GUIDE

Feature Stories

SNOW LION	Language Arts	Math	Science, Health, Social Studies	Motor
Snow Is . . .	●			
Some Like It Hot . . . Some Like It Cold		●	○	○
Caution . . . Ice Ahead!			●	
Please, Don't Melt			●	
What's in Lion's Bag?	●			
Let's Get Away			●	○
Keep a Cool Head			●	
Ribbon Thermometer				●
Fluffy Water		●		
Snowball Toss				●
Shivercise			○	●
Temperature's Rising			●	
Who? Where? What? How?	●			○
Sweat's Wet			●	
Hot Humid Hair Hygrometer			●	
Hand-y Thermometer			●	
Snow Spheres		●		○

SHINGEBISS	Language Arts	Math	Science, Health, Social Studies	Motor
Forming Frost			●	
Hear It Howl	●			
Salt or Slip			●	
Bundle Up			●	
A Comfortable Lodge				●
Creative Catch		●		○
Don't Fan the Fire	●			
Rhyme to the Weather	●			
Beat the Wind		●		
Huddle Up			○	●
Windproof Lodge				●
Ping Pong A-"Long"		●		○
Whooo's the Wind?	●			
Icy Arctic Homes			●	○
Where's the Wind?			●	
The Weather Did It	●			

Instructional Focus: ● Primary   ○ Secondary

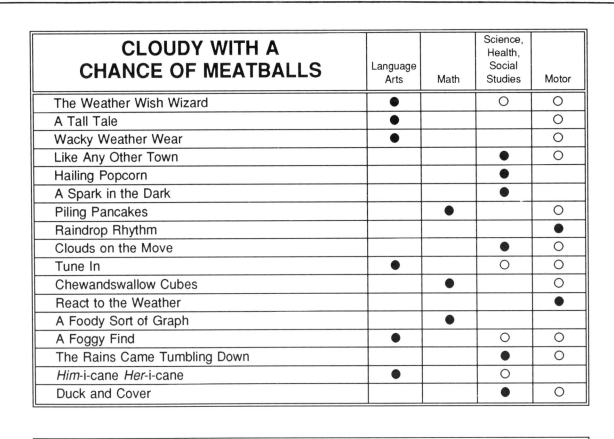

CLOUDY WITH A CHANCE OF MEATBALLS	Language Arts	Math	Science, Health, Social Studies	Motor
The Weather Wish Wizard	●		○	○
A Tall Tale	●			○
Wacky Weather Wear	●			○
Like Any Other Town			●	○
Hailing Popcorn			●	
A Spark in the Dark			●	
Piling Pancakes		●		○
Raindrop Rhythm				●
Clouds on the Move			●	○
Tune In	●		○	○
Chewandswallow Cubes		●		○
React to the Weather				●
A Foody Sort of Graph		●		
A Foggy Find	●		○	○
The Rains Came Tumbling Down			●	○
Him-i-cane *Her*-i-cane	●		○	
Duck and Cover			●	○

UMBRELLA	Language Arts	Math	Science, Health, Social Studies	Motor
Where 'Ya From?			●	
Listen for the Rain	●			○
That's Debatable	●			
Puddle Predictors		●		○
Clap It Out	●	○		
Weather Gear	●			
All Grown Up	●			○
A Cloudful		●		
Pitter Patter	●			
Gauge the Rain		○	●	
The Japanese Way	○		○	●
Watch It Disappear			●	
Windy Rain				●
Worth the Wait	●			
Record the Weather		○	●	
Raining in the Room			●	
Connect the Drops				●
Cloud Watchers			●	○

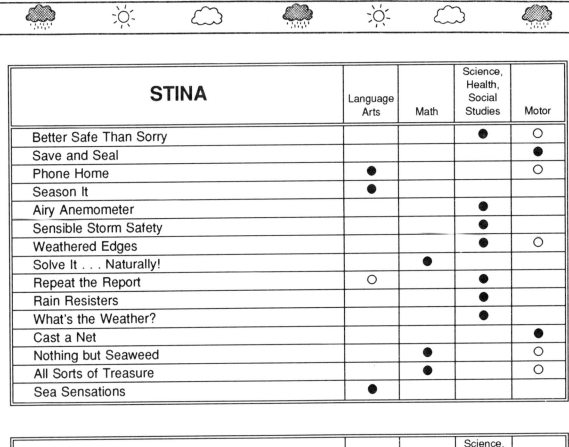

STINA	Language Arts	Math	Science, Health, Social Studies	Motor
Better Safe Than Sorry			●	○
Save and Seal				●
Phone Home	●			○
Season It	●			
Airy Anemometer			●	
Sensible Storm Safety			●	
Weathered Edges			●	○
Solve It . . . Naturally!		●		
Repeat the Report	○		●	
Rain Resisters			●	
What's the Weather?			●	
Cast a Net				●
Nothing but Seaweed		●		○
All Sorts of Treasure		●		○
Sea Sensations	●			

MISCELLANEOUS	Language Arts	Math	Science, Health, Social Studies	Motor
Cool Clothes			●	
Snowflake Inspectors			●	
One of a Kind			○	●
Snowed In			○	●
Zip It, Sip It				●
Fortune Cookie Forecast	○	●	○	
Cloudburst			●	○
The Shocking Truth About Lightning			●	
Snowball Jam		○		●
Thunderpop Relay			○	●
Pine Cone Predictors			●	
What Should I Wear?	●		○	
A Hand-y Graph		●		○
Fuzzy Feelers			●	○
Weather Wear	●			
Contain the Rain			●	○
Foamy the Snowman			●	○
Heavy Bucket		●		
I'm Hot!				●
Thunderation			●	

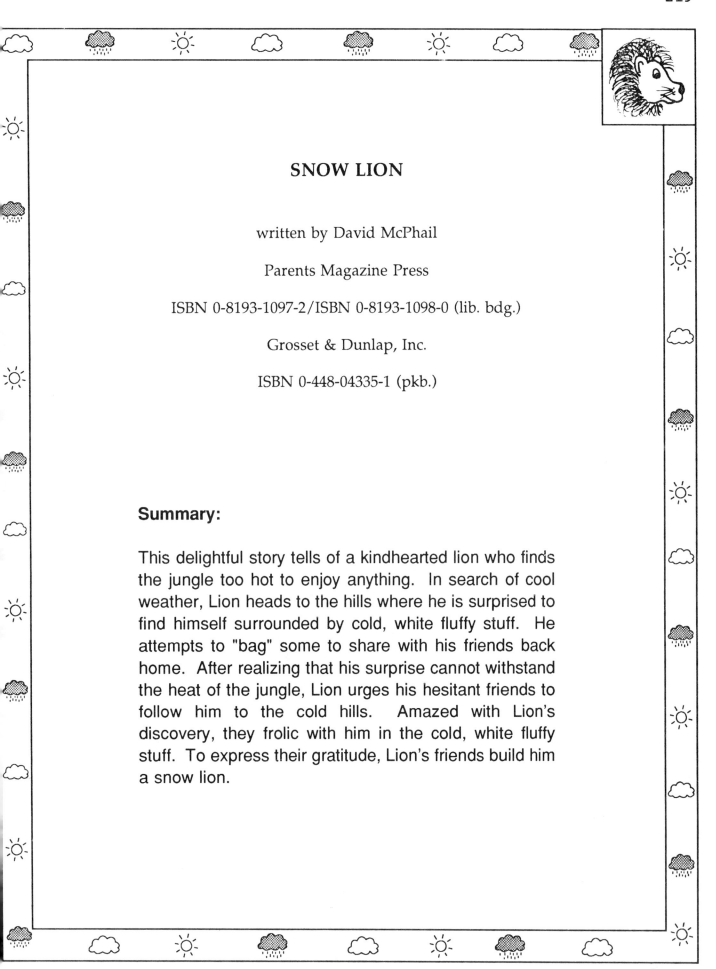

SNOW LION

written by David McPhail

Parents Magazine Press

ISBN 0-8193-1097-2/ISBN 0-8193-1098-0 (lib. bdg.)

Grosset & Dunlap, Inc.

ISBN 0-448-04335-1 (pkb.)

Summary:

This delightful story tells of a kindhearted lion who finds the jungle too hot to enjoy anything. In search of cool weather, Lion heads to the hills where he is surprised to find himself surrounded by cold, white fluffy stuff. He attempts to "bag" some to share with his friends back home. After realizing that his surprise cannot withstand the heat of the jungle, Lion urges his hesitant friends to follow him to the cold hills. Amazed with Lion's discovery, they frolic with him in the cold, white fluffy stuff. To express their gratitude, Lion's friends build him a snow lion.

Snow Is . . .

Ask the children what the white fluffy stuff was that Lion found. On a snowy day, challenge the children to use all of their senses to explore snow. Encourage them to describe how it sounds, looks, smells, tastes, and feels.

Some Like It Hot . . . Some Like It Cold

Recall the reason why Lion left the jungle. Discuss the advantages and disadvantages of hot and cold climates. Ask the children to draw pictures depicting themselves in their favorite climate. Use the illustrations to create a class climate graph.

Variation: Children conduct a survey of family and friends and graph the results. (A climate survey is provided on page 377.)

Caution . . . Ice Ahead!

Ask the children what made Lion slip and go flying. Encourage them to share an experience they have had slipping or falling on ice. Discuss the ways people can get hurt on snowy or icy surfaces. Ask the children to think of ways to prevent accidents in wintry weather.

Please, Don't Melt

Recall what happened to the snow in Lion's bag. Divide the class into small groups and give each a cup of snow. Challenge each group to make their snow last the longest.

What's In Lion's Bag?

Recall the articles Lion packed in his suitcase before he left the jungle. Pack a small suitcase containing items that might be taken on a short journey, such as a stuffed animal, comb, toothbrush, and toothpaste. The children try to identify the item by covering their eyes and feeling inside the suitcase.

Variation: Display objects for the children to view. Remove an object as they close their eyes. Ask the children to guess what is missing.

Let's Get Away

Recall where Lion and his friends went when the jungle got too hot for them. Ask the children why so many people want to visit places such as Florida and Colorado. Ask them to draw a picture of a place they would like to visit where the weather is *just right*.

Keep a Cool Head

Ask the children why Lion wished he had some cold, white fluffy stuff to put on his head. On a hot day, dampen and freeze some white washcloths. To cool off, the children wear the cold white cloths on their heads, pretending to be Lion.

Ribbon Thermometer

Ask the children to pretend to be the mercury inside of a thermometer as they dramatize the words of the following song:

(Tune: *Oh, A-Hunting We Will Go*)

And when I'm up, it's hot!
And when I'm down, it's cold!
And when I'm only halfway up,
It's neither hot nor cold!

Variation: Children manipulate individual ribbon thermometers to correspond with the words in the song. (A pattern and directions for making a ribbon thermometer are provided on page 378.)

Fluffy Water

Recall the reason water was in Lion's suitcase. Fill a bucket with about ten inches of snow. Ask the children to estimate how many inches of water will be in the bucket when the snow has melted. Provide rulers for the children to measure the water level.

Snowball Toss

Take the children outdoors on a snowy day to pack snow into balls, as Lion did. Challenge them to throw the balls at a target, such as a tree trunk or an old tire. If real snow is not available, snowballs can be simulated using yarn, sponge, or wadded paper.

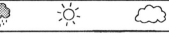

Shivercise

Ask the children what their bodies do when they are cold. On a chilly day when the children are shivering, suggest that they exercise! After exercising for a short time, ask the children if they are still shivering. Explain that shivering is our body's way of moving to warm up.

Temperature's Rising

Place a thermometer in a bowl of icy water for the children to observe the mercury dropping. Ask them to predict what will happen when the thermometer is placed in hot water. Move the thermometer to a bowl of hot water. Encourage the children to observe and discuss the results.

Who? Where? What? How?

Divide a large piece of paper into fourths. Label the sections *Who? Where? What?* and *How?* Ask the children to illustrate the main character, setting, conflict, and solution of the story in the appropriate box.

Sweat's Wet

Recall the reason Lion panted. Ask the children what their bodies do when they are hot. Explain that sweating is our body's way of cooling down. Read the following list of activities and instruct the children to be Lion in the hot jungle and shout, "Yippee!" if the activity named would help to cool them. If it would make them even hotter, they growl.

cuddle (growl)
wear light colored clothing (yippee)
drink hot chocolate (growl)
layer clothing (growl)
be still (yippee)
wear a hat, scarf, and mittens (growl)
blow on hands (growl)
exercise (growl)
sit by a fire (growl)
wear less clothing (yippee)
drink lemonade (yippee)
eat a big breakfast (growl)
open windows for breeze to blow in (yippee)
get wet (yippee)
turn on a fan (yippee)

Yippee!

Grrr!

Hot Humid Hair Hygrometer

Recall the reason why Lion wanted to be left alone. Ask the children if they have ever felt sticky on a hot day.

Make a hygrometer to measure the amount of humidity in the air. Thread a long human hair through the eye of a needle and tie it. Tape the opposite end of the hair to a wall. Draw a line directly under the point of the needle. Encourage the children to observe the needle. When the hair lengthens, dropping the needle below the line, the humidity is high. When the hair shrinks, raising the needle above the line, the humidity is low.

Hand-y Thermometer

Fill three bowls with water—one cold, one warm, and one room temperature. The children take turns holding one hand in the cold water and the other in the warm water for about one minute. Next, have them place both hands in the water that is room temperature and describe how each hand feels. Relate this activity to the reason why people rely on instruments to predict the weather.

Snow Spheres

Ask the children what Lion and Elephant made with the snow. Encourage the children to form snow into spheres of different sizes to make snowmen. If the weather does not bring real snow, use Ivory Snow® mixed with a little water.

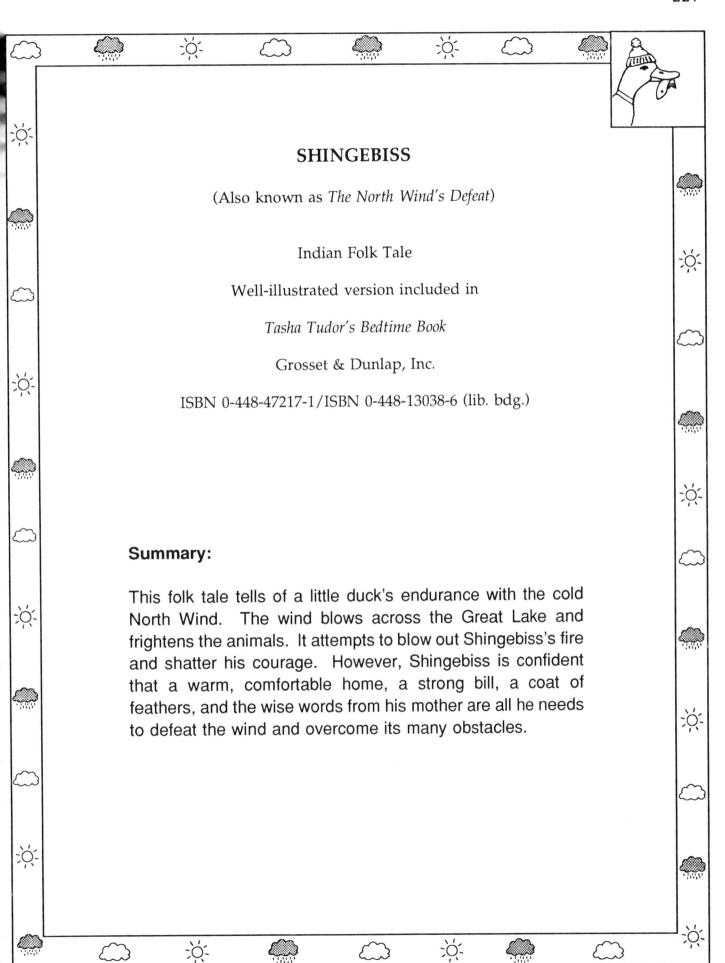

SHINGEBISS

(Also known as *The North Wind's Defeat*)

Indian Folk Tale

Well-illustrated version included in

Tasha Tudor's Bedtime Book

Grosset & Dunlap, Inc.

ISBN 0-448-47217-1/ISBN 0-448-13038-6 (lib. bdg.)

Summary:

This folk tale tells of a little duck's endurance with the cold North Wind. The wind blows across the Great Lake and frightens the animals. It attempts to blow out Shingebiss's fire and shatter his courage. However, Shingebiss is confident that a warm, comfortable home, a strong bill, a coat of feathers, and the wise words from his mother are all he needs to defeat the wind and overcome its many obstacles.

Forming Frost

Fill a can with crushed ice and sprinkle the ice with rock salt. Encourage the children to observe the outside of the can as water from the air collects on it and turns to frost. Ask the children to name other places they have seen frost.

Hear It Howl

Choose one child, "Shingebiss," to stand blindfolded in the center of the classroom. Choose another child, the "wind," to hold a large fan and stand in one corner of the room. The "wind" howls, "Whoo! Whoo! Whoo!" and moves the air with the fan. "Shingebiss" tries to find the "wind."

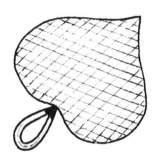

Salt or Slip

Ask the children why they think people put salt on snowy walkways and roads. Fill two cups with four ounces of water. Add a tablespoon of salt to one. Place both cups in the freezer for about two hours. Compare and discuss the results.

Bundle Up

Recall what kept Shingebiss so warm and comfortable when he was outside in the cold. Ask the children what people wear in cold weather to stay warm. Fill two identical lidded containers with hot water. Pull a woolen sock over one. Place both containers in a cold spot. After a short time, feel and compare the water temperature in the containers. Relate this to the reason extra clothing is worn in cold weather.

A Comfortable Lodge

Recall why Shingebiss did not mind the cold weather. Ask the children to describe what they would consider to be a comfortable lodge. Provide blankets or sheets and encourage the children to "build" a comfortable lodge.

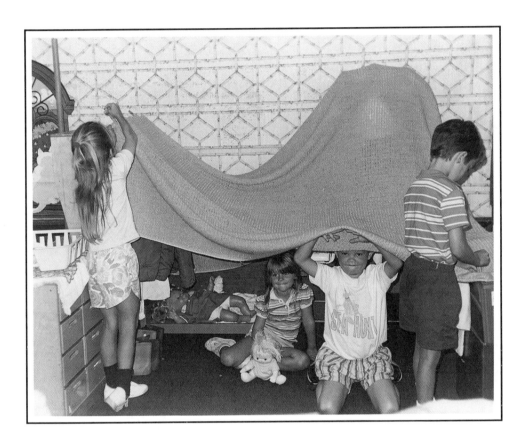

Creative Catch

Ask the children how Shingebiss caught his food. Fill a large container with water. Drop several items, such as metal washers or paper clips, into the water to represent fish. Challenge the children to try different ways to catch the "fish" without getting their hands wet.

Variation: Children "fish" in mud as Shingebiss did.

Don't Fan the Fire

Ask the children what happened to Shingebiss's fire when the wind blew on it. Teach the children the following verse:

"Fire! Fire!"
Cried Mrs. _____. (Drier)

"Where? Where?"
Cried Mr. _____. (Flair)

"On my clothes!"
Cried Mr. _____. (Rose)

"Fan it out!"
Cried Mrs. _____. (Stout)

"That'll make it worse!"
Cried Mrs. _____. (Hurse)

"Why? Why?"
Cried Mrs. _____. (Eli)

"Fire needs air!"
Cried Mr. _____. (Ware)

"What'll we do?"
Cried Mr. _____. (McGoo)

"Stop, drop, and roll!"
Cried Mrs. _____. (Sole)

Choose nine children to role-play the verse. As each character chants the beginning of a line, the remaining children listen and supply the rhyme.

Rhyme to the Weather

Chant the song Shingebiss learned from his mother, omitting the last word in each rhyme. Ask the children to recall the ending. Encourage them to compose their own weather rhymes.

Beat the Wind

One child, representing the North Wind, holds a large paper fan. The "North Wind" stands at one end of the room, "the Arctic." Choose three or four children to sit at the opposite end of the room. Provide each of them with a set of numeral cards, 1 through 10. The "North Wind" chants:

> "I'm going to blow across the lake;
> Ten big steps I'm going to take."

The remaining children watch from the side lines and count the "North Wind's" steps. The children with the numeral cards try to place them in order before the "North Wind" arrives and blows them away.

Variation: Use this activity to review alphabet or picture sequence.

Huddle Up

Ask the children what the deer and rabbits did when the wind blew. Choose four children to represent the four directional winds—north, south, west, and east. Each "wind" stands at the appropriate side of the playing area. The remaining children scatter, pretending to be animals. On a signal, the "winds" chase the "animals" around the playing area. Any "animal" caught must "freeze." The only means of "thawing" is to be hugged by another "animal."

Windproof Lodge

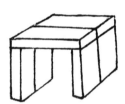

Challenge the children to use classroom materials to build "lodges" that will withstand the wind. To test the construction, the children fan the "lodges" with a large piece of cardboard.

Ping Pong A-"Long"

Position two long strings parallel on the floor to represent a path. Divide the "path" into one-foot sections. Choose one child to represent the wind. Place a ping pong ball at the beginning of the "path." Encourage the "wind" to move the ball as far as possible in just one blow. Measure the distance the ball traveled. Give the "wind" another chance, challenging "it" to blow the ball farther. Measure and compare the difference.

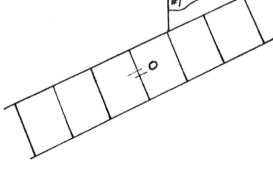

Whooo's the Wind?

Invite the children to take turns imitating the sound of the wind. Record the children's versions. Replay the tape for the children to listen to one another's voices. They will delight in guessing *whooo's* making the sound of the wind.

Icy Arctic Homes

Recall where the North Wind lives. Locate his Arctic home on a globe. Ask the children if they know who else lives in the Arctic. Have them compare the lifestyle of the Eskimos to their own. Fill a variety of containers with water and freeze them. After removing the ice from the containers, encourage the children to pretend to be Eskimos and use the frozen shapes to construct "igloos." Salt can be sprinkled between the layers to help them stick together. If available, packed snow can be used in place of ice.

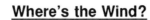

Where's the Wind?

Help the children construct a class weather vane. Mark a one-foot square outdoors on concrete. Make two diagonal lines from corner to corner, forming an **X**. Label each section of the **X** with the appropriate directional symbol—N, S, W, or E.

In the center of the square, place a ball of clay. Push the point of a pencil into the clay so the eraser is at the top. Punch a hole through the middle of the straw. Stick a pin through the hole and into the eraser. Cut a slit on each end of the straw and insert a small cardboard triangle in one end and a fringed cardboard rectangle in the other.

Encourage the children to observe the weather vane to determine the direction of the wind.

The Weather Did It

Ask the children what the weather caused Shingebiss to do differently in the winter than in the summer. Invite them to share how their own lives are affected by different kinds of weather.

CLOUDY WITH A CHANCE OF MEATBALLS

by Judi Barrett

illustrated by Ron Barrett

Macmillan Publishing Company, Inc.

ISBN 0-689-30647-4/ISBN 0-689-70749-5 (pbk.)

Summary:

This entertaining story cleverly combines weather terminology with just plain silliness. When a pancake accidentally lands on Henry's head, Grandpa concocts a most imaginative bedtime story about a town that has the wackiest, most delicious weather, which falls from the sky each day at breakfast, lunch, and dinner. Every day the townspeople watch the weather forecast to know if they should expect a shower of orange juice or perhaps a storm of hamburgers. All is delicious until the weather takes a turn for the worse and the people must evacuate to escape a flood of maple syrup and the strong winds of a tomato tornado.

The Weather Wish Wizard

Make a "weather machine." Cut the top and bottom off of a large appliance box. Decorate it with knobs and buttons. Cut a slot on one side of the box. Put "weather making" props, such as a fan, spray bottle, flashlight, and some styrofoam packing material, inside the box. Provide a chart showing the weather symbols and their corresponding words. (A chart is provided on pages 379–380.)

Choose one child, the Weather Wizard, to go inside the box and operate the props. The children copy a symbol or word from the weather chart. They take turns dropping their wish into the slot on the box for the Weather Wizard to read. Everyone stands back to enjoy the "weather."

A Tall Tale

Recall what kind of bedtime story Grandpa told to Henry and his sister. Write a creative tall tale with the class. Ask the children to make a class book or mural illustrating their tale.

Wacky Weather Wear

Brainstorm types of clothing needed for warm and cold weather. Challenge the children to invent a type of clothing that would protect them from the silly weather in Chewandswallow. Ask the children to illustrate their invention.

Like Any Other Town

Brainstorm things that most towns have in common, such as houses, stores, hospitals, and schools. Encourage the children to build a town using blocks to represent buildings. Challenge them to use their imaginations to make the town unique.

Hailing Popcorn

Recall where the food came from in the tiny town of Chewandswallow. Spread a large sheet on the ground. The children sit around its edges. Position a conventional corn popper in the center of the sheet.

Follow the directions for popping corn but do not cover. The children will delight in watching the corn fly through the sky and land on the sheet. Caution the children to stay off the sheet to prevent the hot grease from splattering them. After the corn has popped, the children can enjoy sampling the delicious "hail."

A Spark in the Dark

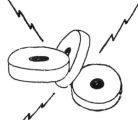

Ask the children if they would like to make a spark of "lightning" in their mouths. Pairs of children sit facing one another. Give each child a wintergreen Life Saver® mint and *completely darken* the room. Instruct the children to chew the mints with their mouths open so they can see sparks in the dark.

Piling Pancakes

Cut one large pancake and many small ones from poster board. Mark a plus sign (+) on one side of the large pancake and a minus sign (–) on the other.

Give each player a plate with a short stack (two pancakes). The children take turns flipping the large pancake with a spatula. If the plus side lands up, one pancake is added to the child's stack. If the minus sign lands up, one pancake is removed from the child's stack and returned to the center pile. The object of the game is to have the most pancakes at the end of a designated time period.

Raindrop Rhythm

Choose one child to be a rainmaker to beat the "rhythm of the rain" on a drum. The remaining children pretend to be raindrops, moving around the room to the drum's tempo.

Clouds on the Move

Ask the children what moves the clouds across the sky. Invite them to act as the wind. Mark a four-foot square on the floor. Label each side with the appropriate directional word—north, south, west, and east. Hang a paper cloud over the center of the square about three feet from the ground.

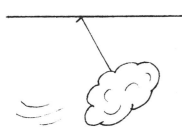

Choose one child to stand on each side of the square. The remaining children take turns calling out one of the four directions. The appropriate "wind" blows on the cloud, making it move.

Tune In

Ask the children why people watch the weather report on television.

Make a "television" from a large box. Cut a hole in the bottom to represent the screen, and add knobs or buttons for the dials. Encourage the children to write a weather forecast. They take turns behind the screen, pretending to be the weather reporter as their friends tune in.

Chewandswallow Cubes

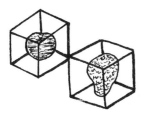

Pour fruit juice into ice cube trays filling a compartment for each child. Have the children match one-to-one as they drop a cherry or strawberry into each compartment. Put the trays into the freezer. When the ice cubes are frozen, each child adds one to a clear drink, watching it float. The children will enjoy their fruity treat.

React to the Weather

Ask the children to pretend they live in the town of Chewandswallow. Pose some weather situations for them to pantomime.

Examples: You are walking to school and find the streets are flooded from last night's rain of maple syrup.

You are playing outside and suddenly it begins to hail meatballs.

You are going swimming and realize the pool is filled with yesterday's shower of spaghetti.

A Foody Sort of Graph

Provide pictures of many different foods. Ask the children to sort the food pictures into the four basic food groups. The pictures can be used to construct a graph. Repeat the activity sorting the pictures into other categories.

A Foggy Find

Ask the children if they have ever walked through clouds. Explain that fog is a cloud that is close to the ground. Have the children pretend to be the townspeople of Chewandswallow walking through the pea soup fog. Blindfold the children, one at a time, and challenge them to find objects named in the following chant.

Use your hands, use your hands,

Feel your way around.

(Amy) walk right through fog

Until a _(book)_ you've found.

The Rains Came Tumbling Down

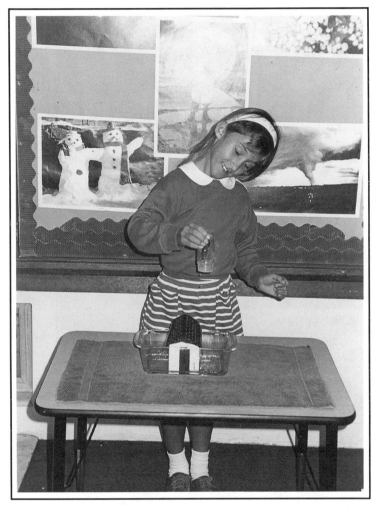

Ask the children what would happen if heavy rains fell every day. Encourage them to create a "flood" in the classroom. Invite the children to make "houses" from construction paper. Instruct them to fold a 3" x 12" strip into fourths. Suggest they draw windows and doors. Tape the ends together and add a 3" x 6" "roof." Place the "house" in a loaf pan. Provide empty spice jars filled with water to use as rain. The children sprinkle "rain" on their "house" and watch as the "rains" come down and the "floods" go up.

Him-i-cane *Her*-i-cane

The children pretend to be meteorologists who watch the oceans for powerful hurricanes to form. Tell them that part of their job is to assign each hurricane a name. Explain that meteorologists create an alphabetical girl/boy pattern of names each year. Ask the children to determine possible names for the current year's hurricanes, following the girl/boy pattern in alphabetical order.

Example: A–Ashley, B–Barry, C–Carol, D–Duke . . .

Duck and Cover

Ask the children what happened during the tomato tornado. Explain that real tornadoes begin on land and can cause considerable damage. Help the children determine where the safest location in the room would be during a real tornado. Demonstrate the "duck and cover" position.

To provide practice for tornado safety, set a timer at different intervals throughout the day. The timer signals the children to stop what they are doing, move to the designated "safe spot," and assume the "duck and cover" position. When an "all clear" signal is given, the children resume their previous activities. Relate the spontaneity of this activity to the sudden occurrence of real tornadoes.

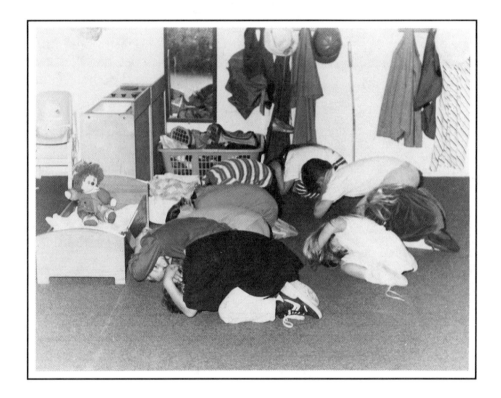

UMBRELLA

written by Taro Yashima

Penguin Books

ISBN 0-14-050240-8 (pbk.)

Summary:

This heartwarming Caldecott Honor Book tells about a little Japanese girl who is pleased to receive an umbrella and boots for her birthday. Momo's anxiety to use her new gifts turns to frustration when the weather refuses to cooperate. After many days of dry weather, she construes other uses for her gifts. Momo's mother continues to encourage her to be patient. When the rain finally arrives, Momo proudly enjoys her gifts as she walks through the rain, listening to its music. Not only is she finally able to use her umbrella and boots, but also for the first time, she walks alone—just like a grownup lady.

Where 'Ya From?

Recall the country where Momo's parents used to live. Locate Japan on a globe or a map and mark it with Momo's name. Encourage the children to ask their parents where their families originated. Place the children's names or photographs on a map to designate their origins.

Listen for the Rain

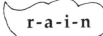

Ask the children what Momo was waiting for. Write the word *rain* on a chalkboard. Give each child a medicine dropper and a cup of water. Name sets of four letters, such as *bfga, prns,* and *rain.* Instruct the children to fill their dropper and listen for the letters that spell the word *rain.* Each time they hear them, the children release the water into their cup to make "rain."

That's Debatable

Have the children form two groups—those who want rain and those who do not. Give each group five minutes to brainstorm reasons for their choice. The groups hold a debate trying to convince each other of their choice.

Puddle Predictors

Provide medicine droppers, cups of water, waxed paper, and permanent markers. Instruct the children to draw a circle, representing a puddle, on a small piece of waxed paper. Ask the children to estimate the number of "raindrops" needed to fill their "puddle." Using the droppers and water, have them check their estimates.

<u>Clap It Out</u>

Write the following words across the top of a chalkboard: *rain*, *Momo,* and *umbrella*. Ask the children to clap the syllables in each word as it is pronounced. Have the class clap the syllables in each child's name. The children write their name on the chalkboard under the word that has the same number of syllables as their name.

<u>Weather Gear</u>

Gather the children in a circle. Place a box containing weather-related clothing and accessories, such as a bathing suit, scarf, boots, mittens, and an umbrella, in the center of the circle. Ask a child to select an item and use its name in a sentence.

Variation: Read sentences containing weather gear words. The children take turns finding a described item in the box.

All Grown Up

Recall how Momo felt when she walked with her new umbrella. Ask the children what makes them feel grown up. Provide dress up clothes for the children to role-play "grown up" situations.

Variation: Children illustrate something they have done that made them feel grown up.

A Cloudful

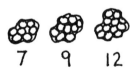

Cut small paper clouds of different shapes. Provide bingo chips to represent raindrops. Ask the children to estimate the number of "raindrops" needed to fill each cloud. Have the children place the bingo chips on the clouds to confirm their guesses. The clouds can then be ordered according to the number of "raindrops" each holds.

247

Pitter Patter

Ask the children to repeat the sounds the rain made on Momo's umbrella. Encourage them to make other sounds such as *buzzzz* and *vrooom* for their classmates to identify.

Gauge the Rain

Attach a ruler to the outside of a clear, cylindrical container. Place the container outside to catch rain. Measure and record the amount of water in the container every day for one month. Discuss how a weather forecaster might use this information.

Variation: Measure the water level using inch blocks or interlocking cubes.

The Japanese Way

Provide several samples of words written in Japanese. Encourage the children to write them in both Japanese and English.

Examples:

sun   rain   lightning   umbrella

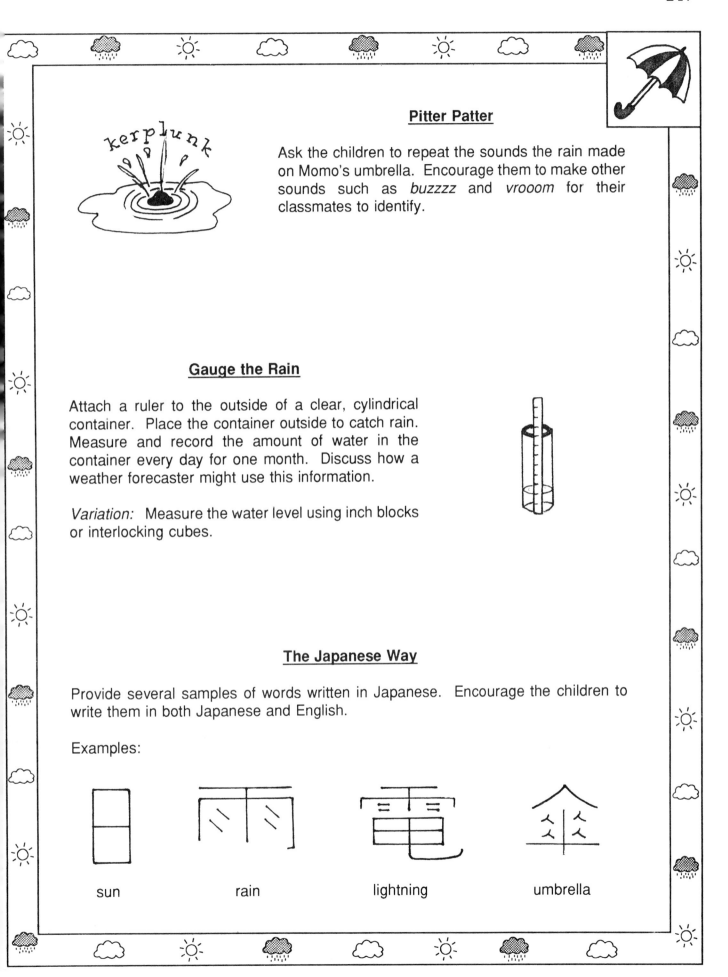

Watch It Disappear

Give each child a small, shallow container. Instruct the children to drip a drop of water in their container and take it outside. Ask them to predict how long it will take for the water to disappear. Have the children sit in a sunny spot and watch their water evaporate.

Variation: After a rainfall, the children trace a puddle with chalk and watch it evaporate.

Windy Rain

One child, representing the wind, holds a fan. The remaining children act as raindrops and scatter around the playing area. Instruct the "wind" to raise and lower the fan, gradually increasing the speed. The "raindrops" *pitter patter* around the room, reacting to the "wind."

Worth the Wait

Recall how Momo felt each day that it did not rain. Ask the children to share an experience they have had waiting for something special.

Record the Weather

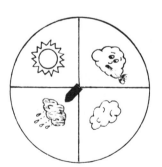

Each day choose a weather reporter to determine the weather. The reporter indicates the weather on a weather wheel or graph. (Symbols and a weather wheel are provided on pages 381 and 388.)

Variation: The weather can be recorded through the year to determine the sunniest, cloudiest, and rainiest months. (A weather calendar is provided on pages 379–380.)

Raining in the Room

Ask the children if they would like it to rain in the classroom. Place a kettle of water on a hot plate. While the water is heating, ask the children to predict what will happen to the hot water. Instruct them to observe the water vapor as it rises.

Ask the children what they think will happen when the water vapor is cooled. Place ice cubes in a baking pan and hold it over the rising steam. The children observe the underside of the pan to see water droplets form. Move the pan over the children so they can feel the "rain" fall.

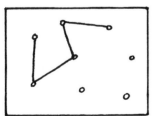

Connect the Drops

Place a chalkboard on a flat surface. One child uses a medicine dropper to drip water onto the board. A second child connects the water droplets by using one finger to draw a line from drop to drop.

Cloud Watchers

Encourage the children to forecast the weather by watching the clouds. Teach them the following poem to help them remember what kind of weather to expect when they see different types of clouds:

A *cirrus cloud* shows a change in the weather.
High in the sky it looks like a feather.

A *cumulus cloud* is fluffy and white.
It shows clear weather is in our sight.

And when a *stratus cloud* looks dark and gray,
We know that rain is on its way.

Provide materials such as feathers, cotton balls, chalk, glue, and paper, for the children to make different kinds of "clouds."

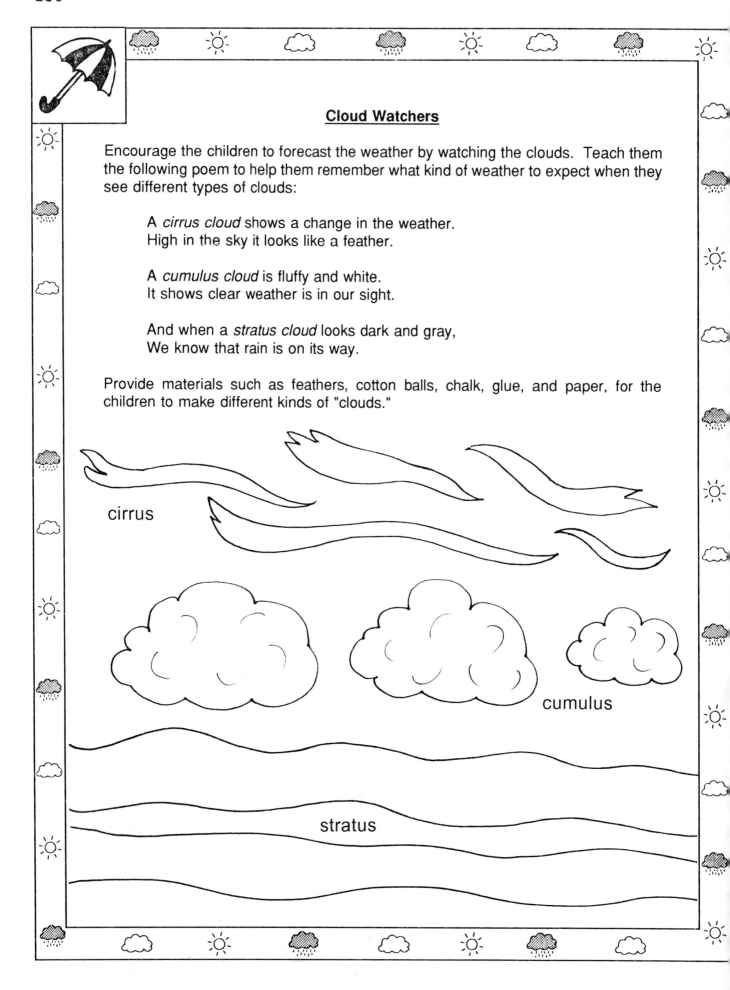

cirrus

cumulus

stratus

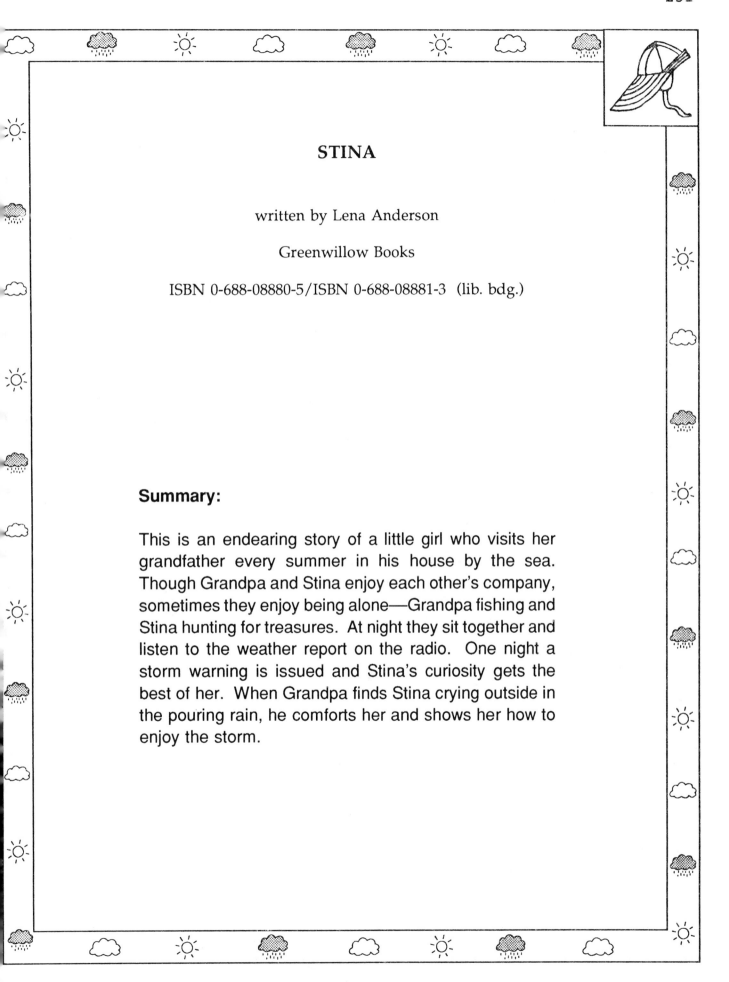

STINA

written by Lena Anderson

Greenwillow Books

ISBN 0-688-08880-5/ISBN 0-688-08881-3 (lib. bdg.)

Summary:

This is an endearing story of a little girl who visits her grandfather every summer in his house by the sea. Though Grandpa and Stina enjoy each other's company, sometimes they enjoy being alone—Grandpa fishing and Stina hunting for treasures. At night they sit together and listen to the weather report on the radio. One night a storm warning is issued and Stina's curiosity gets the best of her. When Grandpa finds Stina crying outside in the pouring rain, he comforts her and shows her how to enjoy the storm.

Better Safe Than Sorry

Ask the children why it was okay for Grandpa and Stina to go out in the storm. Have the children generate a list of ways to be safe during a lightning storm. Use their responses to list storm safety rules. Encourage the children to design and create safety posters.

Save and Seal

Provide treasures from nature such as seeds, flowers, leaves, and feathers. Each child arranges several treasures between two sheets of waxed paper. Cover the design with a piece of cloth and press with a warm iron to seal the paper. The children can border their design with construction paper or mount it to make a greeting card.

Phone Home

Choose one child to be Stina. Ask "Stina" to phone home to tell all about her summer vacation with Grandpa. Encourage the children to share an experience they have had away from home.

Variation: Have the children write or dictate a letter recalling Stina's summer vacation.

Season It

Recall the season in which Stina visited her grandfather. Encourage the children to create a list of words that describe summer. The children use their words to compose a summer story.

Variation: Any of the three remaining seasons can be substituted.

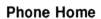

Airy Anemometer

Ask the children what Grandpa meant when he said, "We're in for a real blow." Discuss different wind strengths.

The children make simple anemometers to demonstrate wind strength by attaching a pinwheel to the eraser of an unsharpened pencil. (Directions for making a pinwheel are provided on page 332.) Place a dot on one vane and take the instrument outside. As the wind blows the pinwheel, instruct the children to observe the dot. If they can see the dot, the wind is moving slowly. If the dot is not visible, but a solid, circular line appears, the wind is moving fast. And if their pinwheel blows away, the children better go back inside . . . *You're in for a real blow!*

Sensible Storm Safety

Ask the children why Stina was crying. Reassure them that they don't need to be afraid during a storm if they follow safety precautions. Pose statements about stormy situations for the children to complete.

Examples: If swimming . . . . . . (get out of the water).
If outside . . . . (go inside).
If inside . . . . (stay away from the telephone and bath).
If in an open field . . (get down low).
If in a car . . . . (stay there).

Variation: Write storm safety rules on sentence strips. Cut each strip apart and have the children mix and match the pieces to form safety rules.

Weathered Edges

Recall the many treasures Stina found. Ask the children what they think sea glass is. Drop a small piece of broken glass into a plastic quart bottle. Add just enough salt water to cover the glass. Secure the lid. Have the children take turns shaking the bottle.

Repeat the shaking procedure every day for a week. At the end of the week, pour the water out of the bottle and observe the piece of glass. Ask them how the glass has changed and why.

Solve It . . . Naturally!

The children use collected nature materials to solve number stories.

Examples: If Stina found 3 feathers yesterday and 2 more today, how many would she have altogether?

If Stina collected 4 sticks and a wave washed 2 of them back into the sea, how many would she have left?

If Stina found 6 pieces of sea glass and gave 3 to Grandpa, how many would she have left?

If Stina had 3 rocks but she needed to have 7 for her family, how many more rocks would she have to find?

Repeat the Report

Ask the children how Grandpa knew a storm was coming. Choose a "weather reporter" to go outside to check the weather. Instruct the "reporter" to observe a variety of indicators such as a thermometer, windsock, clouds, and trees. The "reporter" marks the findings on a weather chart. When the "reporter" returns to the classroom, chant the following:

Use your ears, use your ears,

Listen carefully

To the weatherman's report.

Then tell it back to me.

After the weather has been reported, the child who can repeat the report places the correct props on a classroom weather board. (A weather chart, symbols, and doll with accessories are provided on pages 379–380 and 382–386.)

Rain Resisters

Ask the children why Stina and Grandpa did not get wet the second time they went out in the rain. Provide a cup of water, a medicine dropper, and a variety of fabric scraps. Ask the children to predict which scraps of fabric will be the best water resisters. Instruct the children to place the scraps on their arm and drop water on them. As the scraps are removed, the children feel their arm to test their predictions. The scraps can be sorted into two piles—those that resist rain and those that do not.

What's the Weather?

Ask the children why Grandpa and Stina listened to the weather report on the radio. Brainstorm reasons why people need to know the weather. Invite the children to share a time when they were affected by the weather.

Cast a Net

Designate a section of the playing area to represent the sea. Choose four "fishermen" to hold a sheet, representing a net, over the "sea." The remaining children pretend to be fish swimming upstream and downstream. As the children crawl under the "net," the "fishermen" chant:

Big fish, little fish

> in the sea

Better watch out

> or our catch you'll be!

We raise our net

> with all our might.

Then drop it down

> and hold it tight.

When the direction *drop it down* is chanted, the "fishermen" lower their "net" and try to catch some "fish." New "fishermen" can be chosen from the catch.

Nothing But Seaweed

Recall that on some days Grandpa's net was full of fish while on other days it was empty. Put some sinkable items, to represent fish, into a large container filled with water. Add blue tempera to darken the water. Two children take turns using a small fish net to catch the "fish." The object of the game is to have the most "fish" at the end of a designated time period. Add a piece of seaweed to heighten excitement. If a child catches the seaweed, all of the "fish" the child has previously caught must be "thrown" back into the water.

All Sorts of Treasure

Provide a box of treasures similar to the ones Stina collected. After the treasures have been explored, the children sort them into categories, such as those that come from plants and those that come from animals.

Variation: Children go for a walk and collect their own treasures to sort.

Sea Sensations

Ask the children to recall where Stina's grandfather lived. Instruct them to close their eyes and imagine they are at the sea with Stina. Encourage them to describe what they see, hear, smell, taste, and feel.

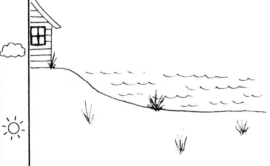

WEATHER

MISCELLANEOUS

Cool Clothes

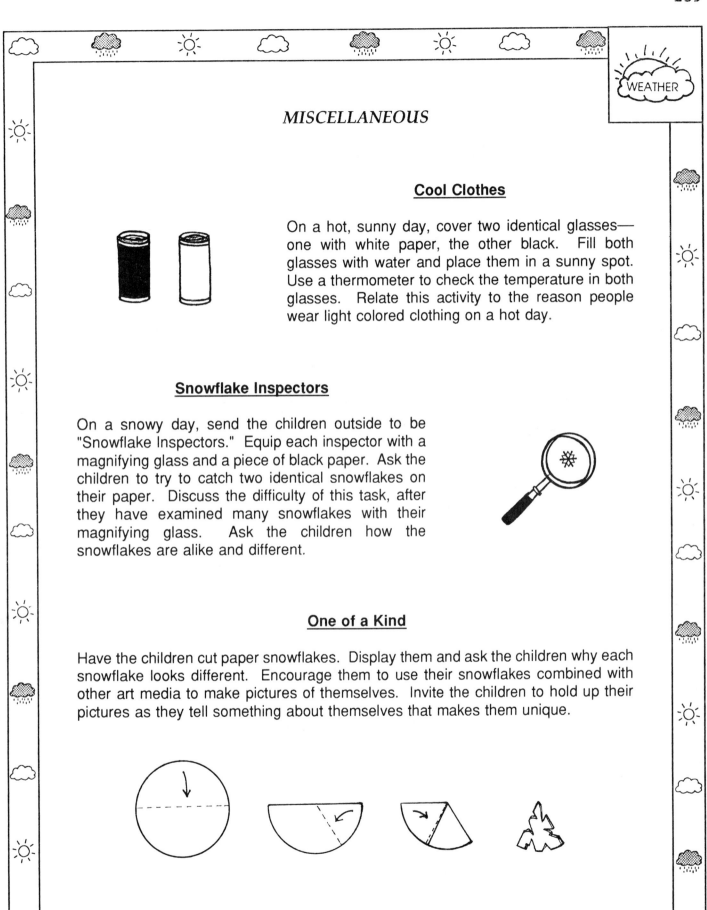

On a hot, sunny day, cover two identical glasses—one with white paper, the other black. Fill both glasses with water and place them in a sunny spot. Use a thermometer to check the temperature in both glasses. Relate this activity to the reason people wear light colored clothing on a hot day.

Snowflake Inspectors

On a snowy day, send the children outside to be "Snowflake Inspectors." Equip each inspector with a magnifying glass and a piece of black paper. Ask the children to try to catch two identical snowflakes on their paper. Discuss the difficulty of this task, after they have examined many snowflakes with their magnifying glass. Ask the children how the snowflakes are alike and different.

One of a Kind

Have the children cut paper snowflakes. Display them and ask the children why each snowflake looks different. Encourage them to use their snowflakes combined with other art media to make pictures of themselves. Invite the children to hold up their pictures as they tell something about themselves that makes them unique.

WEATHER

Snowed In

Children can experience fun in the snow indoors. Fill a water table or a large container with snow. Give the children a variety of utensils, such as spoons, cups, and molds, to enhance their snow play. Encourage the children to explore the snow as it changes from snow to slush to water.

Zip It, Sip It

Pour fruit juice into a small sealable freezer bag. Gently squeeze the air out as the bag is sealed. Partially freeze the juice. Ask the children to knead the bag until the contents are slushy. Slightly open a corner and place a straw inside for the children to sip their slushy treat.

Fortune Cookie Forecast

Give each child a strip of paper approximately 3" x ½". Ask them to write or type a weather prediction for use in the following recipe:

½ cup all-purpose flour	4 tablespoons vegetable oil
4 tablespoons brown sugar	½ teaspoon vanilla extract
2 tablespoons cornstarch	2 egg whites
Dash of salt	6 tablespoons water

Mix the dry ingredients together in a large bowl. Stir in oil until the batter is smooth. Beat the egg whites until stiff and fold them into the batter. Add the vanilla and water. Mix well.

Drop a spoonful of batter onto a greased electric skillet set on medium heat. Spread the batter until a 3" circle is formed. Cook for approximately four minutes or until lightly browned. Turn with a spatula and cook one more minute. Remove from the skillet and quickly place a paper "forecast" in the center of each cookie. Fold the cookies in half and hang them over the edge of a bowl until cool. Place the cookies in empty egg cartons to hold their shape. This recipe makes about two dozen cookies.

The children exchange cookies and enjoy reading each other's weather predictions.

Cloudburst

Choose two children to hold a paper bag at shoulder level to represent a cloud. The remaining children take turns pouring water into the "cloud" until it becomes heavy with "rain." *Be prepared for a real "downpour!"*

The Shocking Truth About Lightning

During dry weather, let the children experience static electricity. Rub a balloon back and forth vigorously on a carpet. Darken the room and ask for a volunteer to touch the balloon. Encourage the children to watch for a small spark of lightning. Explain that a small static spark is not dangerous but that lightning from storm clouds can be.

WEATHER

Snowball Jam

Children sit in a circle. Shape foam soap into a snowball and pass it around the circle as the children sing the following song:

(Tune: *Go In and Out the Window*)

 (One) snowball 'round the circle,

 (One) snowball 'round the circle,

 (One) snowball 'round the circle,

How many can we pass?

Continue to make snowballs, passing them around the circle. Change the number in the song as each new snowball is added. The object of the game is to move as many snowballs around the circle as possible without causing a "snowball jam."

WEATHER

Thunderpop Relay

Divide the class into teams. Designate a starting line and a "thunderpop" line. Place small paper bags, one for each child, at the "thunderpop" line. On a signal, the first child in each line runs to the "thunderpop" line, blows up a bag, pops it, and returns to the team. Play continues until one team has popped all of their bags. (Popped bags can be added to the scrap box or reused in an art project.)

Pine Cone Predictors

Give the children a dry pine cone. Instruct them to immerse the cone in water and observe it as it closes. Explain that the closing of a pine cone is one of nature's many ways of predicting rain.

What Should I Wear?

Display a variety of weather-related clothes and accessories. Read sentences including different types of weather. The children take turns choosing the appropriate gear they should wear.

Examples: The rain has stopped, but there are big puddles on the ground. (galoshes)

My hands are so cold from making snowballs. (mittens, gloves)

The sun is so bright, I can hardly see. (sunglasses)

A Hand-y Graph

On a cold day, ask the children to trace their hands on a piece of paper and color them to show how they came "dressed" for school. Construct a graph using the mittens, gloves, and bare hands.

WEATHER

Fuzzy Feelers

Provide a sack containing such items as a crayon, coin, paper clip, sponge, and an orange. Have the children put mittens on their hands and try to identify the objects by feeling them. Ask the children to remove their mittens and repeat the activity. Discuss why it is easier to identify the objects with bare hands.

Weather Wear

Add weather gear such as a raincoat, scarf, galoshes, mittens, boots, sunglasses, and an umbrella to the housekeeping center. The children will be prepared for all kinds of weather!

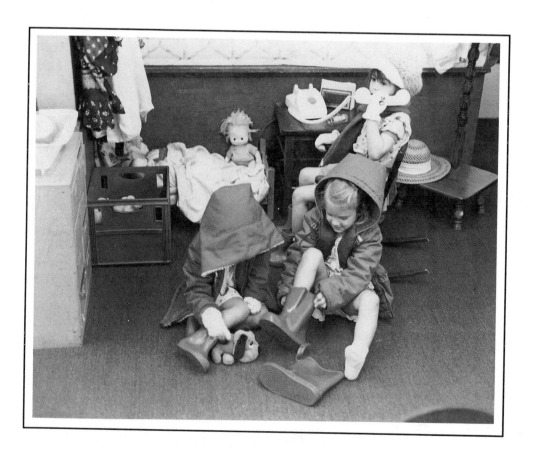

Contain the Rain

Instruct the children to press clay inside the bottom half of a transparent lidded container. Have them make a small indentation in the clay and fill it with water to form a "lake." They can add miniature models to complete their landscape. Place the container in a sunny spot. Encourage the children to observe the water cycle as moisture from the "lake" collects on the lid and "rains" on their landscape.

Foamy the Snowman

Invite the children to create a snowman using foam soap. Use lightweight materials to add facial features to the smallest sphere before placing it on the top. Additional accessories can be added to complete the snowman. Encourage the children to watch as the snowman slowly "melts," leaving his hat, eyes, nose, etc., in a "puddle."

WEATHER

Heavy Bucket

Ask the children to predict which will be heavier—a bucket of water or a bucket of snow. Fill two identical buckets—one with water, the other snow. To confirm their predictions, the children can lift the buckets or weigh them on a scale.

I'm Hot!

Divide the class into two or three teams. Have each team line up behind a hula hoop that contains an oversized coat, scarf, boots, and mittens. Place a cone approximately 15 yards from each team's hula hoop. On a signal, the first player on each team dresses as quickly as possible, runs around the team's cone, returns to the team, and calls out, "I'm hot!" As the first player undresses, the next player begins to dress. The object of the game is to be the first team to dress and undress.

Thunderation

Ask the children if thunder can hurt them. Assure them that thunder is a sound that helps us determine the distance between lightning and thunder. When lightning is seen, ask the children to begin counting until they hear the thunder roar. For every five seconds counted, the lightning is approximately one mile away. Teach the children the following chant to help them remember:

If when I count I get to three,

The storm is really close to me.

But if I count to twenty or more

Before I hear the thunder roar,

That means the storm is not too near

And I have nothing more to fear.

ART

Dab It

Place several cotton balls in the center of a square of porous fabric. Pull up the corners and fasten them with a rubber band. Pour a small amount of white tempera paint into a tray. The children gently dip the bottom of the stuffed square into the paint and dab it onto paper to represent clouds or snow.

Cloud Clues

Fill a bowl with white tempera paint. The children use a coffee scoop or large spoon to drop paint onto blue paper to represent a cumulus cloud. When their "cloud" is dry, ask the children to transform it into an animal or object. Encourage them to complete the sentence, "My cloud looks like . . ."

Art-sy Weather Station

Set up a "weather station" that features a variety of materials for the children to use to depict many kinds of weather. Some suggested materials and uses include:

rice for rain or sleet

cotton balls for clouds

sponges for the sun or clouds

sticky dots for the sun, snowballs, or hail

yarn for sun rays, clouds, snowdrifts, or puddles

Is That a Snowflake I See?

Place a snowflake stencil on dark construction paper. Spatter white tempera paint over the stencil. Remove the stencil and discover a beautiful surprise. Additional splattering can create a snowy effect.

Snowball Throw

Attach a long piece of blue mural paper to a washable wall. Place a "splat" mat on the ground under the paper. Provide several sponge balls and a shallow tray of white tempera paint. The children dip the balls into the paint and throw them at the paper. They will enjoy throwing the snowballs to create a mural that can be used as a background for a class snow scene.

Drop a Drip

Children turn a sunny day picture into a rainy day scene by dropping glue from eyedroppers onto their paper.

Colorful Ice Cubes

Add one of the three primary colors—red, blue, and yellow—to three small containers of water. Ask the children to use a medicine dropper to drop the colored water into ice cube trays. Encourage the children to mix the colors or add water to create different shades. Place the tray into the freezer. When frozen, remove the cubes and invite the children to watch them melt into colorful puddles.

Creamy Clouds

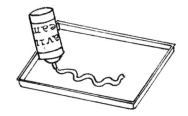

Squirt shaving cream onto a smooth surface such as a table top or tray. Encourage the children to draw with their fingers to design clouds in the cream.

Firsthand Weather

Children go outside during different types of weather to draw pictures of their surroundings. If the weather is too inclement, they can look out of a window while illustrating.

Muddy Memories

After rain has fallen and left behind squishy-squashy mud, invite the children outside to "paint" with it. Not only will they delight in using their hands or feet to create muddy designs, but this sensory experience will long be remembered . . . and this time it is okay to get muddy!

Variation: If the weather does not cooperate, make mud with soil and water.

Foggy Surprises

Children use white paper and white crayons to draw a picture of themselves in an outdoor scene. Collect the pictures and randomly distribute them among the children. Have them apply a coat of diluted gray tempera or watercolor over their classmate's picture. Allow the pictures to dry before displaying. Challenge the children to look at the display and find "themselves" in the "fog."

Snow Sculptures

Children enjoy creating with snow, whether it is real snow, Ivory Snow®, foam soap, or shaving cream. Suggest they create snow sculptures such as snowmen, animals, igloos, or free-form designs.

Drip Drop a Rainbow

Provide cone coffee filters, medicine droppers, and three containers of colored water—red, blue, and yellow. Cut an arc off the bottom of the coffee filters so the bottom is parallel to the top. Snip off the side seam and unfold. The children drop "raindrops" of colored water onto their filters. As the colors drop and explode, colorful "rainbows" will appear.

Lid Print Snowpeople

Saturate a sponge with white tempera paint and place it in a shallow pan. Provide dark blue paper and a variety of round lids. Ask the children to choose three different sized lids to make a snowperson. They press the rim of each lid in the paint and onto their paper. Suggest the children use different sized lids to create a whole family of snowpeople. After the paint has dried, the children can use other materials to complete their snowpeople.

DRAMA

A Picnic in Winter?

Pretend to go on a winter picnic. Read the dramatization and suit actions to the words.

Anyone for a picnic?
Don't you think it's kind of cold?   (Cross arms and rub)
Well, let's give it a try.
Pull on your boots.
Button up your coat.
Tie your scarf around your neck and tuck it down in.
Put on your hat and don't forget your mittens.
Are we ready?
Oops, we're missing something.
I know . . . it must be the food.
Let's pack it in a basket.
What should we take?   (Ask children what foods to pack)
I've got my thermos.
Ready, let's go.   (Pretend to open door and walk in place)
Boy, this is going to be fun.
Uh-oh, look at those dark clouds in the sky.   (Look up)
Plip, plop. Plip, plop . . . RAIN!   (Hold hands out, palms up)
Better run!   (Run in place)
Thunder's roaring.   (Clap hands)
Watch out for the lightning.   (Place hands over head)
Better hurry . . . run faster!   (Continue running)
I see a barn.   (Point ahead)
Can we make it?
Yes, we did.   (Pretend to open door and sigh)
Let's rest awhile.   (Sit and relax)
Look, the rain is stopping.
Now, we can go again.   (Pretend to open door and walk in place)
What's this? Oh, no . . . it's SNOW!
Oh well, let's catch some.   (Stick out tongue)
Mmmmmmmmmmmm!
Hey, let's make angels in the snow.   (Lie on back, moving arms and legs)
How about a snowman?   (Roll snowballs)

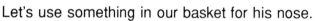

Let's use something in our basket for his nose.
What could we use?   (Ask the children which item would be best)
There!
A snowball battle would be fun.   (Pretend to throw snowballs)
Gotcha! Ouch . . . caught that one in my ear.   (Place hand on ear)
Let's eat! I'm hungry.
Where shall we sit?
Spread out the blanket.
Anyone for hot chocolate?
Yummy! (Pretend to eat and drink)
I'm done.
The food tasted great! (Rub tummy)
Let's shake out the crumbs for the birds.
Better call it a day.
Time to head for home.   (Walk in place)
Wow, the snow is so deep.
Let's slide down the hill.
Wheee! This is fun!
There's our house. We're almost home.
My pants are frozen.
Quick, open the door.
Home at last. (Sigh)
Let's get into some dry clothes.
Come on over and warm up by the fire.   (Rub hands)
Ready for a nap?
I sure am! (Snore)

Skiddy Skating

Children pretend to be ice skaters. Cut waxed paper into 12" squares. Give each child two pieces to use as skates. Invite the children to take off their shoes and "put on their ice skates." Turn on the "tunes" as the children stand on the waxed paper and glide across the carpet. Encourage them to skate forward, backward, or twirl around in circles.

WELL-KNOWN RECORDINGS

Hap Palmer

"Good Morning, Mister Weatherman." Patriotic and Morning Time Songs.

"Fishing Trip." Creative Movement and Rhythmic Expression.

Raffi

"Robin in the Rain." Singable Songs for the Very Young.

Wee Sing

"Rain, Rain, Go Away." Wee Sing.

"There Is Thunder." Wee Sing.

"It's Raining." Wee Sing.

"I'm a Little Snowman." Wee Sing.

"It Ain't Gonna Rain." Wee Sing Silly Songs.

"The North Wind Doth Blow." Wee Sing Nursery Rhymes and Lullabies.

"One Misty, Moisty Morning." Wee Sing Nursery Rhymes and Lullabies.

"Doctor Foster." Wee Sing Nursery Rhymes and Lullabies.

"Three Little Kittens." Wee Sing Nursery Rhymes and Lullabies.

Sharon, Lois & Bram

"It's Raining, It's Pouring." Mainly Mother Goose.

"Rain on the Green Grass." Mainly Mother Goose.

"If All the Raindrops." Mainly Mother Goose.

"Doctor Foster." Mainly Mother Goose.

"Rain, Rain, Go Away." Mainly Mother Goose.

Carole King

Chicken Soup With Rice by Maurice Sendak.

SONGS

WATER, AIR, AND SUN

(Tune: *Head and Shoulders*)

Do you know what makes our weather, makes our weather?
Do you know what makes our weather, makes our weather?
Water and air and sun go together—
That's what helps to make our weather, make our weather.

SPLISHIN', SPLASHIN'

(Tune: *Three Little Fishies*)

Up in the sky in a great big cloud
Lived a family of raindrops, oh so proud!
"Fall," said the mama raindrop, "Fall if you can."
And they fell and they fell all over the land.
Plip, plop, splishin', splashin', rainin' down.
Plip, plop, splishin', splashin', rainin' down.
Plip, plop, splishin', splashin', rainin' down.
And they fell and they fell all over the ground.

IT'S STORMING

(Tune: *The Eensy Weensy Spider*)

The dark storm clouds are rolling in—watch them floating by.
See lightning flash and brighten up the sky.
Hear thunder roar and make a crashing sound
As the rain begins to pour and pound upon the ground.

NOT TOO HOT, NOT TOO COLD

(Tune: *A-Hunting We Will Go*)

The temperature we know,
The temperature we know,
A thermometer will show
The temperature we know.

When red is at the top,
When red is at the top,
We know it will be hot
When red is at the top.

When red has dropped below,
When red has dropped below,
We know that it might snow
When red has dropped below.

When not too cold or hot,
When not too cold or hot,
Red is in the middle spot
When not too cold or hot.

In snow or wind or sun,
In snow or wind or sun,
The weather can be fun
In snow or wind or sun.

THE FOG ROLLS IN

(Tune: *Down by the Bay*)

Down by the ground
Where the thick fog rolls,
I could not see
The groundhog holes.
But later that day,
The fog rolled away;
High in the sky
Drifting on by,
Clouds on their way.

DO YOU KNOW WHAT TO DO?

(Tune: *Have You Ever Gone A-Fishing?*)

Do you know what to do on a stormy kind of day
If you look up in the sky and the clouds look gray?
Then the raindrops fall and the sky turns black
And the thunder rumbles and the lightning cracks.

Yes, I know what to do on a stormy kind of day.
If I am inside that is where I'll stay.
I will not take a bath or a shower at all
And I won't use the telephone to make a call.

I DON'T CARE

(Tune: *Jimmy Crack Corn*)

The cool wind blows, but I don't care.
The cool wind blows, but I don't care.
The cool wind blows, but I don't care.
It blows my kite up high.

The clouds turn gray, but I don't care.
The clouds turn gray, but I don't care.
The clouds turn gray, but I don't care.
See pictures in the sky.

The snow is cold, but I don't care.
The snow is cold, but I don't care.
The snow is cold, but I don't care.
My mittens keep me warm.

The rain pours down, but I don't care.
The rain pours down, but I don't care.
The rain pours down, but I don't care.
My raincoat keeps me dry.

The thunder roars, but I don't care.
The thunder roars, but I don't care.
The thunder roars, but I don't care.
That rumblin' can't hurt me.

The lightning flashes, and now I care.
The lightning flashes, and now I care.
The lightning flashes, and now I care.
It might strike you or me.

POEMS AND ACTION RHYMES

WEATHER   (Anonymous)

Whether the weather be fine

Or whether the weather be not,

Weather the weather be cold

Or whether the weather be hot,

We'll weather the weather

Whatever the weather,

Whether we like it or not.

APRIL   (Author Unknown)

Two little clouds one April day

Went sailing across the sky.

They went so fast that they bumped their heads,

And both began to cry.

The big round sun came out and said,

"Oh, never mind, my dears,

I'll send all my sunbeams down

To dry your fallen tears."

The raindrops got together

And formed a big dark cloud.

The raindrops got so heavy

They all came tumbling down.

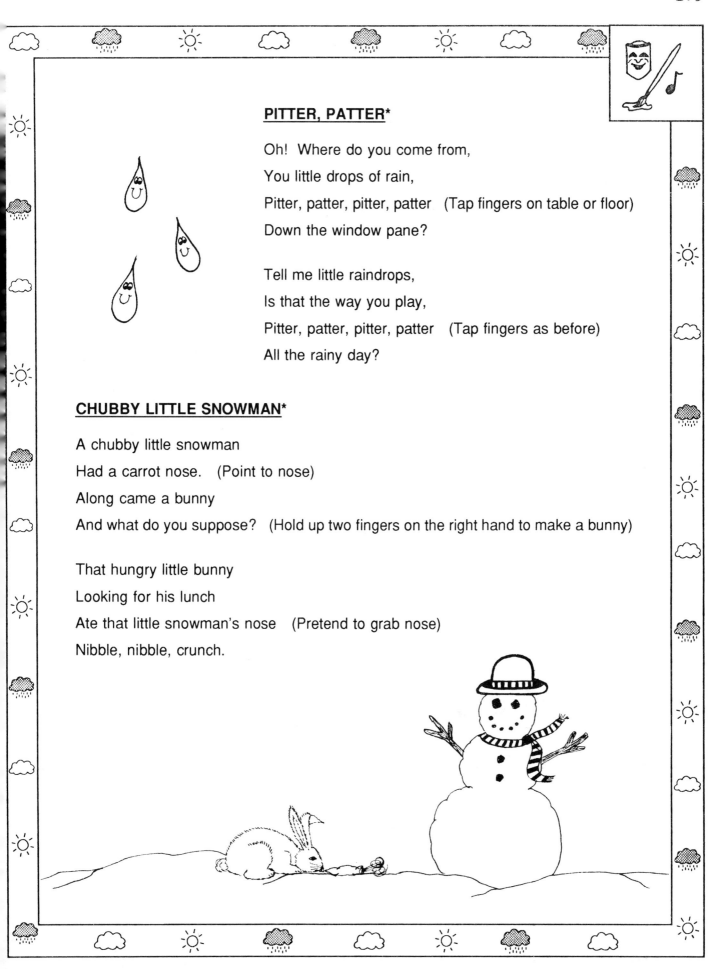

PITTER, PATTER*

Oh! Where do you come from,
You little drops of rain,
Pitter, patter, pitter, patter   (Tap fingers on table or floor)
Down the window pane?

Tell me little raindrops,
Is that the way you play,
Pitter, patter, pitter, patter   (Tap fingers as before)
All the rainy day?

CHUBBY LITTLE SNOWMAN*

A chubby little snowman
Had a carrot nose.   (Point to nose)
Along came a bunny
And what do you suppose?   (Hold up two fingers on the right hand to make a bunny)

That hungry little bunny
Looking for his lunch
Ate that little snowman's nose   (Pretend to grab nose)
Nibble, nibble, crunch.

CLOUDS   (Author Unknown)

What's fluffy white and floats up high   (Point upward)

Like piles of ice cream in the sky?   (Rub stomach)

And when the wind blows hard and strong,   (Move hands slowly through air)

What brings the rain?   (Flutter fingers downward)

What brings the snow?   (Flutter fingers downward)

That showers down on us below?   (Point to friends and self)

NATURE'S WASH DAY   (Author Unknown)

Mother Nature had a wash day

And called upon the showers

To bathe the dusty faces

Of the little roadside flowers.

She scrubbed the green grass carpet

Until it shone like new.

She washed the faded dresses

Of oaks and maples too.

No shady nook or corner

Escaped her searching eye,

And then she sent the friendly sun

To shine and make them dry.

JACK FROST*

Jack Frost is a fairy small,   (Show smallness with thumb and pointer finger)

I'm sure he is out today.

He nipped my nose   (Point to nose)

And pinched my toes   (Point to toes)

When I went out to play.

FIVE LITTLE SNOWMEN   (Author Unknown)

Five little snowmen, standing in a row,   (Hold up fingers)

Each with a hat   (Point to head)

And a bright red bow. (Make bow under chin)

Five little snowmen dressed for a show.   (Hold up fingers)

Now they are ready. Where will they go?

Wait till the sun shines. (Make circle above head)

Soon they will go

Down through the field with the melting snow.

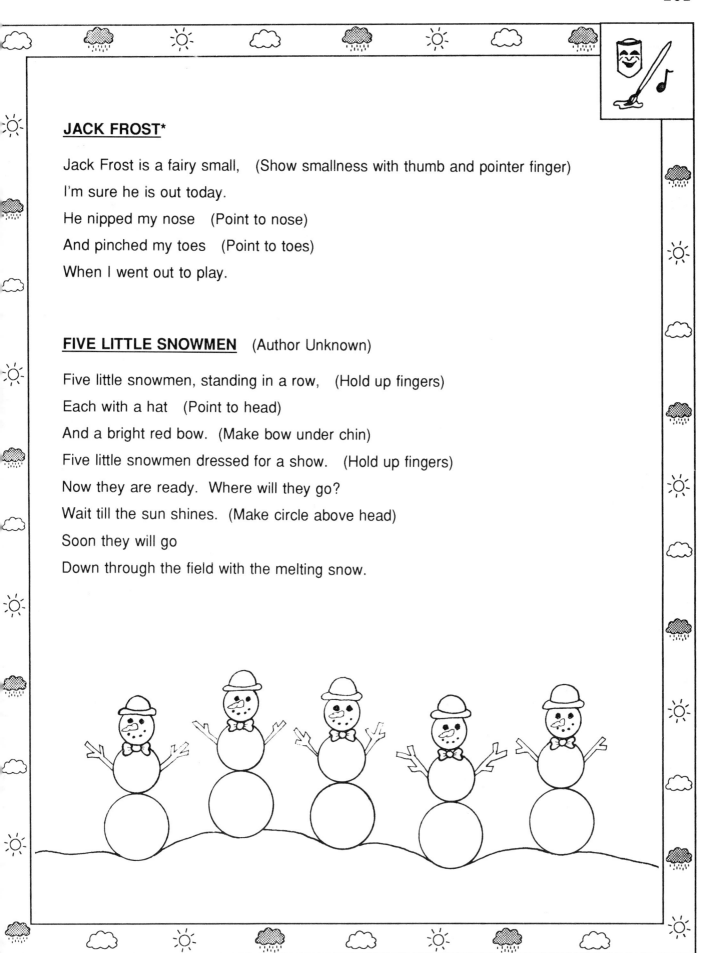

FALLING SNOW   (Author Unknown)

See the pretty snowflakes
　　Falling from the sky;
On the walk and housetop
　　Soft and thick they lie.

On the window ledges
　　On the branches bare;
Now how fast they gather,
　　Filling all the air.

THE WIND*

Feel the strong wind, it almost blows me down.   (Bend body, almost falling)

Hear it whistle through the trees and all around.   (Cup hand to ear)

Try to see the wind as it howls and blows.   (Hands over eyebrows)

But what the wind looks like? Nobody knows!   (Shrug shoulders, palms up)

THE RAIN*

I sit before the window now   (Seat yourself, if possible)

And look out at the rain.   (Shade eyes and look around)

It means no play outside today   (Shake head, shrug)

So inside I remain.   (Rest chin on fist, look sorrowful)

I watch the water dribble down (Follow up-to-down
　　　　　　　　　　　　　　　movements with eyes)

And turn the brown grass green.   (Sit up, take notice)

And after a while I start to smile

At Nature's washing machine.   (Smile, lean back, relax)

STORY BOOKS

Rain Drop Splash by Alvin Tresselt

This book shows rain traveling from raindrop to puddle to pond to lake to river to sea.

Will It Rain? by Holly Keller

The animals around the pond notice changes in the air and sky as they anticipate an approaching storm.

It Looked Like Spilt Milk by Charles G. Shaw

Simplistic white "blobs" depict some of the interesting shapes clouds make.

Hide and Seek Fog by Alvin Tresselt

Only the children find fun during the three foggiest days a little village has seen in twenty years.

Thundercake by Patricia Polacco

When a storm approaches, Grandma comforts her granddaughter by teaching her to bake a "thundercake" as they track the storm's distance.

Winter Fun by Rita Schlacter

Rabbit teaches Turtle that February's weather can be as much fun as June's if he will only give it a chance.

The Snowman by Raymond Briggs

A little boy finds a friend when his snowman suddenly comes to life.

Snow by Roy McKie and P. D. Eastman

This easy reader depicts children's excitement as they play in the snow.

It's Ground Hog Day! by Steven Kroll

Not everyone is anxious for an early spring; for Roland Raccoon, it means losing his business; therefore, he tries to prevent Godfrey Groundhog from looking for his shadow.

Forecast by Malcom Hall

After Stan Groundhog retires as the weather forecaster for the town's newspaper, Caroline Porcupine tries to convince everyone that she's the right one for the job.

Frog and Toad All Year by Arnold Lobel

Frog and Toad share the year together experiencing the weather each season brings.

Ida Fanfanny by Dick Gackenbach

After a peddler sells Ida magical paintings of the seasons, she experiences weather for the first time.

Fair-Weather Friends by Jack Gantos and Nicole Rubel

When best friends find that their weather preferences are opposite, they realize they must live apart for each one to be truly happy.

The Rain Cloud by Mary Rayner

A little rain cloud tries to find someone who really wants his rain to fall.

The First Snowfall by Anne and Harlow Rockwell

This simplistic book follows a little girl's exploration of a snowy day from the kinds of clothes she must wear to the kinds of things she can do.

Hold My Hand by Charlotte Zolotow

The friendship of two little girls radiates through a cold winter's afternoon.

The Winter Picnic by Robert Welber

A little boy's persistence pays off in the end when he shows his mother that a winter picnic is possible.

Bonnie Bess The Weathervane Horse by Alvin Tresselt

A weathervane horse plays an important role in helping the farmers determine the weather.

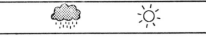

Tar Beach by Arthur Getz

Living in the city during hot weather, a brother and sister explore different ways of cooling off to beat the heat.

Storm in the Night by Mary Stolz

When left in the dark during a bad thunderstorm, a grandfather shares his childhood fear of storms with his grandson.

The Perfect Picnic by Betsy Maestro

The changing weather causes Goose and her friends to make many decisions about their planned afternoon picnic.

Katy and the Big Snow by Virginia Lee Burton

The big red tractor with the snow plow comes to a town's rescue during a big snowstorm.

The Snowy Day by Ezra Jack Keats

A little boy experiences the joys of playing outside on a snowy day.

In the Middle of the Puddle by Mike Thaler

As the rain falls and makes an ocean out of their puddle, a frog and a turtle watch the sun take over and dry up the water.

Come a Tide by George Ella Lyon

A little girl shares her story of how the spring floods affected her rural family.

Haircuts for the Woolseys by Tomie dePaola

After spring haircuts, the weather takes a turn for the worse; but thanks to Granny, the Woolsey lambs can still have fun playing outdoors.

The Big Snow by Berta and Elmer Hader

As winter approaches, the forest animals make the necessary preparations for cold weather.

Lost in the Storm by Carol Carrick

When his dog is lost during a storm, a little boy spends a restless night worrying.

Where Does the Butterfly Go When It Rains? by May Garelick

Questions about where many animals go during the rain are answered but where the butterfly goes remains a mystery.

The Jacket I Wear in the Snow by Shirley Neitzel

A little girl goes through the process of dressing and undressing for snowplay in this rhythmic rhyme.

Bringing the Rain to Kapiti Plain by Verna Aardema

This cumulative rhyme tells about an African boy who finds a way to change the dry weather and end the drought.

Sadie and the Snowman by Allen Morgan

All winter long, a little girl builds and rebuilds a snowman, decorating him with different foods until he becomes too small for anything except a plastic bag in her freezer.

White Snow, Bright Snow by Alvin Tresselt

All over town, everyone adjusts to the snowy winter weather and watch for the sunny spring weather to arrive.

Will Spring Be Early? or Will Spring Be Late? by Crockett Johnson

Groundhog waits patiently for his big prediction day only to find that spring might have already come.

CONCEPT BOOKS

What Makes the Weather by Janet Palazzo; *Now I Know* series

Colorful illustrations and easy text show the sky as a way of predicting many kinds of weather.

Hot and Cold and In Between by Robert Froman

Simple experiments help to explain why things feel hot and cold in different situations.

Weather Forecasting by Gail Gibbons

A behind-the-scenes look shows meteorologists using instruments and other means to predict the weather.

Rain by David Bennett; *Bear Facts* series

A clear and easy-to-understand book that explains rain.

Rain and Hail by Franklyn M. Branley; *Let's Read and Find Out Science* series

A look at the water cycle bringing rain and hail is offered in this informative book.

Clouds by Roy Wandelmaier; *Now I Know* series

Through colorful illustrations and simplistic wording, this book shows the different types of clouds and what kind of weather they bring.

Tornado Alert by Franklyn M. Branley; *Let's-Read-and-Find-Out* series

The many different aspects of tornadoes, including the damage they can cause, are presented in this informative book.

What Makes It Rain? The Story of a Raindrop by Keith Brandt

Raindrops are followed as they go through the water cycle.

Weather Words and What They Mean by Gail Gibbons

This book provides a basic understanding of weather terms and concepts.

Hurricane Watch by Franklyn M. Branley; *Let's-Read-and-Find-Out* series

A complete look at hurricanes is offered from the way they are formed to what safety steps are required.

Weather All Around by Tillie S. Pine and Joseph Levine

Answers to many questions about different kinds of weather, in addition to directions for making weather instruments, are included in this informative book.

Snow Is Falling by Franklyn M. Branley; *Let's-Read-and-Find-Out* series

The good and the bad affects of snow are presented through easy terms and simplistic illustrations.

The Cloud Book by Tomie dePaola

Kinds of clouds and different sayings about how they help us predict the weather are offered in this informative book.

Why Is It Hot? by Chris Arvetis and Carole Palmer; *Just Ask* series

Christopher Mouse learns about humidity and why weather is sometimes so hot.

Why Does It Snow? by Chris Arvetis and Carole Palmer; *Just Ask* series

Many facts about snow are taught to Christopher Mouse and his forest friends.

Why Does It Rain? by Chris Arvetis and Carole Palmer; *Just Ask* series

Christopher Mouse travels through rain clouds to learn more about evaporation and rainfall.

What Is a Cloud? by Chris Arvetis and Carole Palmer; *Just Ask* series

Christopher Mouse learns how clouds are made and the kind of weather they bring.

<u>Why Does It Thunder and Lightning?</u> by Chris Arvetis and Carole Palmer; *Just Ask* series

Magnets are used to help Christopher Mouse understand the cause of lightning and thunder.

<u>Why Is It Cold?</u> by Chris Arvetis and Carole Palmer; *Just Ask* series

Christopher Mouse learns about cold weather and how instruments can help us make a forecast.

<u>Weather or Not</u> by Rick and Ann Walton

A humorous, yet factual description of weather is provided in this riddle book about rain and shine.

<u>What Makes the Wind?</u> by Laurence Santrey

This informative book explains the different types of wind and their many effects.

<u>Storms</u> by Melvin Berger; *Science Is What and Why* Book

Types and causes of storms, in addition to safety precautions, are explained in this informative text.

<u>Flash, Crash, Rumble, and Roll</u> by Franklyn M. Branley; *Let's-Read-and-Find-Out* series

Many different aspects of thunderstorms are presented in this informative book, including steps to follow to keep safe.

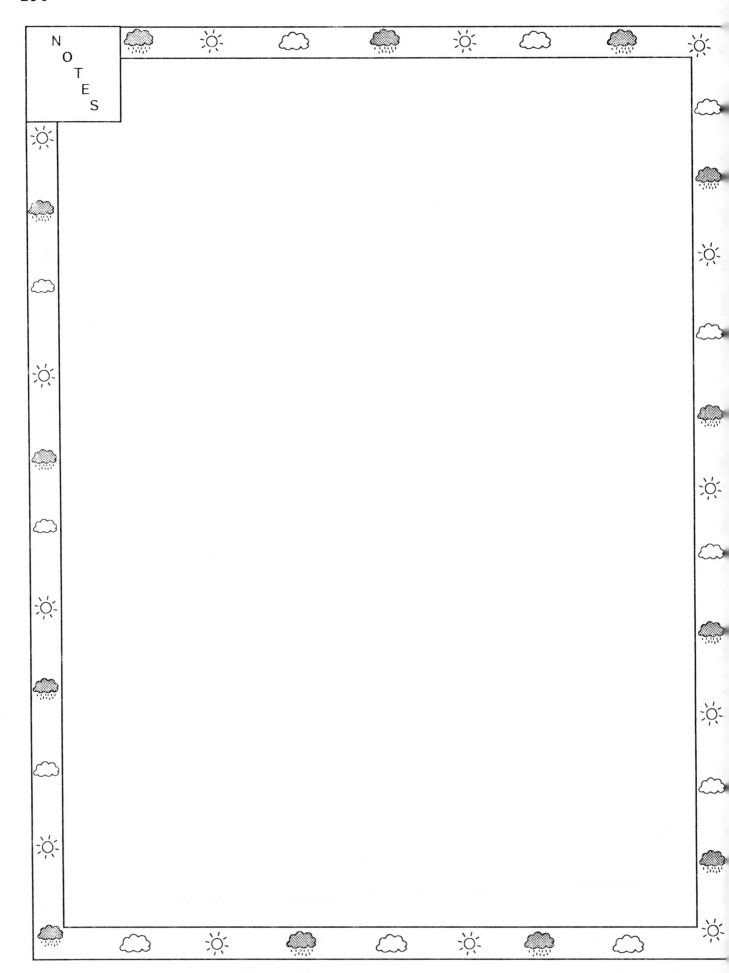

NOTES

NOTES

NOTES

REPRODUCIBLES

The activity sheets and patterns included in this section are provided to supplement the four units. Directions are suggested on each sheet with a reference to unit activities when applicable. The sheets can be reproduced for large group, small group, or individual instruction. Lamination of the sheets will aid durability for center use.

 The Story O'Mimus sheets are designed for the children to share their special friend at home. They can be reproduced for classroom use, such as bulletin boards, rewards, or center labels.

Story O'Mimus Reading in Rocker Picture: Use as a motivational aid.

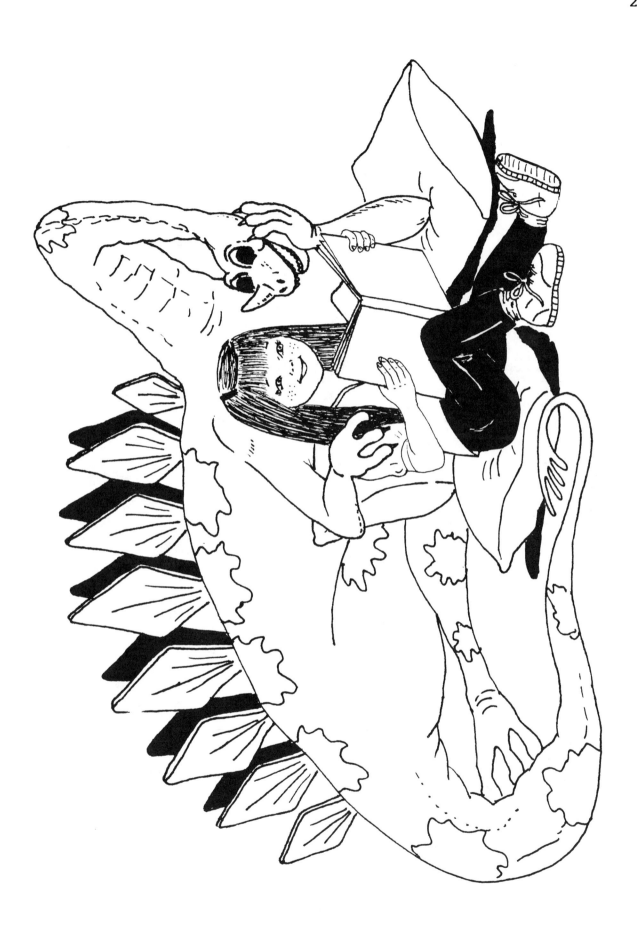

Story O'Mimus Reading with Friend Picture: Use as a follow-up to the Story O'Mimus story.

Figure 1

Figure 2

Figure 3

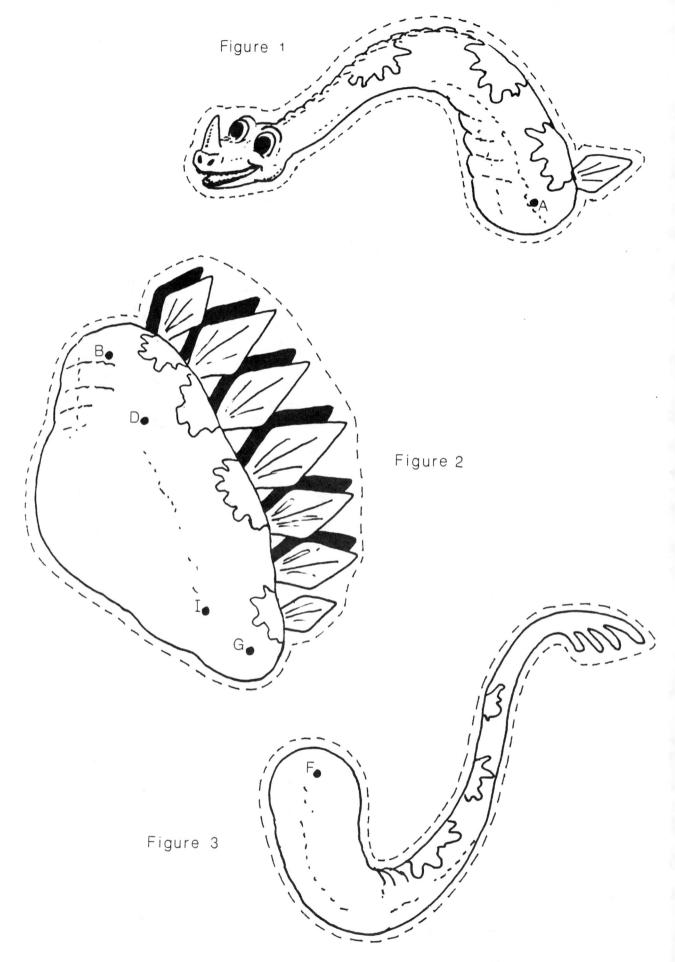

Story O'Mimus Puppet: Children color, cut out, and attach the body parts in alphabetical order with paper fasteners.

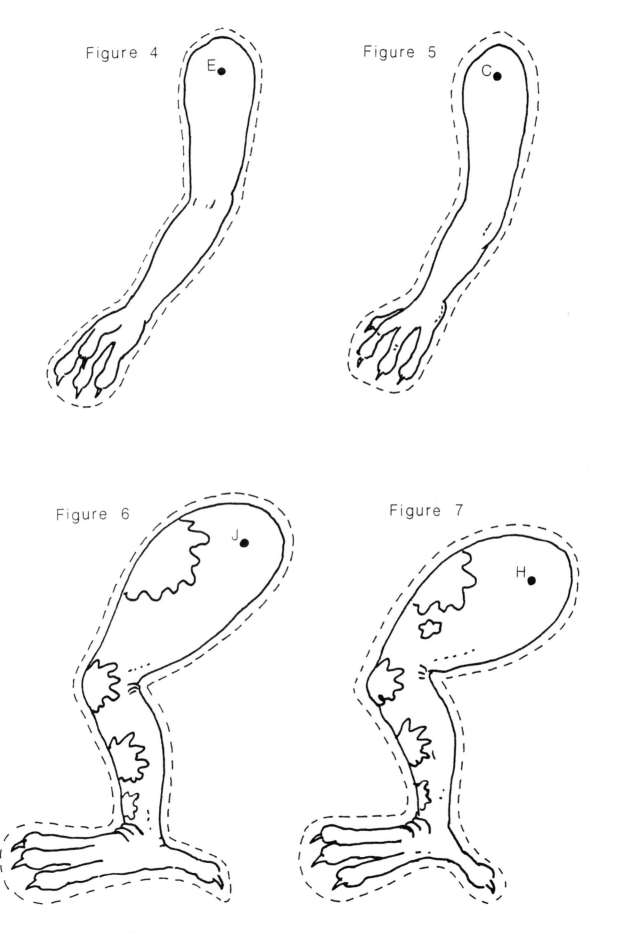

Figure 4

Figure 5

Figure 6

Figure 7

Story O'Mimus Puppet: Children color, cut out, and attach the body parts in alphabetical order with paper fasteners.

STORY O'MIMUS

The Story Mimic

Story O'Mimus Bookmark: Children illustrate or list their favorite stories.

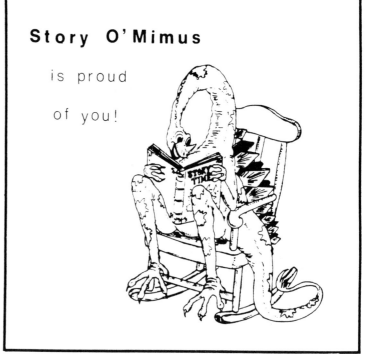

Story O'Mimus

is proud

of you!

Story O'Mimus Reward: Use as a motivational reward.

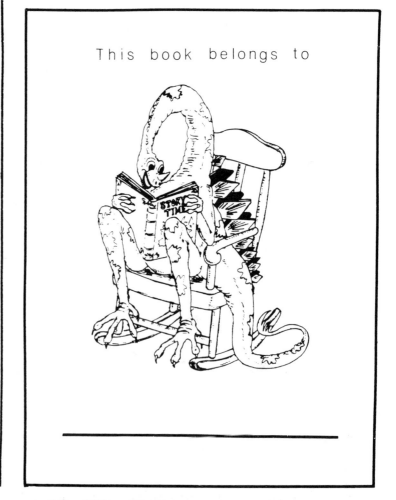

This book belongs to

Story O'Mimus Bookplate: Use to label a favorite book.

Name _____

Water, Water, Water

Water is all around us. We play in salty ocean water and swim in fresh pool water. Jumping in water puddles is great fun. Frozen water can help make popsicles that are good for licking.

We must be careful not to waste water because it is used in so many ways. All living things need water to grow. We wash ourselves with water in the bathtub. 'Round and 'round goes the water in the washing machine to clean our clothes. A cold drink of water tastes good and cools us down on a hot day. Our dishes are "whooshed" clean with water in the dishwasher. We cook with water. We try to help scrub the floor, but it's hard because the pail of water is so heavy to carry. Firemen use water to put out fires. Water is important to everyone.

Water Story: Children draw wavy lines under the word **water** each time it appears.

Story O'Mimus Water Picture: Children locate water-related items.

Water Patterning Pictures: Children color, cut apart, and use the pictures to create or repeat patterns.

Water Sorting Pictures: Children color, cut apart, and sort the pictures into categories.

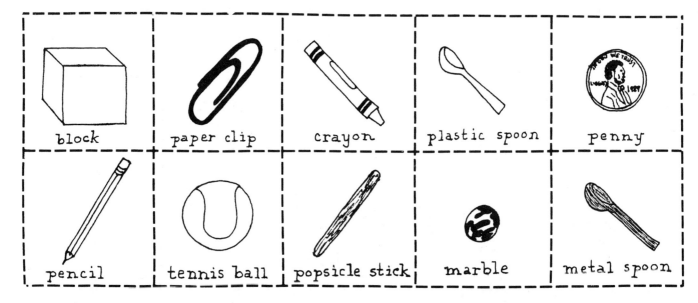

block	paper clip	crayon	plastic spoon	penny
pencil	tennis ball	popsicle stick	marble	metal spoon

Sink/Float Pictures: Children color, cut apart, and sort the pictures into two categories—those that sink and those that float. The pictures can be pasted on the Sink/Float Mat.

Sink

Float

Sink/Float Mat: Children record the Sink/Float Pictures on the mat or use as described on page 37.

Water Bookmark: Children illustrate or list their favorite water stories.

Water Gameboard: Children paste the <u>Patterning/Sorting Pictures</u> on the board to create a bingo or lotto card.

Name _____

water	waiter	water	wanted	wait
pool	pool	loop	pole	doll
ice	icy	nice	ice	ace
splash	splish	splash	smash	space
wet	met	wit	wet	ten
float	float	flute	tools	loot
sink	sank	ink	kiss	sink
vapor	viper	vapor	radar	paver
drip	drop	bird	dip	drip
swim	miss	swim	swan	swam
wash	mash	wish	wash	waste
soak	sock	oaks	sick	soak

Water Word Match: Children look at the first word in each row and circle the word that is the same.

306

Name _____

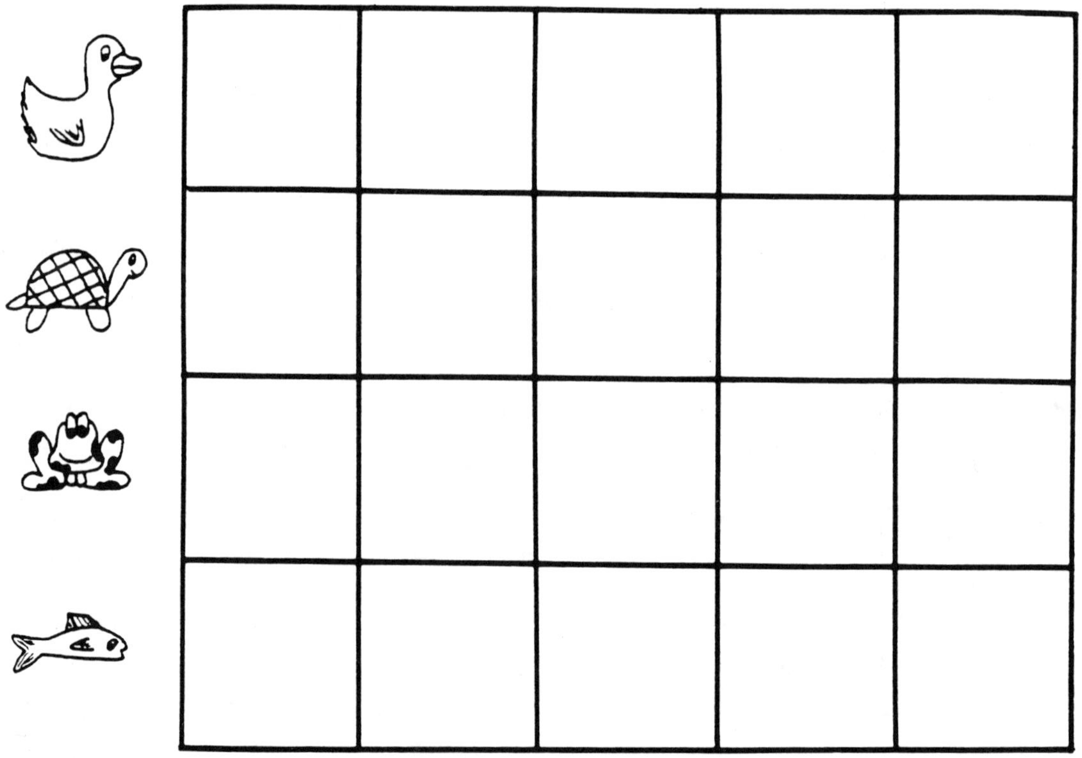

1 2 3 4 5

Water Graph: Children record the number of items on the graph.

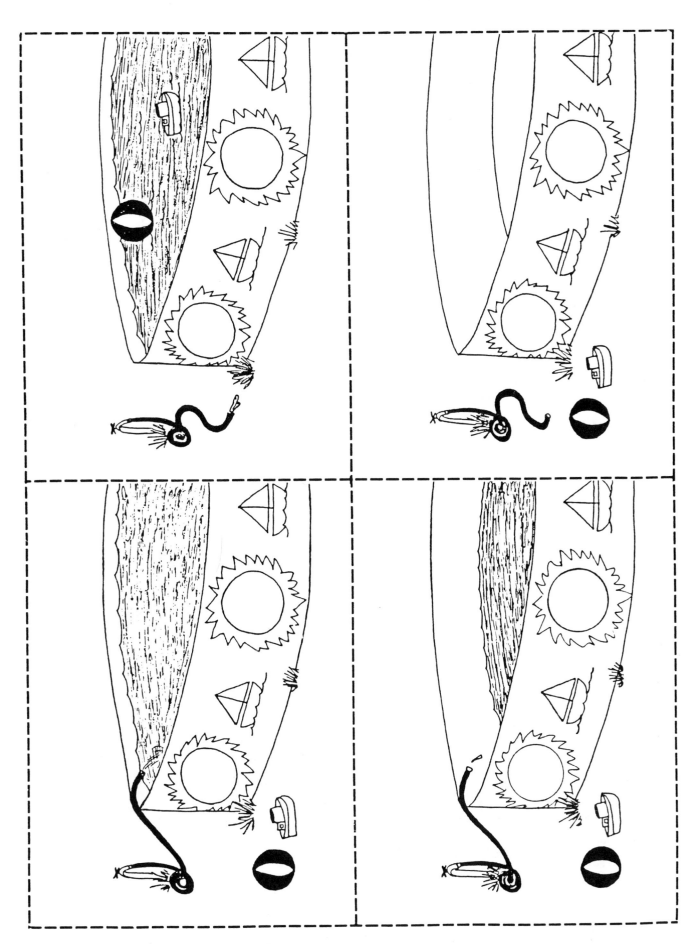

Water Picture Sequence: Children color, cut apart, and sequence the pictures to tell a story.

308

Water Mat: Children use as a background to act out number stories, follow positional directions, or use as described on page 48.

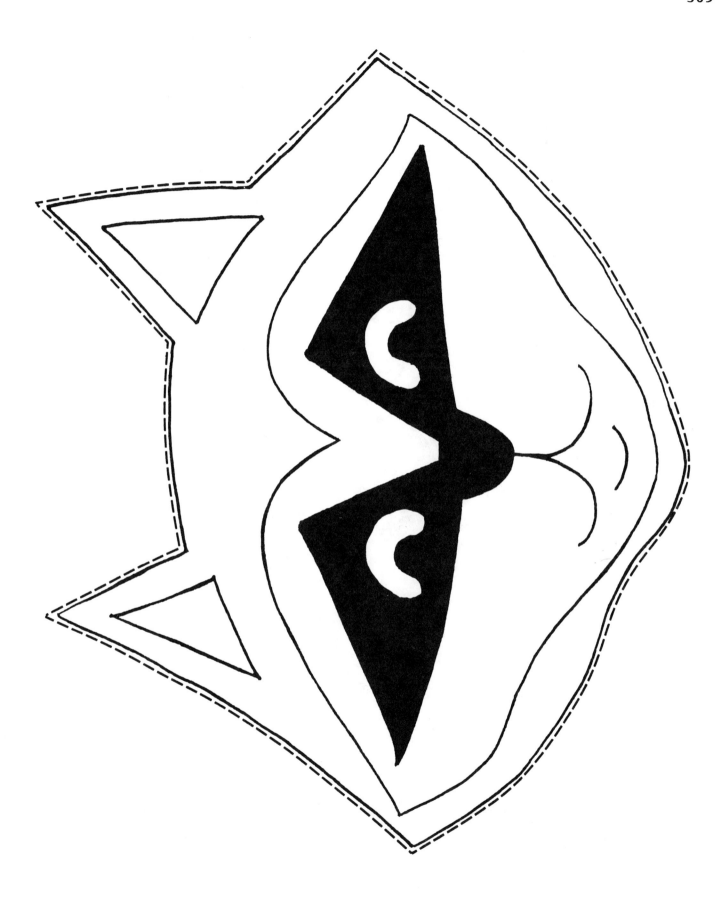

Raccoon Pattern: Children color and cut on the dotted lines. To make a puppet, attach a stick. To make a mask, add a headband and slit or remove the eyes. Use as described on page 16.

310

Rabbit Pattern: Children color and cut on the dotted lines. To make a puppet, attach a stick. To make a mask, add a headband and slit or remove the eyes. Use as described on page 16.

Skunk Pattern: Children color and cut on the dotted lines. To make a puppet, attach a stick. To make a mask, add a headband and slit or remove the eyes. Use as described on page 16.

Porcupine Pattern: Children color and cut on the dotted lines. To make a puppet, attach a stick. To make a mask, add a headband and slit or remove the eyes. Use as described on page 16.

Water Story Character Cards: Children can use the cards for puppets, games and graphs. Use the penguin pattern as described on pages 42 and 46.

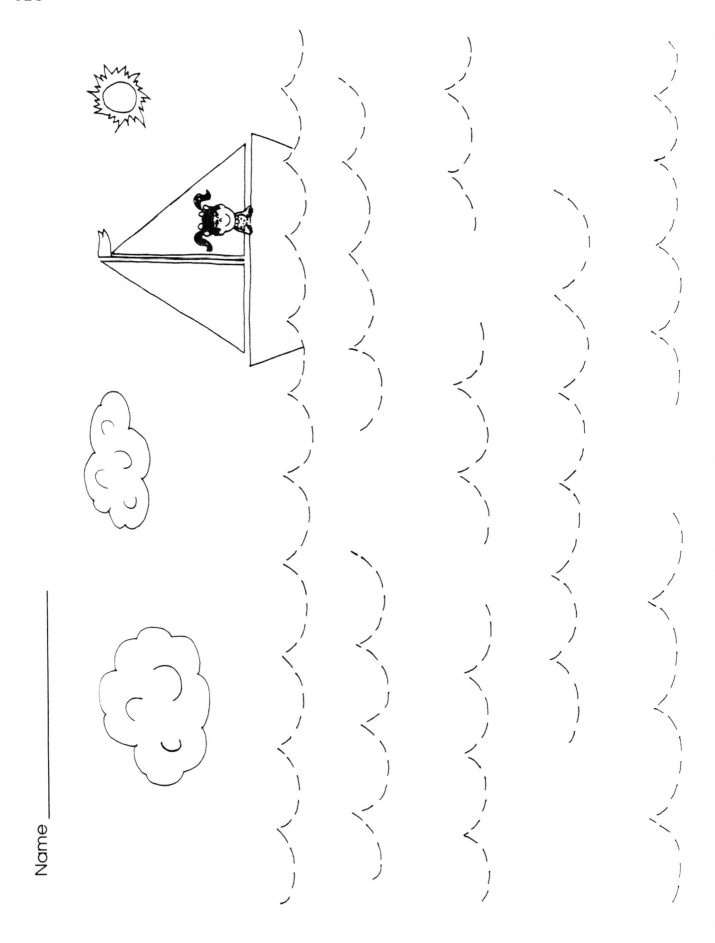

Name

Wavy Water Lines: Children trace the waves to practice writing curved lines.

Penguin Ice Match: Children cut out the lower case letters and paste them under the corresponding capital letters.

Name _____

Air, Air, Air

Air is almost everywhere. We cannot see air, but we can see things that are moved by air. Moving air, called wind, blows the leaves off of a tree or makes a sailboat move across a lake. We can feel air as it ruffles our hair or blows on our wet skin.

A ball filled with air makes a fun playmate. Air fills a balloon or helps sail a kite high above the clouds. Air in a raft helps us float on a hot summer day.

We breathe air into our lungs. We use the air inside of us to blow out our birthday candles. A horn cannot make a sound until we blow air into it.

All living things need air to stay alive. We must keep our air clean to help us stay healthy.

Air Story: Children draw a bubble around the word *air* each time it appears.

Story O'Mimus Air Picture: Children locate air-related items.

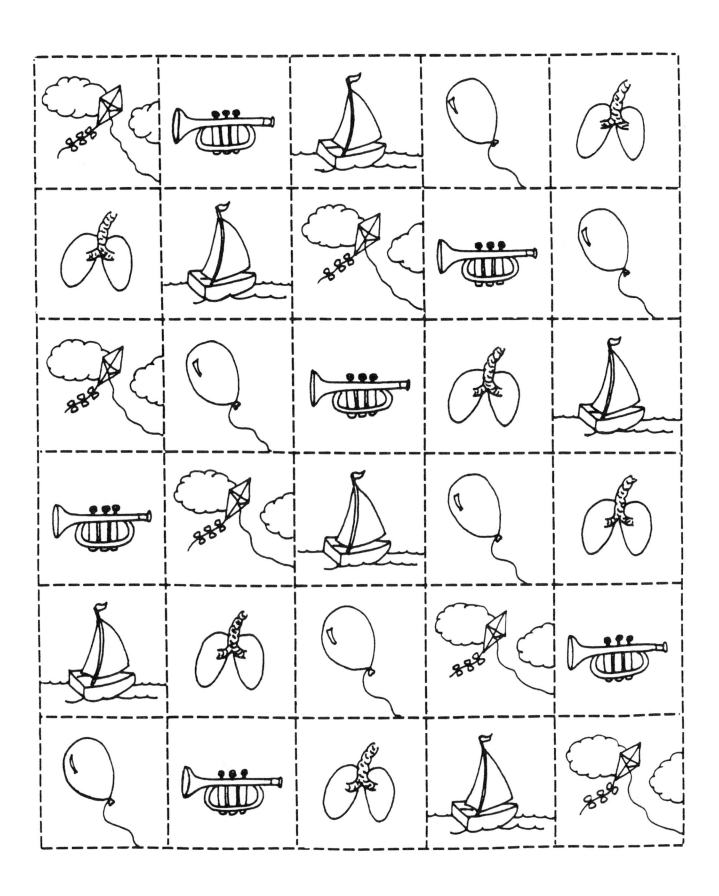

Air Patterning Pictures: Children color, cut apart, and use the pictures to create or repeat patterns.

Air Sorting Pictures: Children color, cut apart, and sort the pictures into categories.

Filled with Air/Moved by Air Pictures: Children color, cut apart, and sort the pictures into two categories—those filled with air and those moved by air. The pictures can be pasted on the Filled with Air/Moved by Air Mat.

Filled with Air

Moved by Air

Filled with Air/Moved by Air Mat: Children record the <u>Filled with Air/Moved by Air Pictures</u> on the mat.

Air Bookmark: Children illustrate or list their favorite air stories.

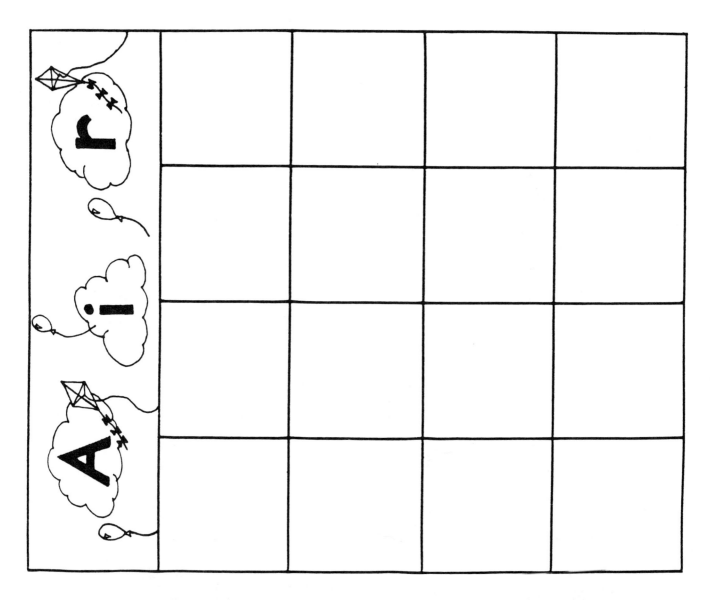

Air Gameboard: Children paste the <u>Patterning/Sorting Pictures</u> on the board to create a bingo or lotto card.

Name _____

boat	boot	boat	toad	coat
wind	win	wand	wind	dawn
fan	hot	fin	tan	fan
kite	bite	kit	kite	tick
ball	doll	ball	lab	bale
smoke	smoke	smack	snore	smack

Air Word Match: Children look at the first word in each row and circle the word that is the same.

Name _____

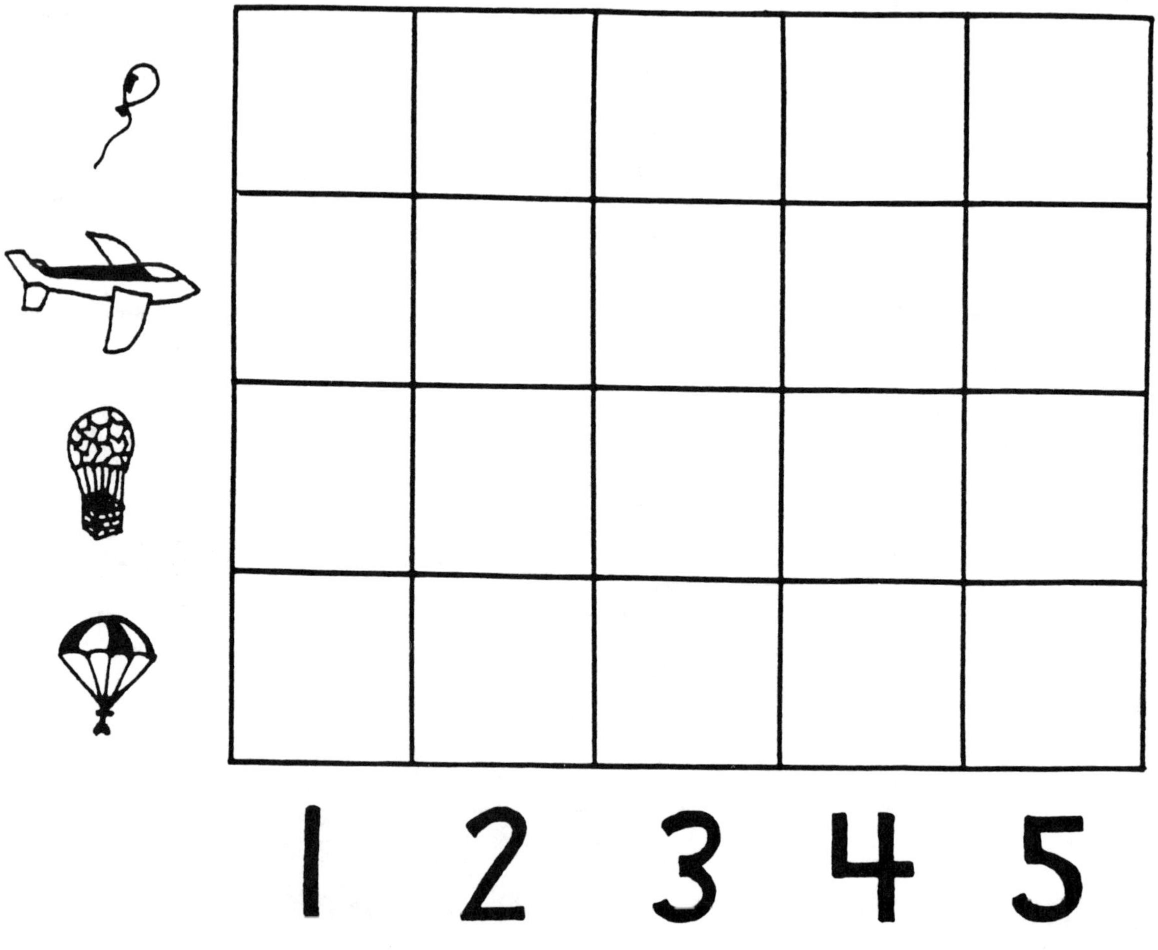

1 2 3 4 5

Air Graph: Children record the number of items on the graph.

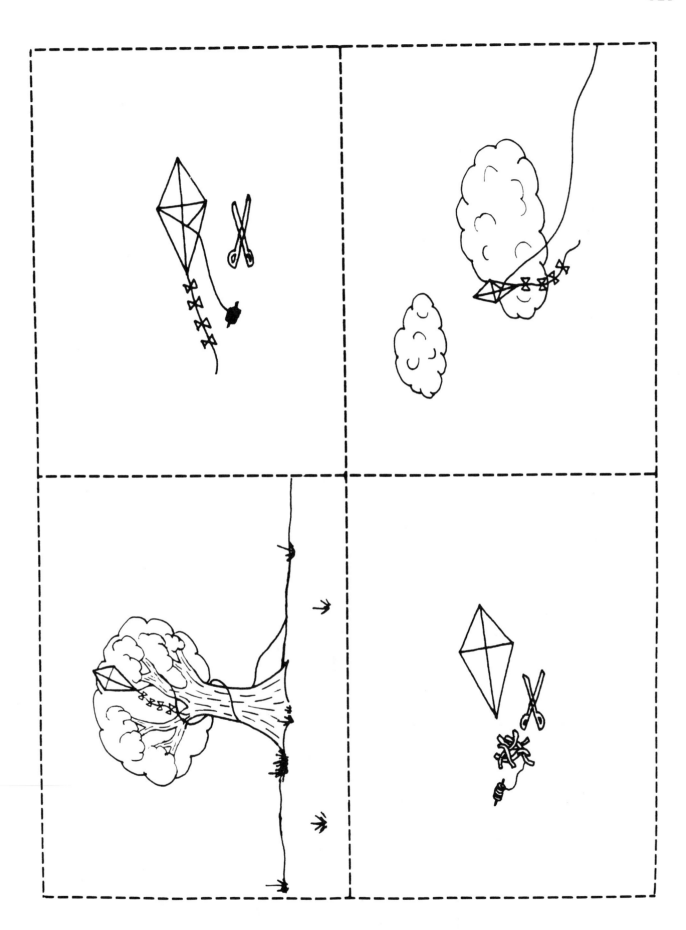

Air Picture Sequence: Children color, cut apart, and sequence the pictures to tell a story.

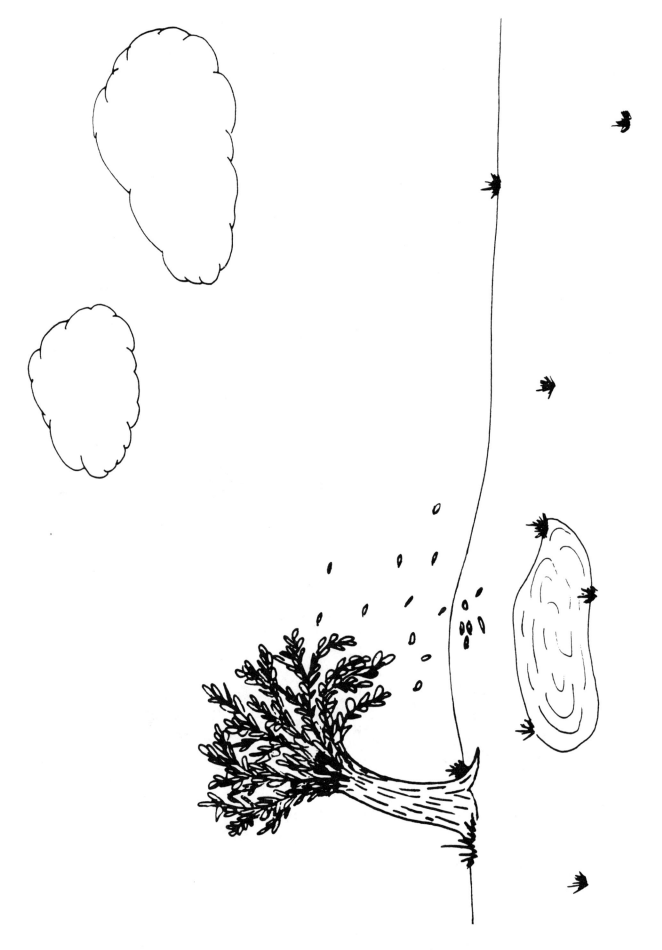

Air Mat: Children use as a background to act out number stories or follow positional directions.

Pig Pattern: Children color and cut on the dotted lines. To make a puppet, attach a stick. To make a mask, add a headband and slit or remove the eyes. Use as described on pages 84 and 88.

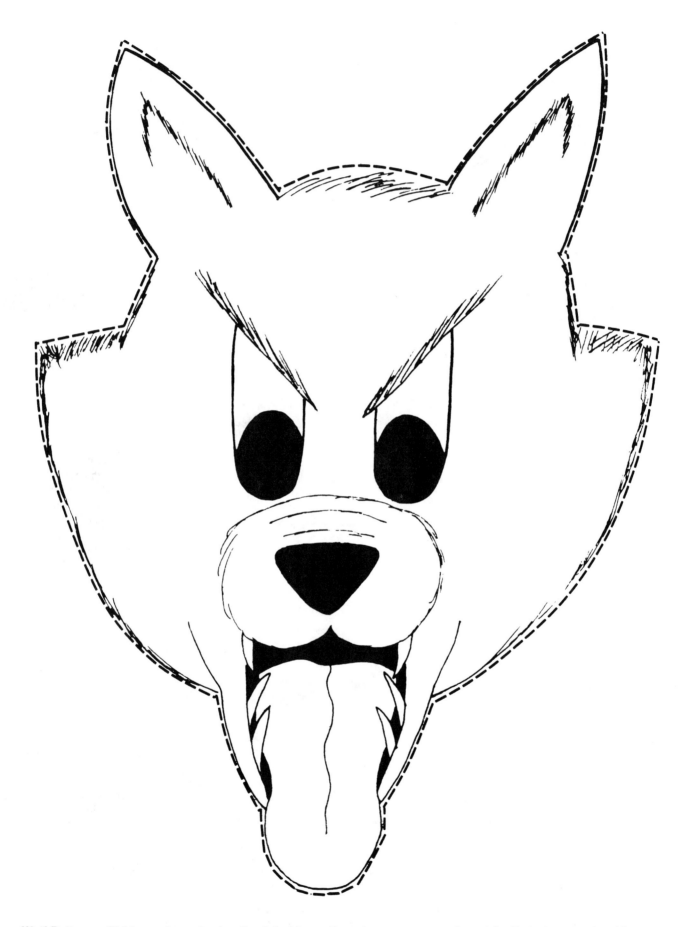

Wolf Pattern: Children color and cut on the dotted lines. To make a puppet, attach a stick. To make a mask, add a headband and slit or remove the eyes. Use as described on pages 84 and 88.

Air Pathway Mat: Use as described on page 85.

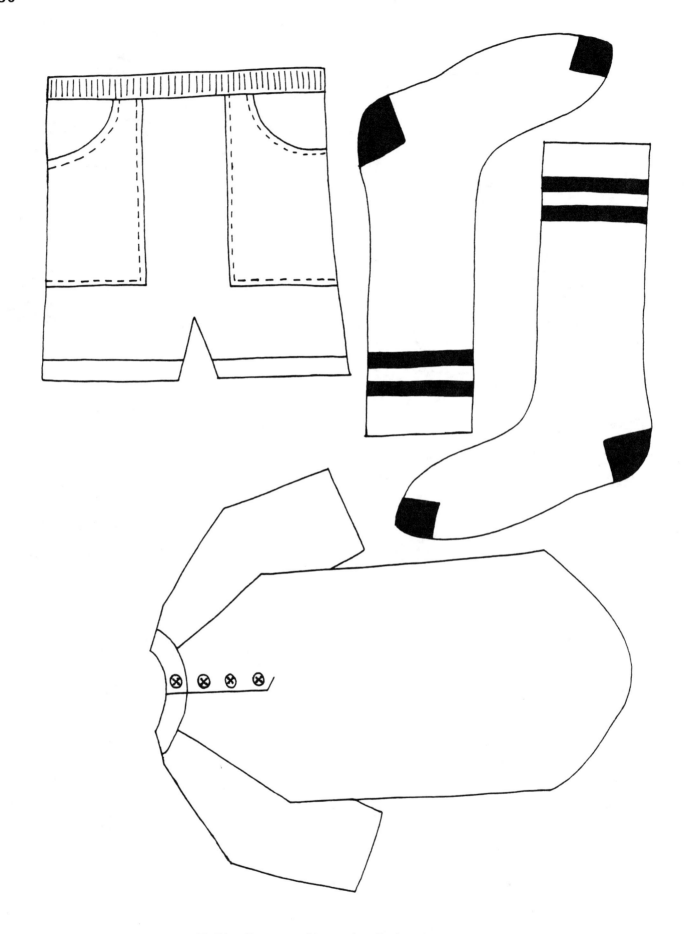

Clothing Patterns: Use as described on page 91.

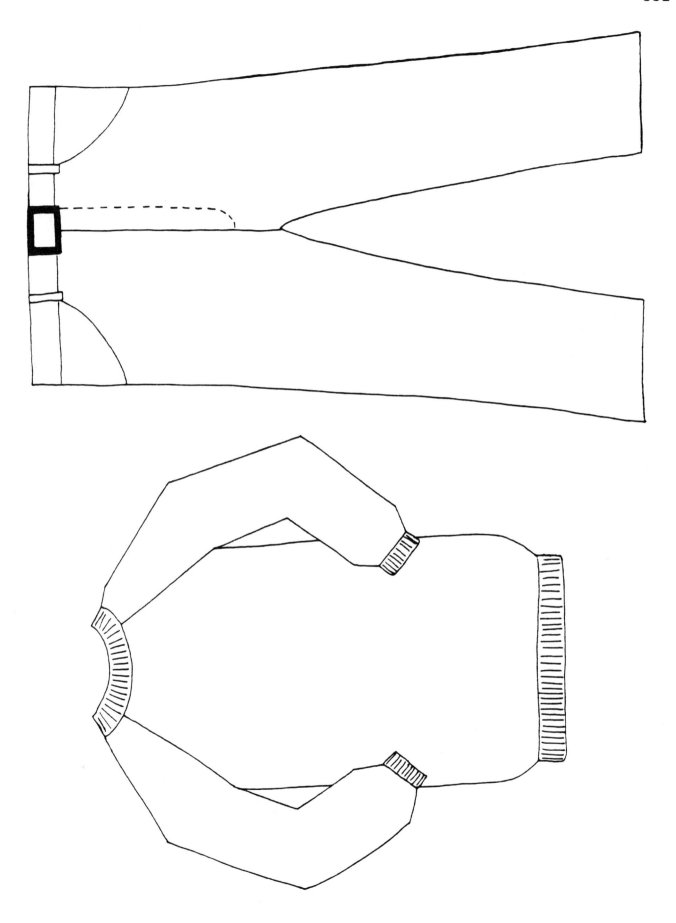

Clothing Patterns: Use as described on page 91.

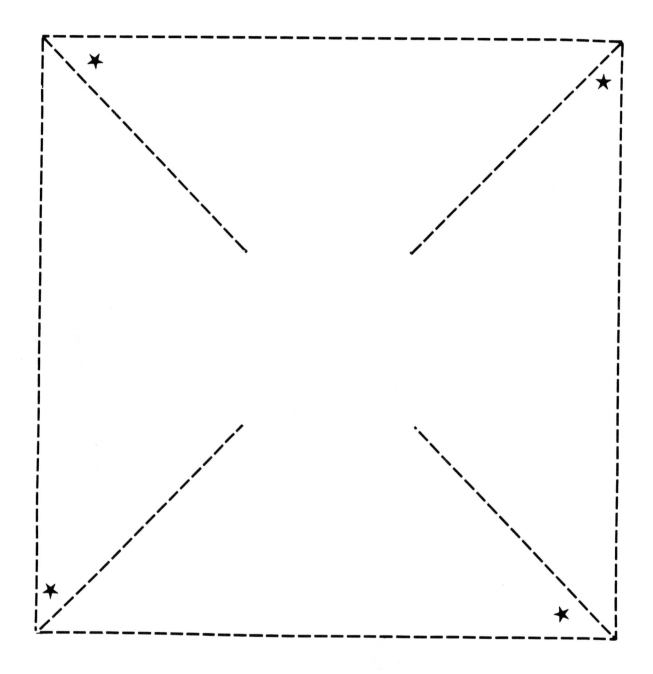

Pinwheel Pattern: Children cut on the dotted lines. Bend and overlap each of the four starred corners into the center and push a straight pin through the stars. To help the pinwheel spin freely, place a bead or a small section of straw on the pin. Push the pin into the eraser of an unsharpened pencil and use as described on page 253 or as described on page 93.

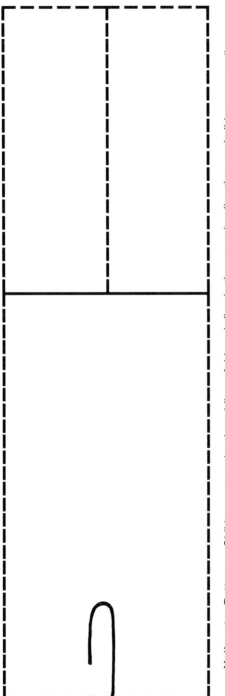

Helicopter Pattern: Children cut on the dotted lines, fold each flap in the opposite direction, and slide a paper clip onto the helicopter before tossing it into the air. Use as described on page 98.

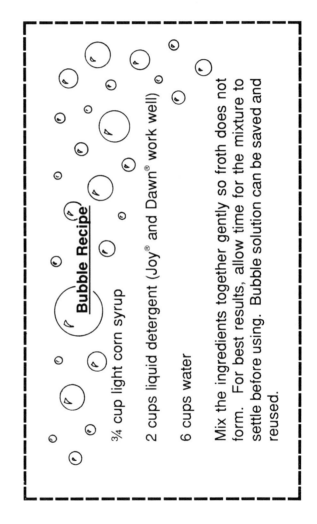

Bubble Recipe

¾ cup light corn syrup

2 cups liquid detergent (Joy® and Dawn® work well)

6 cups water

Mix the ingredients together gently so froth does not form. For best results, allow time for the mixture to settle before using. Bubble solution can be saved and reused.

Bubble Recipe Card: Use as described on pages 82, 96, and 177. The card can be sent home with the children.

Name _____

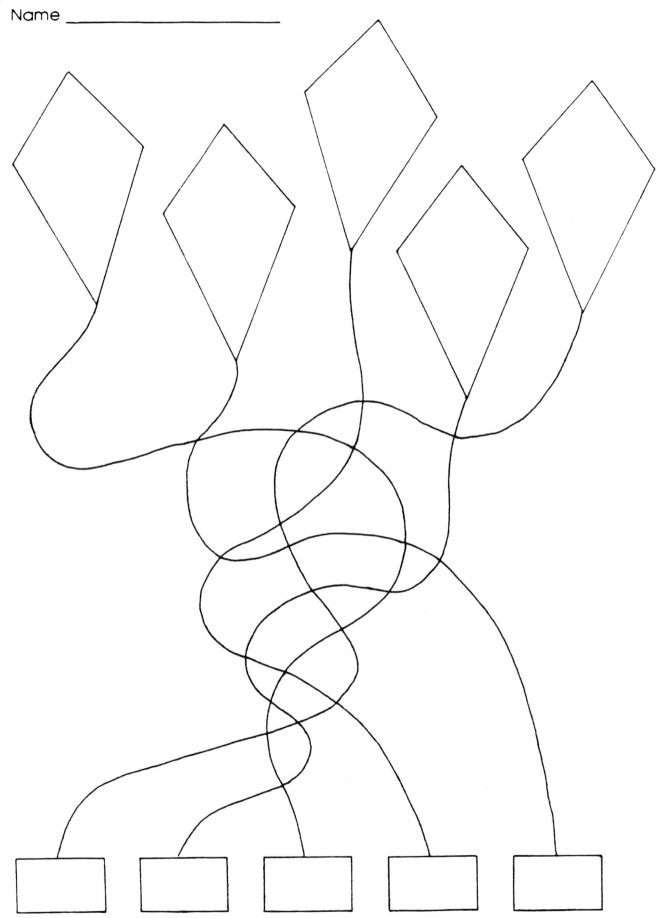

Tangled Kite String Sheet: Use as described on page 106.

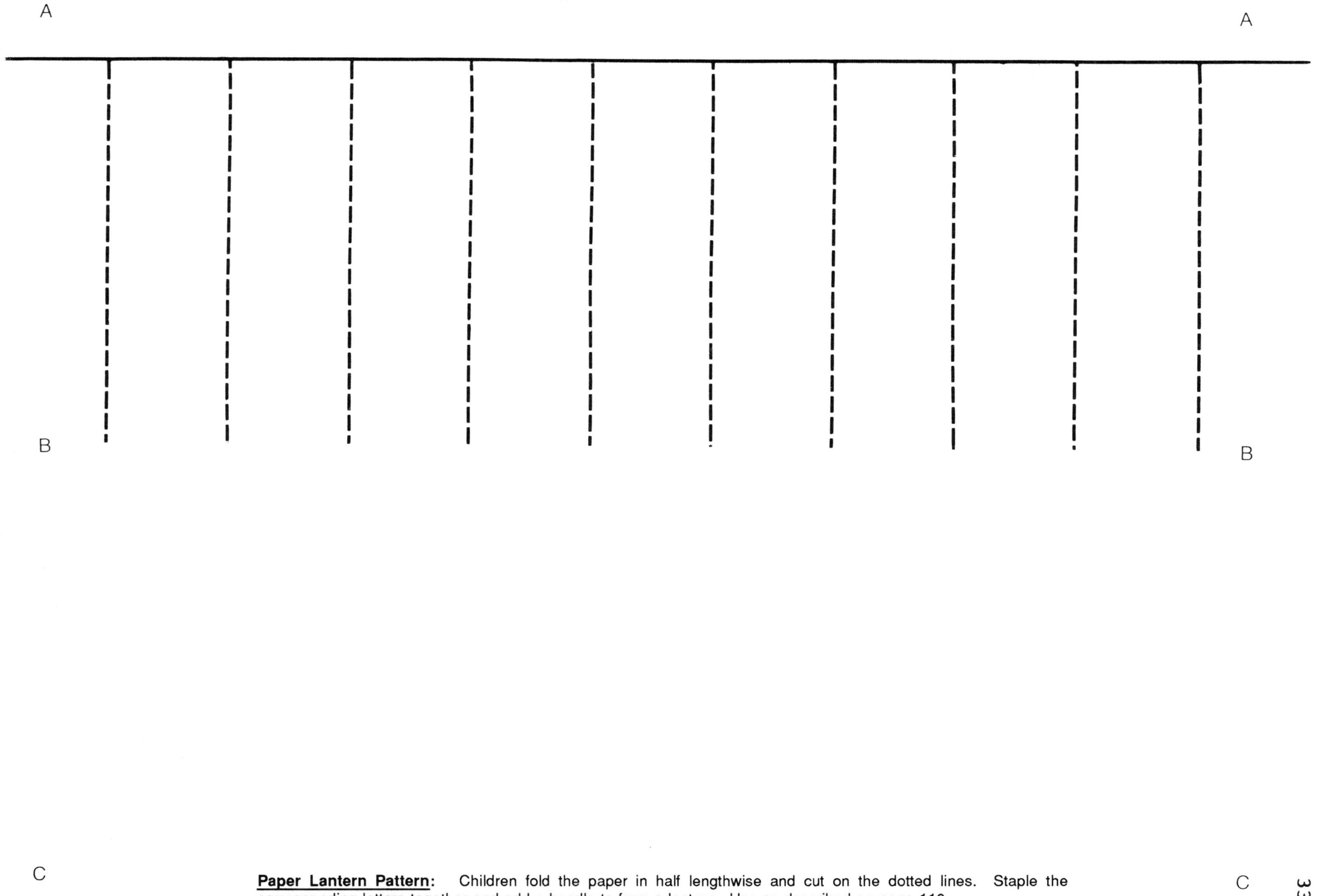

A

B

C

335

Paper Lantern Pattern: Children fold the paper in half lengthwise and cut on the dotted lines. Staple the corresponding letters together and add a handle to form a lantern. Use as described on page 110.

A

B

C

336

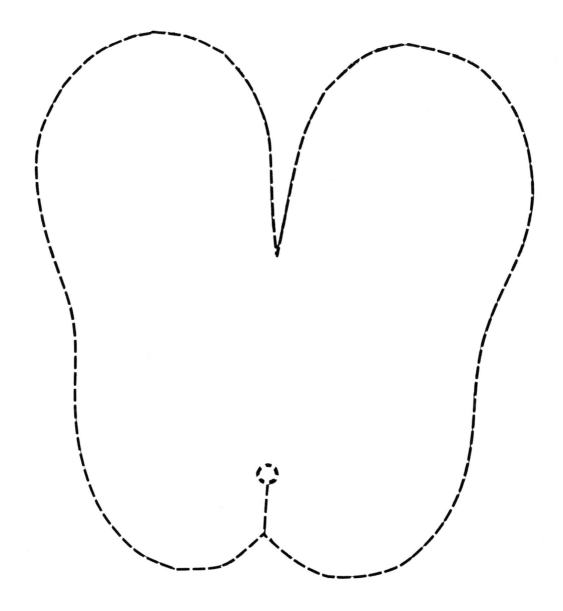

Shoe Pattern: Children color, cut on the dotted line, and use as described on page 122.

Name _____

Balloon String Sheet: Children predict, then use a piece of twine to determine the length of each balloon string.

Name _____

Sun, Sun, Sun

Our earth is heated by the sun.

The sun gives us light 'til day is done.

The sun helps plants and animals live.

The sun has so very much to give.

The sun is a star up in the sky.

Without the sun, we all would die.

The sun will never disappear.

The sun will be there—have no fear.

Our earth revolves around the sun

And brings four seasons full of fun.

The sun doesn't move, so you see,

What really moves is you and me!

Sun Story: Children draw a sun around the word **sun** each time it appears.

Story O'Mimus Sun Picture: Children locate sun-related items.

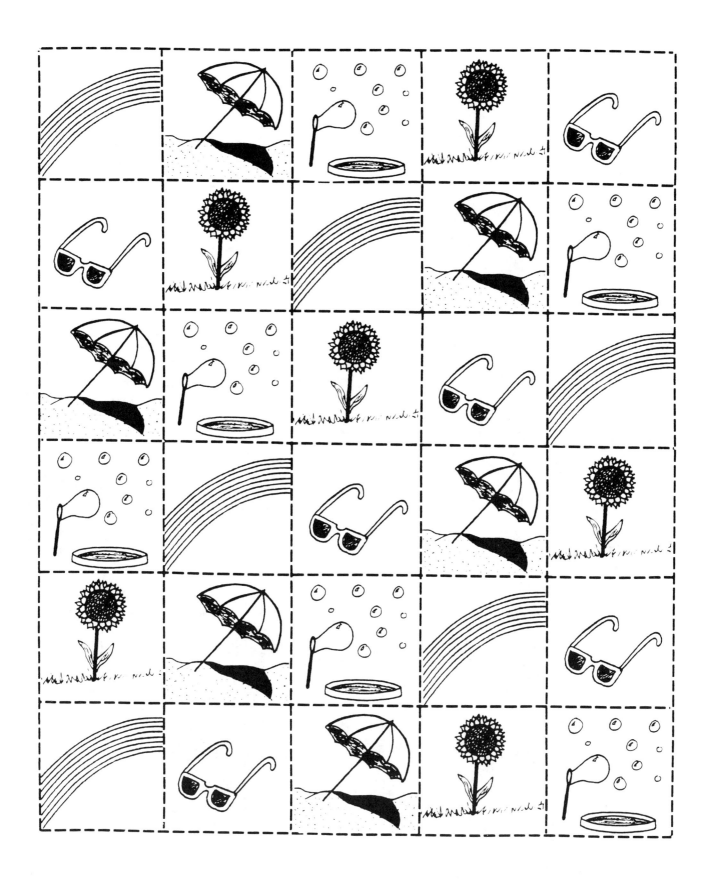

Sun Patterning Pictures: Children color, cut apart, and use the pictures to create or repeat patterns.

Sun Sorting Pictures: Children color, cut apart, and sort the pictures into categories.

Day/Night Pictures: Children color, cut apart, and sort the pictures into two categories—those that represent day and those that represent night. The pictures can be pasted on the Day/Night Mat.

Night

Day

Day/Night Mat: Children record the <u>Day/Night Pictures</u> on the mat.

Sun Bookmark: Children illustrate or list their favorite sun stories.

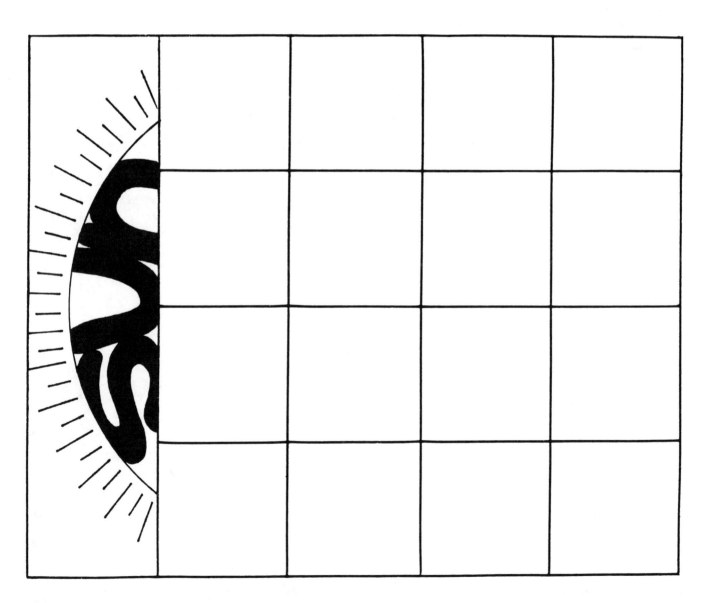

Sun Gameboard: Children paste the Patterning/Sorting Pictures on the board to create a bingo or lotto card.

Name _____

sun	The sun keeps plants and animals alive.
shines	The sun always shines.
heat	The sun's heat warms us.
day	The sun starts my day.
night	At night I can't see the sun.
star	The sun is our daytime star.
light	The sun gives us light.
energy	I get energy from the sun.
shadow	I can see my shadow on a sunny day.
time	The sun helps us tell time.

Sun Word Match: Children look at the first word in each row and circle the word that is the same.

Name _____

Sun Graph: Children record the number of items on the graph.

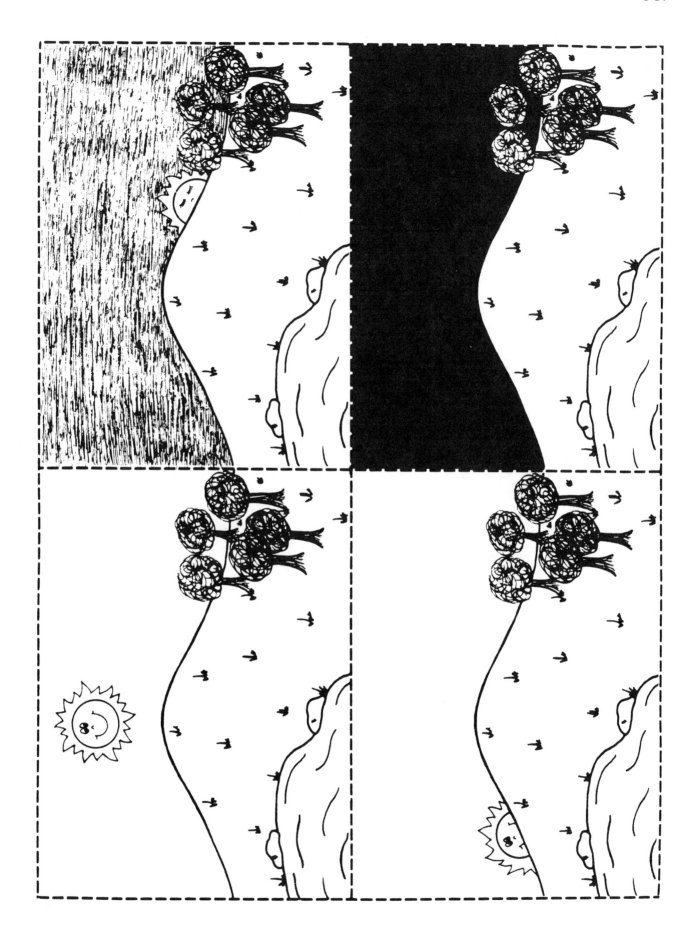

Sun Picture Sequence: Children color, cut apart, and sequence the pictures to tell a story.

Sun Mat: Children use as a background to act out number stories or follow positional directions.

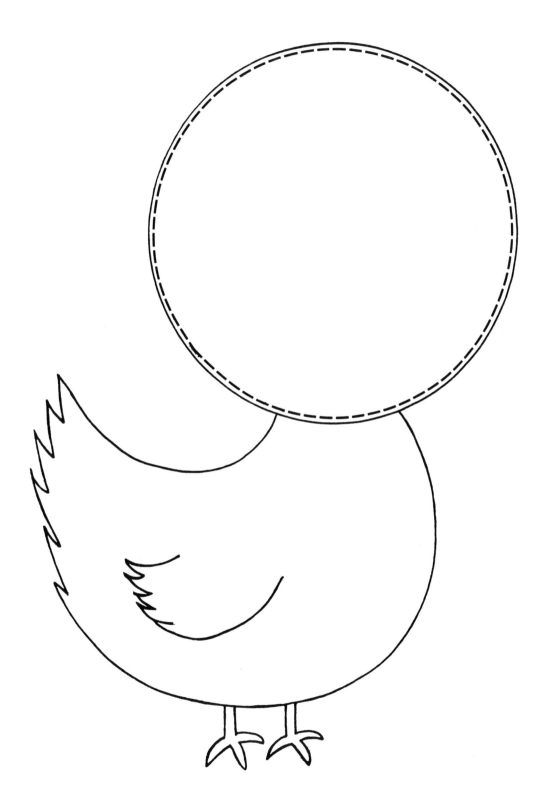

Chick Puppet: Children color, cut on the dotted lines, and use as described on page 158.

Rooster Puppet: Children color, cut on the dotted lines, and use as described on page 158.

Cow Puppet: Children color, cut on the dotted lines, and use as described on page 158.

352

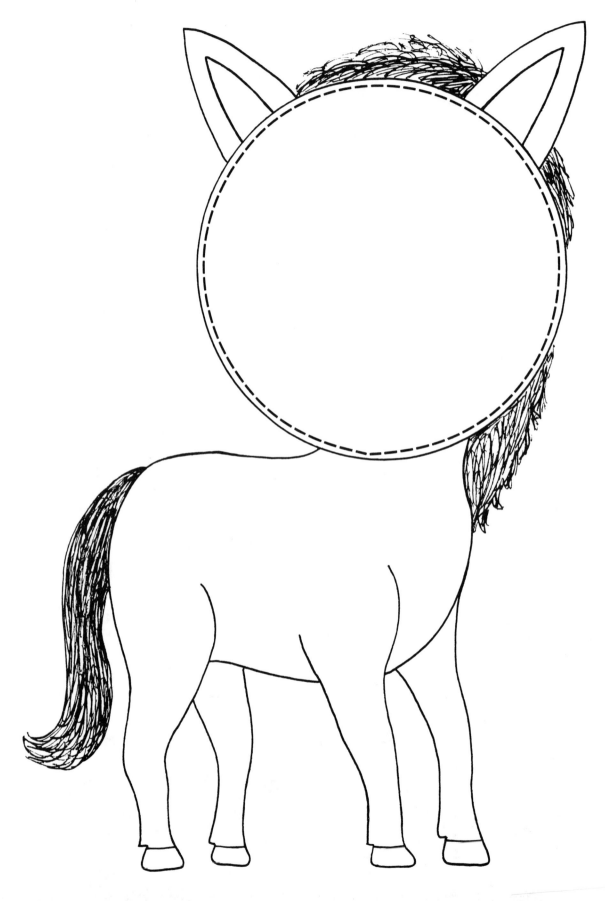

Horse Puppet: Children color, cut on the dotted lines, and use as described on page 158.

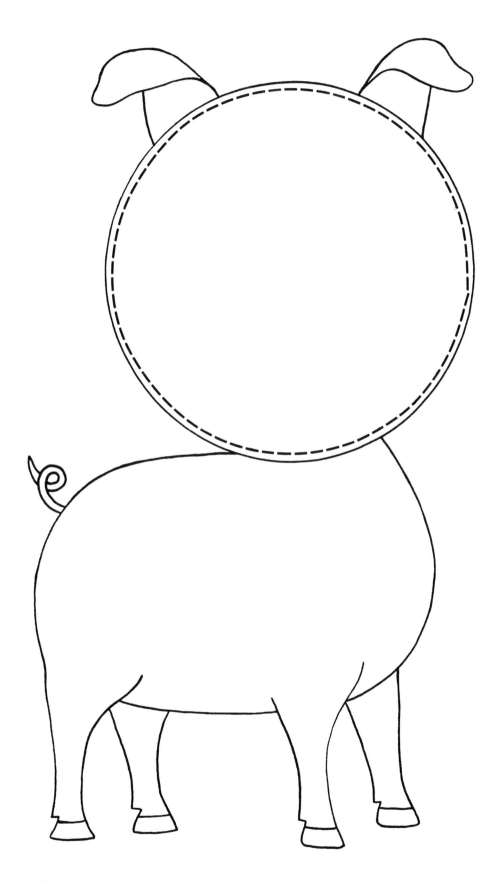

Pig Puppet: Children color, cut on the dotted lines, and use as described on page 158.

Jointed Bear Puppet: Children color, cut out, and attach the body parts with paper fasteners. Use as described on page 169.

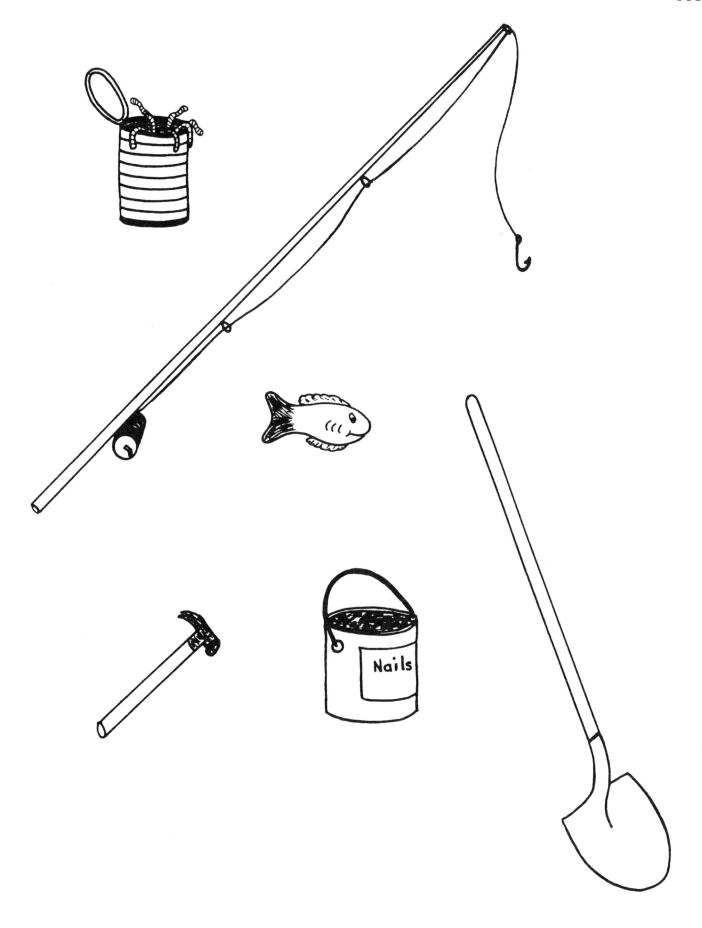

Bear Shadow Story Props: Use as described on page 169.

356

Fish Patterns: Use as described on page 169.

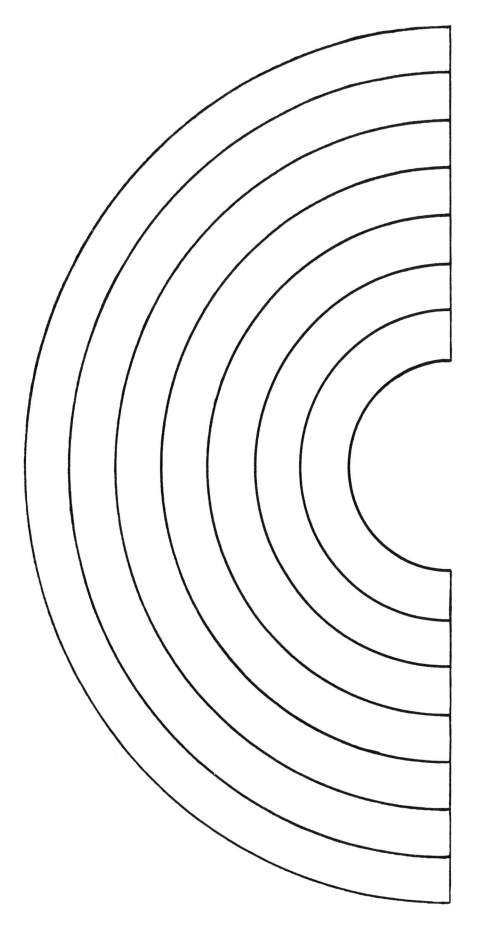

Rainbow Pattern: Use as described on pages 172–175 and 193.

358

Beach Umbrella Pattern: Use as described on page 182.

Sun Visor Pattern: Use as described on page 188.

360

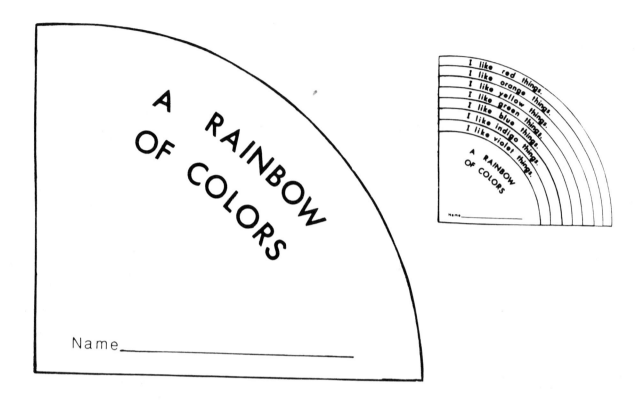

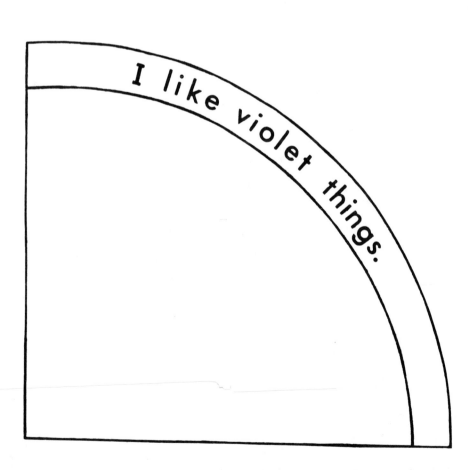

Rainbow Color Book: Use as described on page 178.

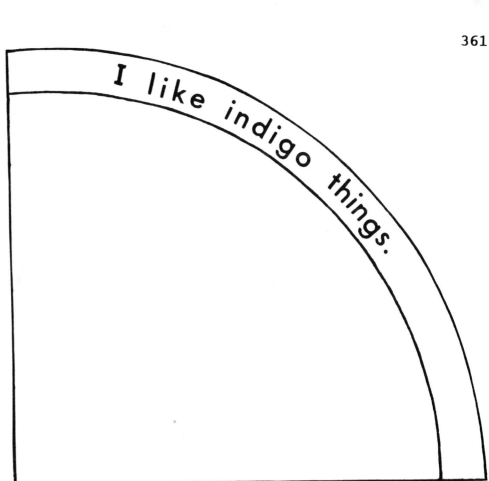

I like indigo things.

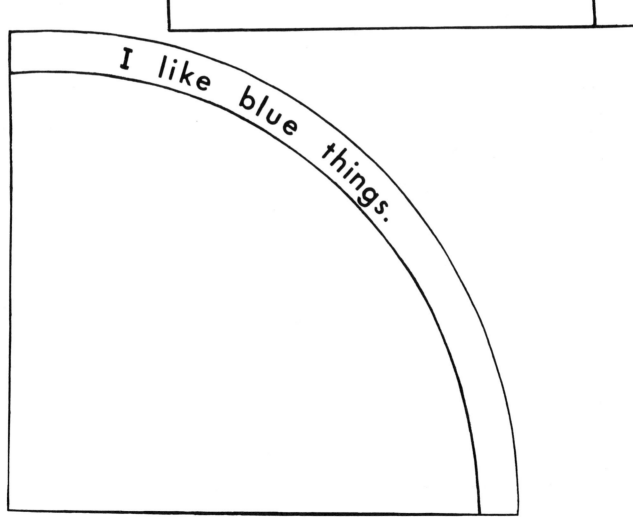

I like blue things.

Rainbow Color Book: Use as described on page 178.

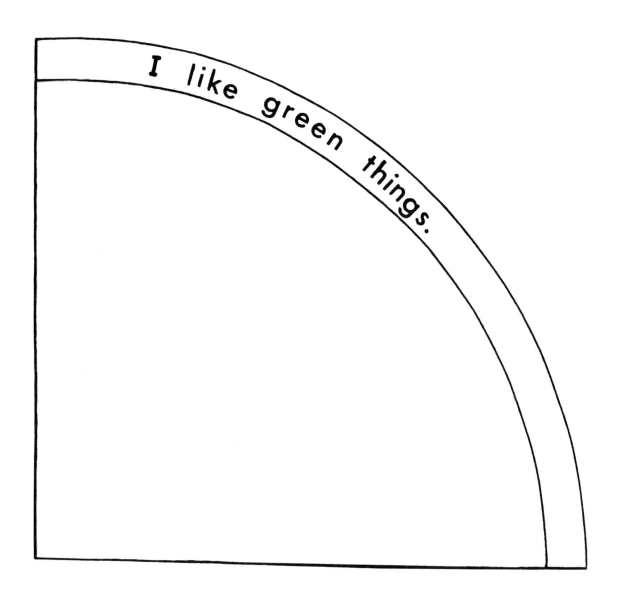

I like green things.

Rainbow Color Book: Use as described on page 178.

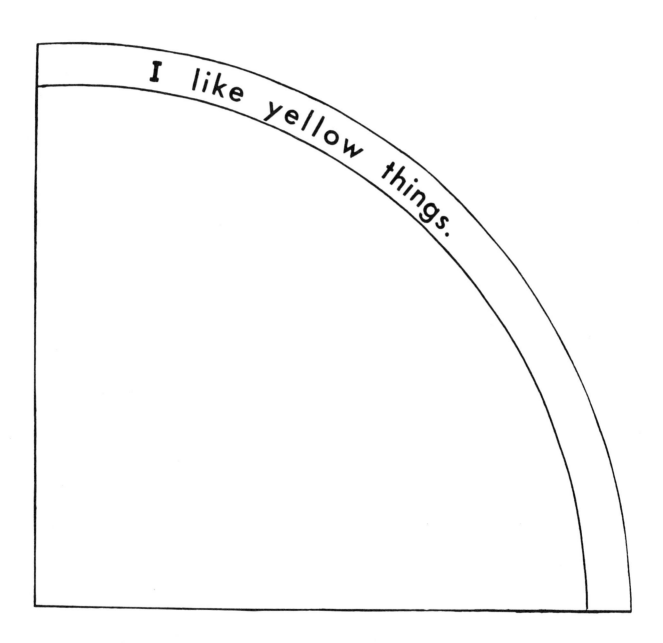

I like yellow things.

Rainbow Color Book: Use as described on page 178.

364

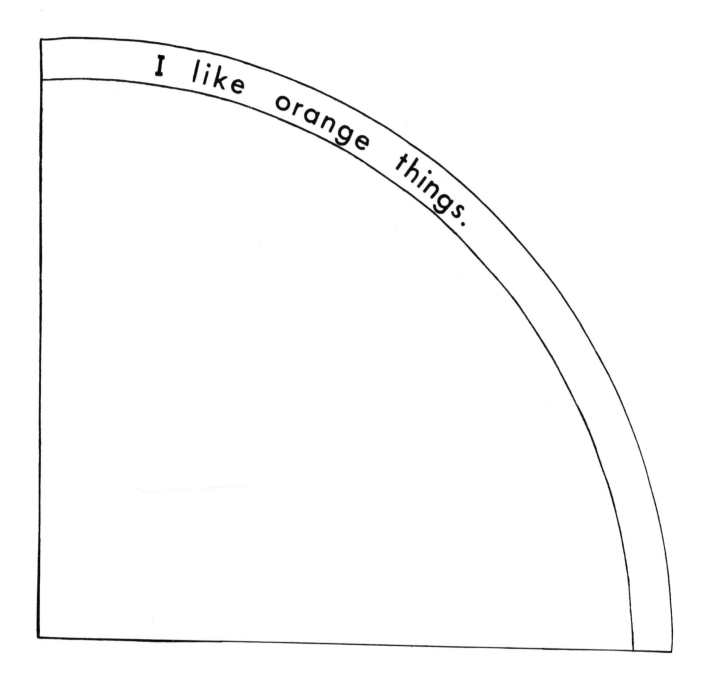

I like orange things.

Rainbow Color Book: Use as described on page 178.

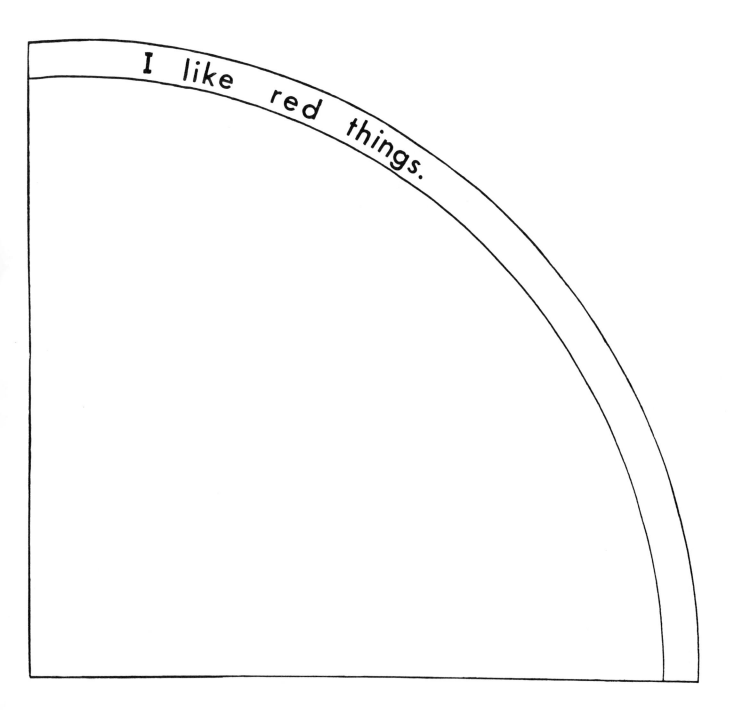

I like red things.

Rainbow Color Book: Use as described on page 178.

Name _____

Weather, Weather, Weather

The ☀ , ☁ , and ⛈ work together to make the weather. There are many kinds of weather. Sometimes the weather is hot and ☀ -ny. Other times the weather is ☁ -y or 🌬 -y. ⛈ -y weather can bring ⚡ and BOOM- . Winter weather can be cold and ❄ -y. It is important to listen to weather reports, so we know what to wear and what we can do. It would be dangerous to go out in stormy weather. But most of the time the weather helps us have fun.

Weather Story: Children draw a circle around the word **weather** each time it appears.

Story O'Mimus Weather Picture: Children locate weather-related items.

Weather Patterning Pictures: Children color, cut apart, and use the pictures to create or repeat patterns.

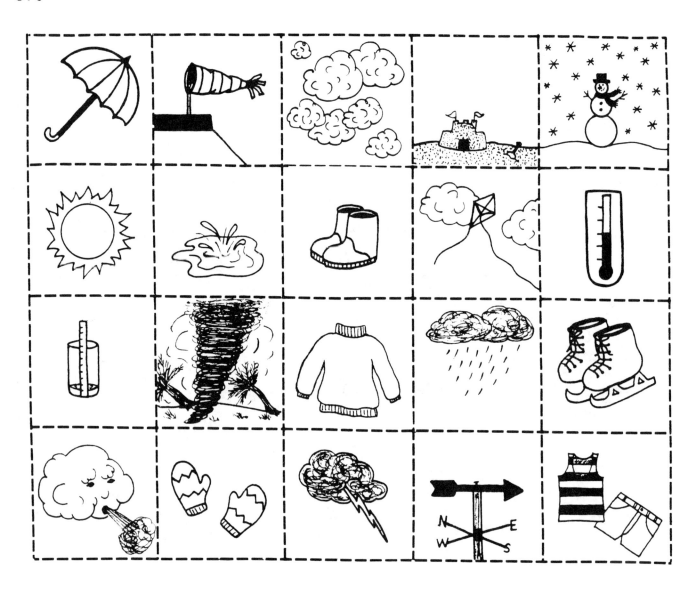

Weather Sorting Pictures: Children color, cut apart, and sort the pictures into categories.

Sun/Rain Pictures: Children color, cut apart, and sort the pictures into two categories—those that represent the sun and those that represent rain. The pictures can be pasted on the <u>Sun/Rain Mat</u>.

Rain

Sun

Sun/Rain Mat: Children record the Sun/Rain Pictures on the mat.

372

Weather Bookmark: Children illustrate or list their favorite weather stories.

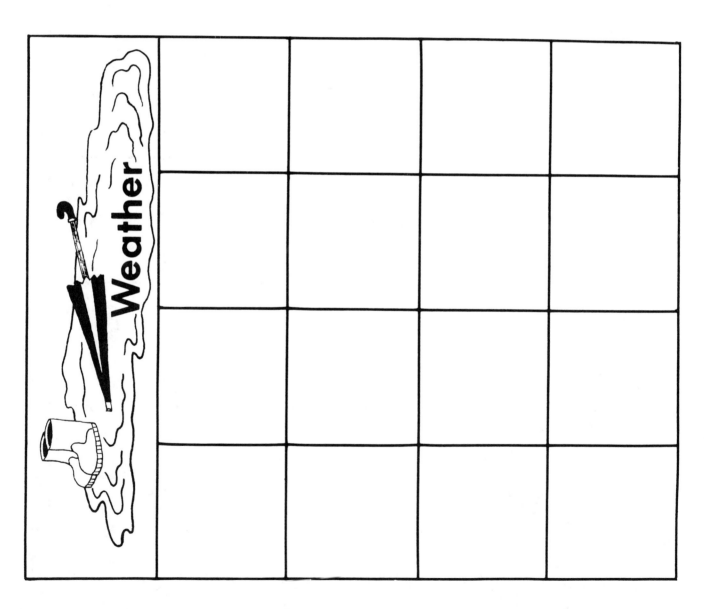

Weather Gameboard: Children paste the <u>Patterning/Sorting Pictures</u> on the board to create a bingo or lotto card.

Name _____

	dog	sun	scooter	nice
	cloud	vacuum	kitten	floor
	rope	rain	shine	noise
	bug	sing	lamp	lightning
	won	dig	snow	shovel
	wind	water	dinner	gum

Weather Word Match: Children look at the picture in each row and circle the word that matches.

374

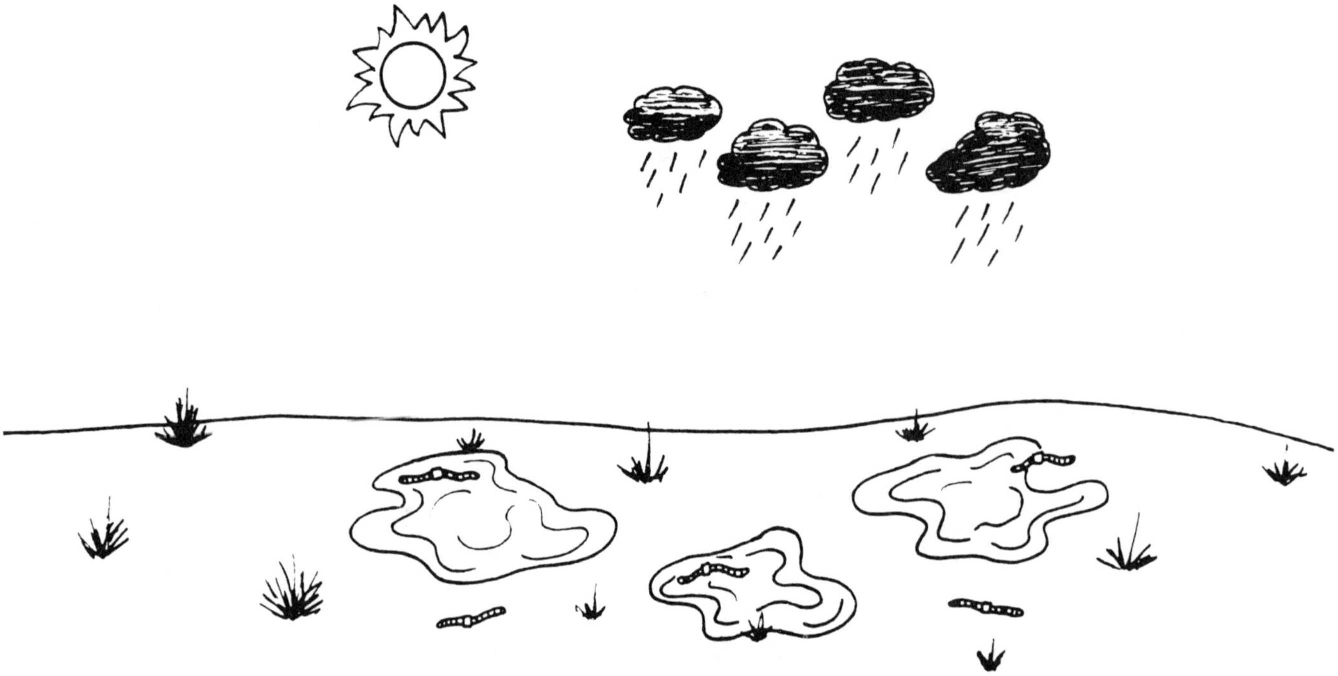

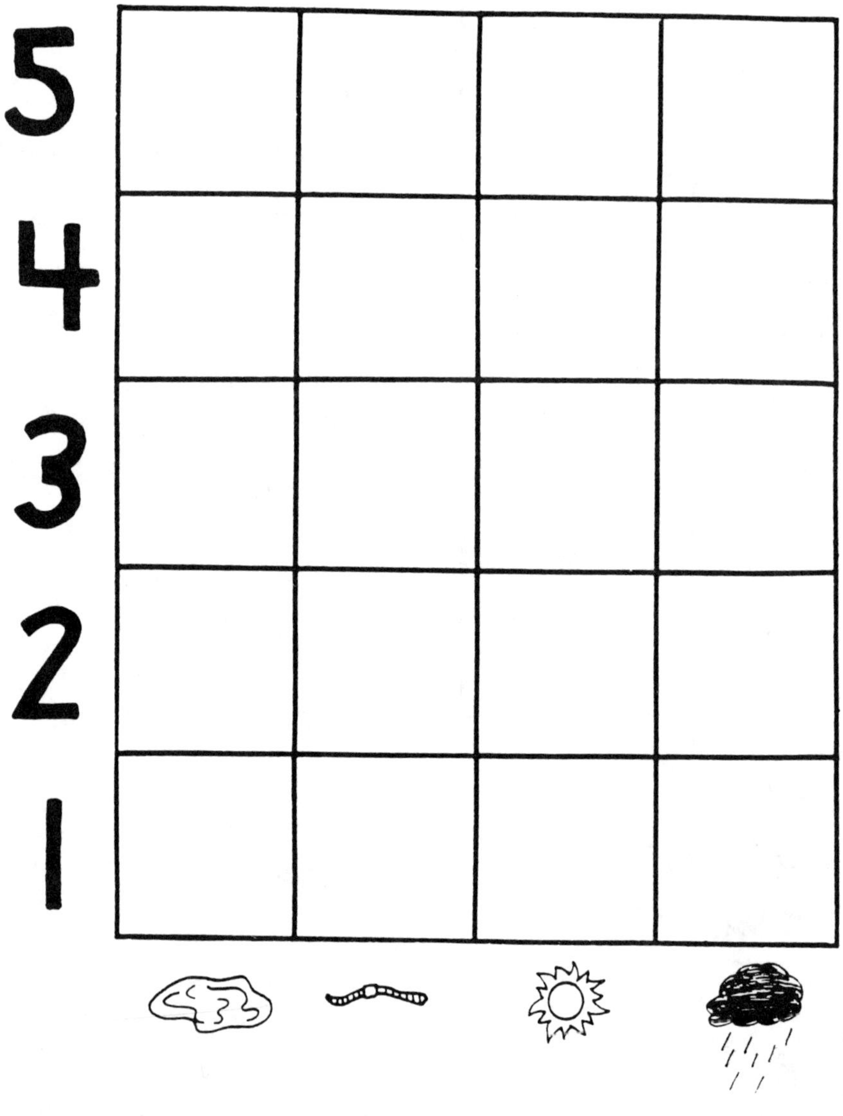

Name _____

5
4
3
2
1

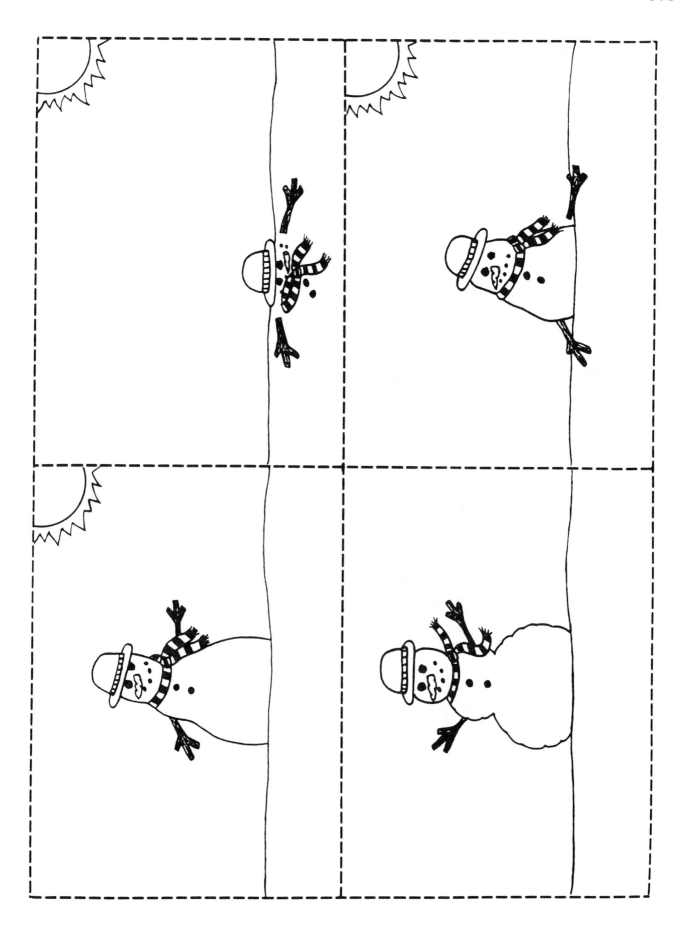

Weather Picture Sequence: Children color, cut apart, and sequence the pictures to tell a story.

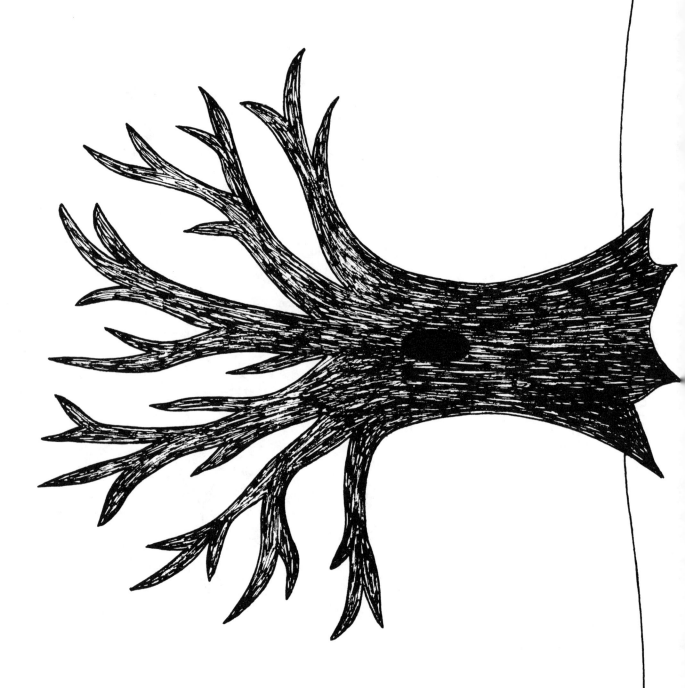

Weather Mat: Children use as a background to act out number stories or follow positional directions.

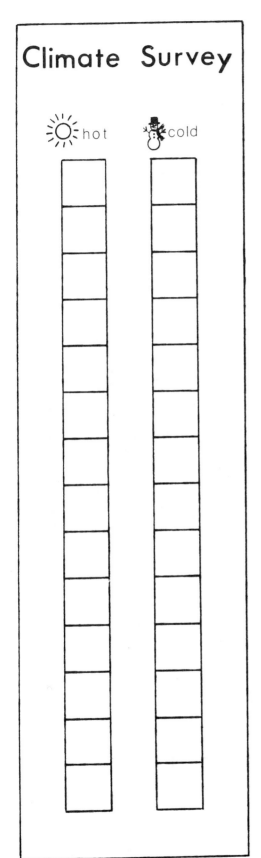

Climate Survey

☀ hot   ⛄ cold

Climate Survey: Use as described on page 220.

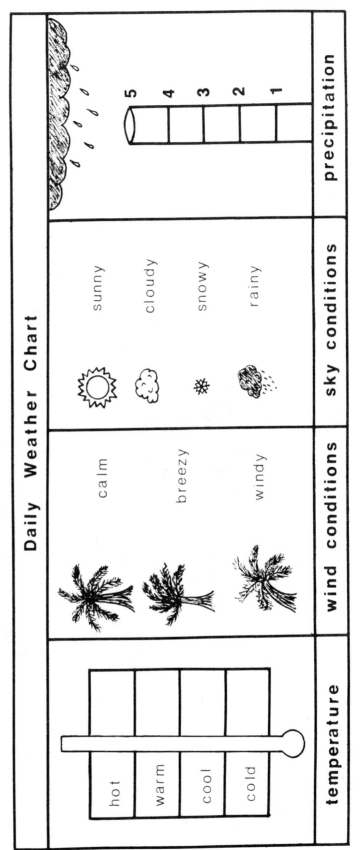

Daily Weather Chart

precipitation

5 4 3 2 1

sky conditions

sunny

cloudy

snowy

rainy

wind conditions

calm

breezy

windy

temperature

hot

warm

cool

cold

Daily Weather Chart: Use as described on page 255.

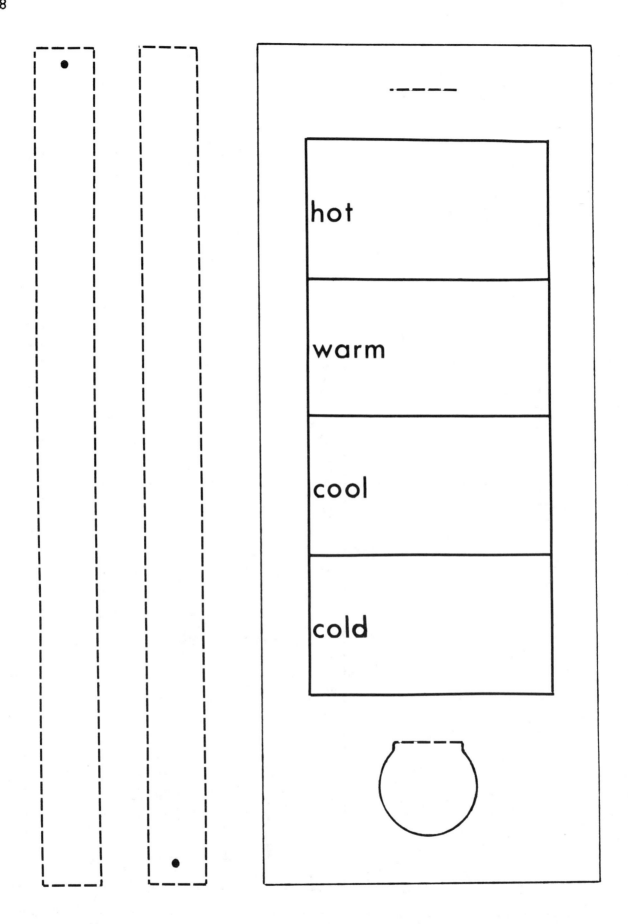

Ribbon Thermometer: Cut out the thermometer and slit on the dotted lines. Children cut out the strips. Color one strip and the bulb of the thermometer red. Glue the strips together at the dots and insert through the slits of the thermometer. Use as described on page 222.

 sun

 rain

 wind

 clouds

Weather Wizard Chart: Use as described on page 236.

 lightning

 thunder

 snow

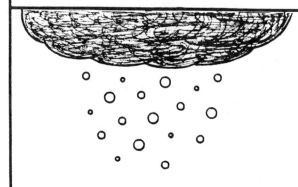 hail

Weather Wizard Chart: Use as described on page 236.

Weather Symbols: Use as described on pages 248 and 255.

Weather Doll Pattern: Use as described on page 255.

Weather Doll Accessories: Use as described on page 255.

384

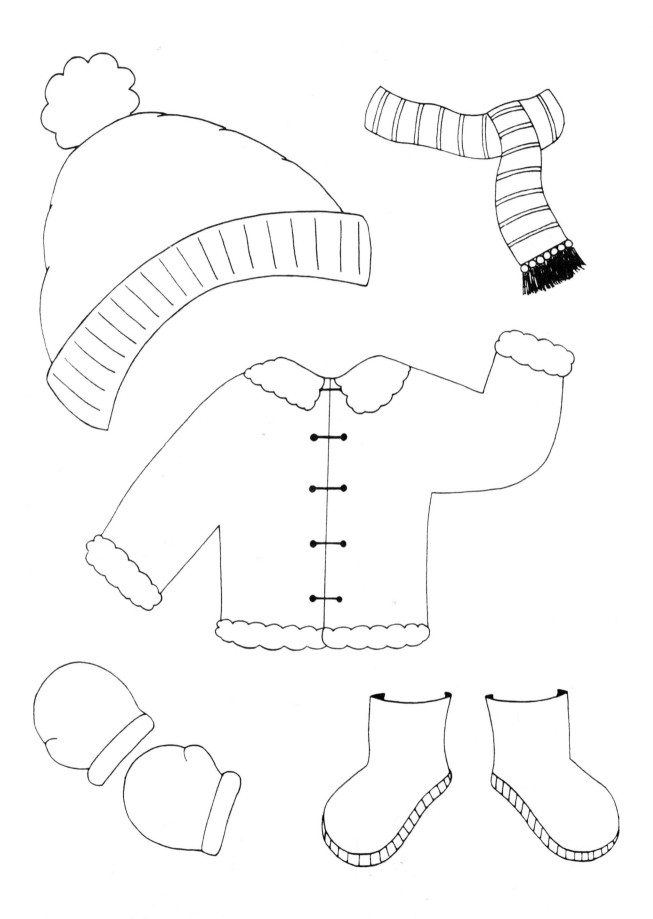

Weather Doll Accessories: Use as described on page 255.

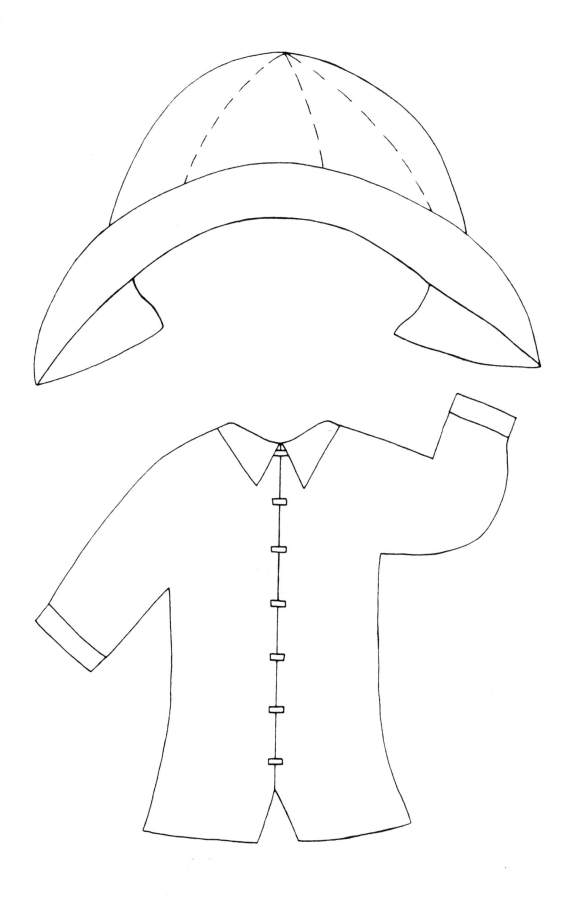

Weather Doll Accessories: Use as described on page 255.

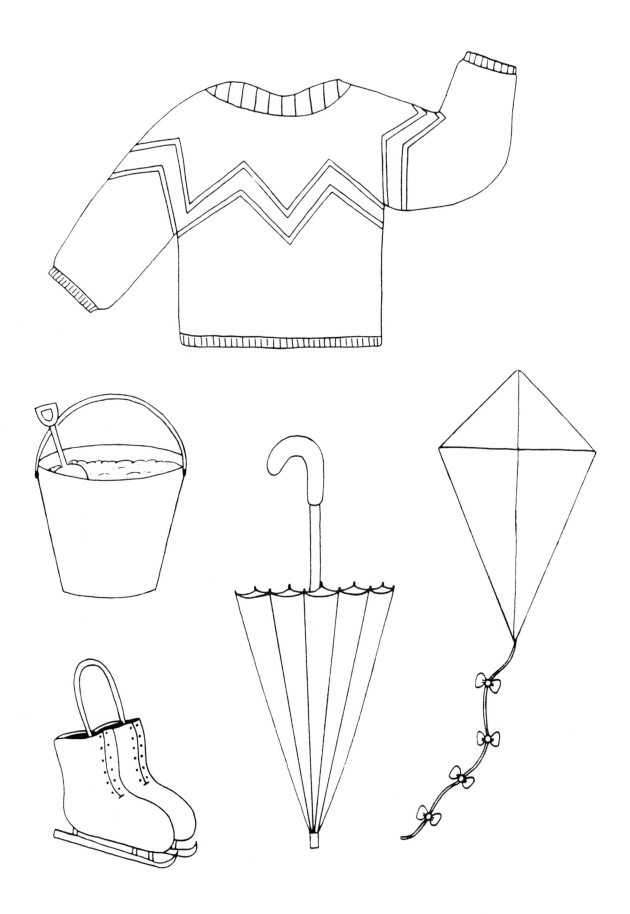

Weather Doll Accessories: Use as described on page 255.

Sunday	Monday	Tuesday	Wednesday	Thursday	Friday	Saturday

Monthly Weather Calendar: Use as described on page 248.

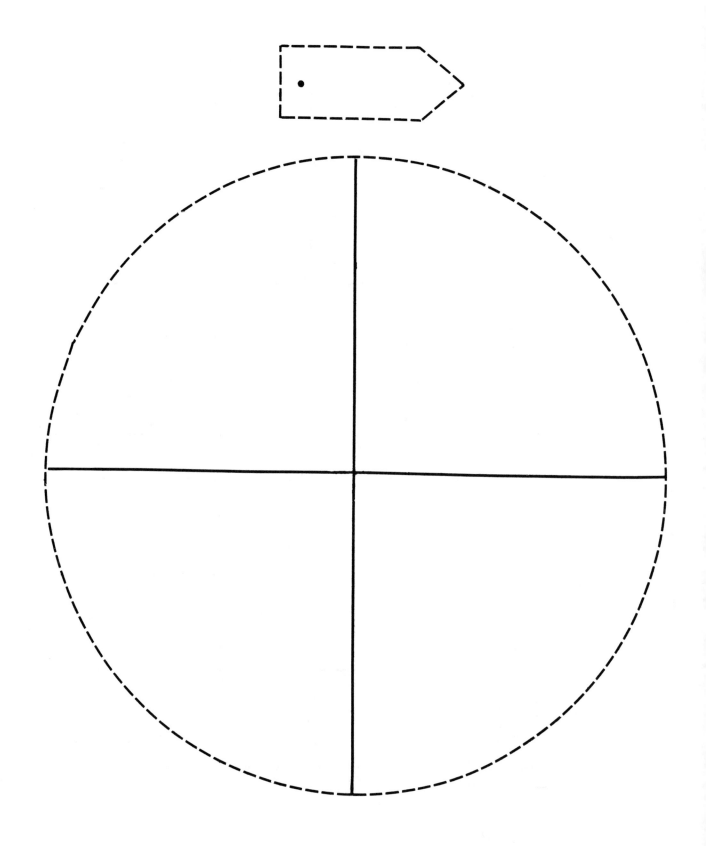

Daily Weather Wheel: Use as described on page 248.

Name _____

Color the following letters to reveal a secret message.

B   C   F   J   Q   V   X   Y   Z

B	X	W	A	T	E	R	Z	F	Y	A	I	R	V	Z	J
A	N	D	Q	B	Y	J	X	S	U	N	C	Z	B	F	Q
X	G	O	C	J	T	O	G	E	T	H	E	R	Z	C	X
T	O	B	V	F	Y	C	M	A	K	E	Z	F	O	U	R
J	Q	X	W	E	A	T	H	E	R	B	V	Y	J	C	Z

Write the message.

___ ___ ___ ___ ___ , ___ ___ ___ , ___ ___ ___

___ ___ ___ ___ ___ ___ ___ ___ ___ ___ ___ ___

___ ___ ___ ___ ___ ___ ___ ___ ___

___ ___ ___ ___ ___ ___ ___ .

Secret Weather Message: Children follow written directions.

INDEX